FAMILY
RECORD
OF

CHATTANOOGA'S
ROBERT SPARKS
WALKER

The UNCONVENTIONAL LIFE *of an*
EAST TENNESSEE NATURALIST

Alexandra Walker Clark

natural

HISTORY
PRESS

Published by Natural History Press
A Division of The History Press
Charleston, SC 29403
www.historypress.net

Back cover image courtesy of Yoshitaka Hamada.

All images are from the Walker family collection unless otherwise noted.

First published 2013

ISBN 9781540221902

Library of Congress CIP data applied for.

Notice: The information in this book is true and complete to the best of our knowledge. It is offered without guarantee on the part of the author or The History Press. The author and The History Press disclaim all liability in connection with the use of this book.

For family, friends and all lovers of the natural world

Special thanks to:
Elizabeth Dixon
Jerry Hill
Kyle Simpson
Yoshitaka Hamada

CONTENTS

Foreword, by Jerry Hill and Kyle Simpson   9
Preface   11
Prologue. Hawkins County, Tennessee, 1870   13

1. Dona Bell Walker, 1878–1897   17
2. Robert Sparks Walker, 1899–1903   41
3. 1904–1915   59
4. 1916–1924   87
5. 1925–1928   107
6. 1929–1935   135
7. 1936–1941   159
8. 1942–1960   185

Epilogue. Madeline, 1960   201
About the Author   223

FOREWORD

Native Americans once inhabited these woods and waters, appreciating the animals, birds and other creatures Mother Nature provided for them. In the 1870s, the Walkers moved here, farming and raising a family.

One of the Walkers was especially drawn to the area's natural wonder and loved teaching and instilling the beauty of nature to many young hearts and minds. Robert Sparks Walker's legacy remains not only in his writings but also here on this pristine land.

Few of Chattanooga's sons or daughters have left a gift as rich, diverse and lasting. Difficult to summarize and impossible to measure, his contribution is written across thousands of pages in the publications he authored and the countless lives he inspired.

But his most tangible memorial is found in the quiet pocket of green hidden amidst the bustle of a thriving city. Once his home, it is known today as Audubon Acres.

JERRY HILL
President, Board of Directors, Chattanooga Audubon Association

KYLE SIMPSON
Sanctuary Manager, Chattanooga Audubon Association

PREFACE

W e set out down the old familiar road, a crease worn deep in the earth's red face, his worn-out shoes flapping, my bare feet pressing against every cold, smooth stone for the sheer joy of sliding over it. Granddad's face was set like a flint toward our destination, a short journey through dense woods sprinkled with light and songs of winged creatures. Good land, good earth, a good trail with a promise at its end, we traveled to the Ford of Youth, the ford of his youth and now mine. Past deep ditches of stagnant overflow, past tangled gnarls of roots swept clean from spring flooding, now the music of its rippling filled our ears.

"Listen!" He paused, turned his good ear toward the melodic splashing. "It says its name: Chickamauga, Chickamauga."

I heard the ancient stream speaking, bidding my eager feet frolic in its shoals. I loosed his hand then, giving rein to childhood glee, delighting in the miracle of living waters swirling at my feet. Granddad waded into the hasty current, old man and old river lifelong friends, nodding a familiar greeting in mutual respect. He sat down on a half-drowned log and drew out his pocketknife, whittling on sassafras as he spoke.

"This is the most beautiful place on earth. The Creator made it to keep you young, for it is a place of great strength." A smile crinkled the corners of his eyes. "Keep this place in your heart, and you will never grow old. This is who we are, you know."

Many years later I hold his words close, close as the tiny glass vial of Chickamauga red earth I often wear if I am in peril of forgetting who

I am. It reminds me I am still full of the hope he imparted, the joy of living things that he taught and the trust in a sure destiny. Just as he was, I am alive and moving with a purpose like our wise and timeless friend, Chickamauga.

HAWKINS COUNTY, TENNESSEE, 1870

In late December, William Thomas Walker set out for Hamilton County in a covered wagon with a cow tied on behind. He had spent his twenty-two years in Hawkins County working his father's farm, growing wheat and corn that was carried down steep hills by sled. Hawkins County is made of picturesque, stony hills, where it was said the Creator had too much earth left over and piled it into fantastic shapes, its sheep and goats having pointed noses to bite grass from the crevices.

The Civil War ravaged the land, and the Walkers, Union sympathizers, had their share of hardships. In 1864, both elder sons, John and Preston, joined other Hawkins County boys, hiking on foot through the Cumberland Gap to enlist in the Union army at Fort Dick, Kentucky. William Thomas, known as Tom, was only twelve, too young to enlist. Besides, he was assured, he was needed at home to protect his parents and younger brother Gabriel and care for the farm.

Tom's father, Edward, had bought an old Kentucky long rifle from a neighbor, John Beckner. It was a flintlock converted to percussion and might have been used during the Revolution, helping purchase freedom from the British back in Virginia, where many Hawkins County residents traced their roots. At twelve, Tom was tall and rangy, becoming an excellent marksman, shooting squirrels and other small game in the eye for a quick kill that didn't tear up the meat. Tom took his new duties seriously.

His father had set aside a section of his farm as a cemetery for the tiny community of Otes. As Tom crossed into neighboring Greene County with his wagon, he reflected on that graveyard and those resting there. He once had a friend his age, Jim Stewart, whose family owned a neighboring farm.

During the Great War, Confederate raiders roamed the hills, stealing food and harassing families whose sons fought for the Union. Mounted riders had been to the Walker farmhouse before, looking for Tom, and once shot up the Seth Thomas clock on the mantel. They often sought teenage boys to shoot or hang before they became old enough to join the Union army. Tom's mother, Elizabeth Bryant Walker, knew what to expect. As horses drew into her yard, she lifted the floorboard near the fireplace and shooed Tom under the house. Replacing the board, she pulled a rug over it, placed her rocker on it, sat down and commenced knitting.

When Confederates burst into the house, demanding her son, she said they were welcome to look around, but she hadn't been able to find him either and was worried. They barged through, broke some things and angrily stormed off. When they were out of sight, Elizabeth released Tom from his hiding place. They soon heard gunfire coming from the Stewart farm; Elizabeth told Tom to get the sled. They knew his friend Jim had been found and shot.

With a heavy heart, Tom went to the Stewart farm, finding his friend dead. He laid the boy's body on the sled and was towing his tragic burden home when he encountered mounted Confederates who asked where he was going. He defiantly said he was going to bury his friend they had just killed. Years later, Tom would tell his son Robert that he never knew why the Confederates hadn't just shot him too. He speculated that seeing the murdered boy being towed to the graveyard might have sparked their twinge of conscience.

Possibly Jim might be coming with him now, had he lived, Tom mused. As it was, another neighbor, Mr. Sanders, was traveling this miserable trail that passed for a road. Sanders's wagon was towing three cows. They were both seeking good farmland. Tom had heard Hamilton County was a place of green fields and plenty of water.

After returning from the War, brother John Walker became a Baptist preacher, with Preston due to inherit the house and farm when their father passed. But as a younger son, Tom's portion was a rocky, poor-yielding piece. He now had a wife and two children.

Tom had been following a plow when Sanders came by, saying he was moving to Hamilton County. Tom decided to go too, presenting the matter to his wife, Mary. She agreed, but her father, William Anderson Moore, said, "Any man's children do better when they move off to themselves, but the place you have chosen I fear is overrun with chills."

Tom's brother Preston strongly opposed the idea, accusing Sanders of persuading Tom to leave. He pleaded that Tom stay for their mother's sake, but Tom replied he could not support a family off his poor ground.

Edward, Tom's father, also opposed Tom's leaving and convinced him to leave his wife and children behind until he got set up. Edward promised to then bring them all down on the train. Tom agreed and was glad his children weren't with him now, as an icy wind blew snow in his face.

Sanders's wagon pulled off for him to tuck in early and sleep in his wagon. Tom did the same. Two nights later, they met a man near Lenoir City who invited them to stay at his warm house. Tom would not forget this man's kindness to two traveling strangers. The rest of the journey, they stayed in their wagons, arriving in Hamilton County on New Year's Day. Then they went separate ways.

Tom came to the Shallowford, east of Missionary Ridge. Before him was a bridge across the Chickamauga, and near its banks was a single-room log house, roof almost gone. Tom began repairing it, staying with the project through winter. Once it was done to his satisfaction, he sent for his wife and children in late 1871. They arrived by train with Edward, as promised. Tom met them at Tyner Station, his father laughing at the tiny building in which they all had to live.

Tom soon learned of another piece of land John Ellis was selling: a 120-acre tract along Chickamauga Creek. It also had a cabin built by the Cherokees in the 1700s that needed work but was larger and better than the one he had. Tom bought the creek farm, moving his family there in 1872.

Chapter 1

DONA BELL WALKER, 1878–1897

Concord Churchyard, East Brainerd, Tennessee, 1902

Only the land remembers when we all lived together on it, putting by the memories of our bare feet against its cheeks and the streams of children's laughter pouring through those woodlands, clear and strong, constant as the Chickamauga. Our days as a family there are held in trust forever, stored in the stones of the riverbanks, wrapped in the soft green shawl of field and forest, locked in the silence of its eternal secrets. It was no more than a flicker of time, our days together on that land, but if you close your eyes and listen hard, you can still hear the shouts of my brothers chucking corn cobs at each other and the soft, crushed rustle of Momma's skirts drifting through the high, nodding grasses.

My pa, Tom Walker, would be at work before sunup, my brothers too; they could show our old rooster a thing or two about early rising. Pa kept our little farm humming; nobody knew land better. He could look at the dirt and tell you what ought to be planted and how good a crop you might expect.

I was proud to be the first of us born in our cabin. My brother John came a year later, followed by Robert Sparks—whom we all called Bob—and then Mary Agnes. Chess and Charlie didn't show up till Pa moved us to a bigger house a few miles from our creek farm. I always felt special to be the first one born in our cabin, built by Cherokees over a hundred years before.

Sometimes I'd think of those unknown Indians who'd come before us, pouring their hearts and lives into this land, just like us, only to be torn off it like weeds that didn't matter at all. Wasn't a thing I could do about it, but whenever I'd sit a spell on the porch with Momma, watching breezes play tag in the treetops at the foot of the hill or counting constellations of lightning bugs twinkling up from the woods, I'd remember those Cherokees, and my heart would hurt for them.

Then I'd think—suppose some Washington big shot made up a law that all white Scotch-Irish folks like me had to pick up and move on foot to Oklahoma? It was just wrong, that was all! Momma said to count my blessings. We were blessed, I knew that. We weren't rich, but we were happy.

Momma was sweet but no coward. Sometimes we got her to tell about the War in Hawkins County, when she and her parents were left home while her brothers were fighting for the Union. Confederate raiders roamed the countryside, robbing families of food and livestock, and many were shot trying to protect their belongings. Once Momma saw soldiers coming toward their homestead, likely after what little the Moores had left, which was one bushel of corn. These renegades were armed, having the reputation as killers, but Momma snatched up a double-bladed axe, barred the corncrib with her body and dared anyone to advance. After one look at Momma, those skunks and their horses disappeared.

She was born July 8, 1846, and educated in Hawkins County. She married Pa on April 25, 1867, at her parents' home, William Anderson and Agnes Crozier Moore. Her grandfather was also named William Anderson Moore, from Botetourt County, Virginia. Momma's great-grandfather was John Crozier, and her maternal grandfather was William Arnot, both from Botetourt County. That's about all I know of her family.

Years after the War, an old bachelor became friends with Pa, but Momma was sure he'd been among the thieves who terrorized the Moores. He had settled in Hamilton County and become a good citizen. When she asked him if he'd been one of the soldiers who robbed her family, he refused to answer. Even after he married a good woman and they proved to be good neighbors, Momma and I never trusted him.

She would gather us up and take us to a dry branch running through the flatwood nearby. Wild plum trees grew there, and how happy we were gathering as much fruit as we could carry. Bob especially liked these adventures.

Our father taught us to respect the animals that served us. When one died, unlike neighbors who just dragged off the carcass and left it exposed,

Pa never let animals be so degraded. Horses, cows, dogs, even fowls were given burial in our meadow. Bob and John made it their solemn duty to erect markers. I reckon there might yet be a crude tombstone in that field yonder, put up by those two for some beloved old mule or dog.

Once when Momma's geese cropped off Pa's newly sprouted corn, he ordered Bob to have our dog kill the culprits. Old Rover and Bob took Pa's orders to heart, and Rover slayed a gander. When they proudly returned, it came clear Pa hadn't really wanted his instructions followed so closely. Momma never said a word, except to call us for baked goose the next day. Rover even got a share of goose hash.

In 1873, Pa'd hand-dug a well near the cabin, walled in with chert rock from a nearby hill. After that, there was always good drinking water at the cabin—about eight feet of it, even in dry spells.

Around 1876, Pa tried his hand making maple sugar and syrup, as he'd located a small stand of sugar maples near our spring. He pounded spigots into their bark, hung buckets to collect sap, boiling it all down, but I reckon it was more work than it was worth. My older brother, Will, said you need lots of trees to make that process pay. There was more profit from other crops, so Pa decided to buy sugar. But he hated to waste any resource the Almighty sent.

As we got older, Mary Agnes and I helped with laundry. It wasn't easy, but there was contentment seeing those clothes come up clean, watching them fly like kites from tree branches where we hung them. Pa put up a line for bedding and quilts, and nothing ever smelled so sweet as those crisp, clean things after drying in the wind and sun. I used to think the threads of the cloth soaked up the light, that our little cabin was perfumed by pure sunshine. Its sweetness in my nostrils was worth the redness of my hands.

Momma's soap was important, made outside in batches in the big kettle. Pa built an ash hopper for lye, and we'd boil down rendered fat from hogs we raised and butchered, adding lye to that. It was Momma's own recipe, likely handed down from the Moores. Pa used to brag about it, and it was real important for a woman to know, if she hoped to marry.

I remember stirring that stuff in the yard. We'd fill the hopper with ashes, put a bed of straw under it, pour water over that and it would filter down to the tilted trough, running into a crock below. That was liquid lye. We'd cook it with lard, put that in a pan and cut it into cakes. Without enough lye, clothes wouldn't come clean; too much, it would take hide off your hands.

Skill with a needle was nearly as important, but a woman who made good soap, she was a true prize, Pa said. Momma taught us her secret recipe, and by the time I was thirteen, I could turn out pretty good soap.

Dona Bell Walker, circa 1896.

While us womenfolk were busy at chores, Pa and my brothers were plowing fields, sowing crops, feeding hogs, milking cows and splitting wood. The work never ended, but it all got done—but that's easier when there's a lot of you, and you all pull in the same direction.

We never minded the train running smack through our front yard and, in fact, took pleasure in its mournful whistle and rumble. The Western and

Atlantic Railroad owned the track just below the red dirt bluff our cabin perched on. From our porch, between two sycamores, we could see the engine approaching. If one of us was lucky enough to have a cent on him, there was just enough time to fly down the hill, lay that penny on the tracks and jump back to safety before the locomotive barreled over it and spread it thin enough to nearly see through. My brothers called these prostrated pennies "lucky pieces." I say the only luck they got was getting out of the way so they didn't end up the same. But flattening pocket change wasn't the only amusement my brothers devised with our rail-bound visitor.

They'd spear fruit with a pole or branch, hanging it out for the brakeman to grab as he flew past. I think they thought they were making influential friends. Sometimes they'd break an entire limb off our fruit trees and stick it out for trainmen to snag.

I liked that train too—the way it flew around the bend in a big hurry to get somewhere important. I used to think of riding one of them someday and find out where they were going in such a great rush.

The railroad was a thoroughfare to lots of folks, hardly a day going by but one or many passed our place on foot, following the rails. Pa believed the Good Book where it says entertain strangers, as some might be angels, so he'd invite them for dinner or to stay the night, especially if they looked tired and hungry. Momma and us girls would set a plate for them at the table, then fix them a place to lay down for the night. Pa said a man had taken him in once when he was traveling, and he never forgot it. We hosted lots of folks; in fact, by the time I was thirteen, we'd counted up to five hundred guests at our table, folks Pa asked in to rest from "tamping ties." But if any of them was ever an angel, I never knew it.

Some traveled with livestock, and I'd be hard pressed to say how many goats and heifers, even sheep—horses too—we put up in our barn while their owners snoozed under our roof! It was a great relief to me that Pa never asked in the man traveling with a music box and a live bear, though my brothers were disappointed. Once or twice we saw a family of Italians coming with a monkey, which I thought might be interesting to see up close. But they never stayed with us either.

The old trains burned wood, and Pa split up cordwood and stacked it next to the tracks, where the work train would collect it on its way past. Once a month, the pay train would pay whatever they owed him. He soon sold enough to pay for our place. He'd earned his first dollar cutting firewood as a boy, selling it to steamboats when they ran short of coal.

The bad side to the trains was losing livestock. It was sad to watch a poor creature try to outrun one, too simple to know all it had to do was get off the tracks. There wasn't a family along the rails who hadn't lost stock, but the Western and Atlantic always paid for losses. I sometimes thought folks might stick a sickly animal on the tracks, settling its future in a financially advantageous way, if you know what I mean.

The first time we saw ice in the summer was when a big block fell off a car bolting down the tracks. That was fair reward for all those apples and peaches offered from sticks and poles. We even saw Presidents Cleveland and Harrison wave to us from their cars. That made us feel right important and might've spurred my brothers on to higher goals a while. Unfortunately, the train carrying a load of melons did not have as uplifting an effect, for I cannot tell how many ways I overheard them plotting to wreck it to get their hands on those melons in the heat. Boys are easily influenced by opportunity, for good or ill, and it's up to us womenfolk to keep them on a straight track. At least Momma and me, and my sisters, we thought so, and did our best to watch for their weaknesses.

Pa kept his boys so busy they didn't have opportunity to get in trouble. If it wasn't a Sabbath, the rule was work, work, even on Saturday. Sometimes he'd let them go into town for a baseball game. And they always managed a dip with the Woods boys in the Chickamauga's swimming hole.

I helped with milking. For a stool, we had a wooden spool barbed wire came on. I liked it for being steadier than those three-legged things. It was a good idea, if you were milking, to bring a corn nubbin for the cow, keeping her occupied so she didn't pay much attention to what you were doing.

The sound of milk hitting the bucket brought out the cats. Sometimes I'd squirt some their way, for it tickled me to see them lick off their whiskers. They earned their keep, keeping after rats and mice, so they deserved a treat. I enjoyed milking, unless the cow got edgy and stepped in the pail and the milk had to be thrown out. But the cats liked when this happened; they'd watch that old cow, just hoping something would happen. I could almost hear them daring her to take a step forward and give them a feast. The other unpleasant part was having your face swatted by the cow's tail, but generally, milking was kind of a restful occupation.

We had sheep. Men sheared, but us womenfolk took the wool to wash, card and spin into yarn. Carding wool was right tedious, but it was pleasant to watch that raw wool spin itself into a tight thread, though it made my neck stiff to sit so long. We'd knit it into socks and scarves. Momma taught us to do all that; she could make nearly anything.

Those sheep provided wool, sheepskins, delicious mutton and tallow for candles and treating boots. We'd set tallow by the fire to melt, then rub it in to make the boots waterproof. Bob said sometimes he'd look down where his boots were and see the cat licking off tallow. That cat knew where to find the good stuff!

Pa was the strongest, finest man I ever saw, standing nearly six-foot-four in his bare feet. I thought him a giant. All us youngsters adored him, and if there ever was an honest man, he was it. Abe Lincoln might've walked fourteen miles to return a dollar, but Pa would've gone a hundred miles to return fourteen cents. Folks trusted and respected him.

He was strong but peace-loving. I reckon that's how come he was elected to court all those years. Shortly after he bought our creek farm, a kind of quarrelsome neighbor took a notion Pa'd put in a crop on land belonging to him. Everyone knew Pa would never do such a thing, but this man decided to sue Pa for his narrow strip of land connecting their properties. "If he feels that strongly, I'll just give it to him," Pa said, and did. He believed in folks getting along, thus ending the matter. When the old man died and his grandson inherited the place, Pa showed the new owner the survey and regained his property without a fuss.

Pa was raised Primitive Baptist, who believe in footwashing, but Momma was Presbyterian, so there was opportunity for discord, but they came to peaceful compromise, attending Concord Baptist Church close by. We all grew up in this church, learning the Gospel, reverence for our Creator and gratitude for living on His earth. The church was mostly the center of our lives, outside of home. I still recall those all-day singings.

Bob loved singing near as much as dinner. He hardly missed a chance to join his voice with the musically inclined, traveling over East Tennessee and northern Georgia to attend a good singing. Churches held them, and some in people's homes, too. It was a good way to meet folks our age; I liked going to them.

Pa was particular about preachers. He valued time as one's most precious possession, attending church only when an educated minister gave a worthwhile message. If he thought a preacher poor, he'd stay home and read his Bible or sermons of respected ministers. But he lived what he believed. If I hadn't with my own eyes seen Pa fulfill the command "love your enemies, do good to those that hate you," I might've considered this impossible.

One year after Pa won a seat in the court, a neighbor got sore over something—I can't recall what—and decided to run against Pa for his seat. This man canvassed the whole district, spreading rumors against Pa, who ignored him. Pa's mean-tempered opponent took in less than a half dozen votes and turned out penniless with his family in bad shape. Pa gave him a home on our farm, furnishing him with tools for cultivating. He was "heaping coals on his enemy's head" and was abiding by his creed. None of us missed the lesson.

Pa was tall by most standards, cutting a fine figure on horseback, toting his long rifle to squirrel hunt with my brothers. I tried to hoist that thing onto my shoulder once and liked to have fallen over. Pa just laughed. I reckon you have to be a long man to shoot a long rifle.

Besides fruits and vegetables, we grew oats and wheat. Back then the only way to get wheat from the field and into the thresher was cut it with a cradle—not a cradle you'd put a baby in, though they're similar shaped. The wheat cradle has long wood fingers on one end, a sharp, narrow blade inside and it's operated by a man swinging it from one side to the other, in a kind of half-circle.

It takes strength and endurance to use one. Pa could cradle wheat all day and be the only man standing at day's end. It's a beautiful thing to behold! I still see those golden, nodding fields of wheat, half cut, men swinging their cradles in the most graceful dance, knees bent, bodies turning side to side all in one sweep, wheat falling ripe beneath each stroke.

Now and then they'd stop to sharpen their blades. Pa kept a whetstone in his pocket to hone his blade, then resumed the rhythmic swinging. A wheat cradle to Pa was like a musical instrument to a great artist. He loved this work above all other, and everyone knew nobody could cradle wheat anywhere near as good. My brothers said it was because he was such a tall man, and strong, that the work tired a shorter man. I couldn't say, but he sure did look like the finest athlete standing there, his long, lean, muscular arms tanned and sweaty, dust from chaff flying around him. There was something unearthly and dreamlike about it; it was so lovely.

I'd sometimes catch Momma looking at him out the corner of her eye as she set out lunch for the men. She did admire her husband when he cradled wheat! She never spoke it, but she didn't need to. It was all over her face.

Bringing in wheat was hot, dusty work, the men working up an appetite. Us women would cook all morning, set out the biggest spread you ever saw and before you could blink, it was gone like it was hit by locusts. They'd go back to work, and we'd make another big meal at day's end.

While menfolk cut wheat down, my brothers ran after them, collecting stalks, tying them in neat little bundles. They'd stand ten bundles in a circle to form a shock of wheat, stuff two more bundles down the middle and spread out their heads to cover the tops of the first ten. That way, if it rained before it got threshed, most of the grain wouldn't get wet and rot. It also helped keep birds off.

We knew a man, Wash Brotherton, who owned a threshing machine, and he'd come to your farm with it. Farmers paid him to thresh wheat right in their own fields. My brothers sometimes rode on one of the horses that turned the thresher, and you would've thought they were at a circus.

We had other animal life on our place besides my brothers. We had pigs, goats, chickens, mules and horses too, but I wasn't much of a rider. Pa wouldn't let anyone but his oldest boys and himself ride Sharp, who had been a race horse and never got over it. He had a superior attitude and liked to kick, but Fortune was the horse we all loved. Pa taught us to ride, but I seldom went to town for things. That generally fell to my brothers.

One of our best pastimes—really a job, but we didn't know it—was collecting eggs. It was a treasure hunt, since you never knew where those foolish ducks would lay theirs. They favored the barn loft and horse stalls, but our greatest challenge was finding guinea eggs. Those crazy birds were half-wild, smart as humans. They hid their nests, so we had to be detectives. A male sentinel was always stalking around like a soldier on guard duty. If we found a nest, we'd race to the house for Momma to hand us a spoon and basket, as the scent of humans would make the hen move her nest and make us more work. We "spooned" out the eggs, leaving a few, and every year at least one old guinea would bring her troop of babies by the house, as if to say, "You weren't so smart! You missed a few!"

We weren't the only ones after those eggs. Crows flying overhead were looking just as hard. One of the funniest things I ever saw was a crow flying silently by, a guinea egg spreading his mouth wide. One caw would have cost his prize.

Momma and us girls made rough aprons from tow sacks, tied them on and sat under the trees to pluck ducks and geese for pillows. It fell to Bob to herd these birds into a fence corner or stall where us pickers could get at them. Sometimes to show appreciation, we'd let him draw out a few feathers, which he seemed to think a great honor. We never could figure out that boy's mind.

For a time, our baby brother kept a little "shop" under our hawthorn tree, leading Momma—optimist as she was—to predict that someday Bob would own a blacksmith shop. He really liked tools but seemed to have less enthusiasm for the actual application of them. Maybe he was saving his efforts for other things.

As we prospered, we cleared more fields for cultivation. Pa would kill a tree by girdling it near the bottom with his axe, then take it down after it died. But there was one old beech Pa cut into without girdling or killing. This was

W.T. Walker's initials on an old beech tree, 1998.

a beech tree standing sentry at the edge of a deep riverbank overlooking the Chickamauga, leaning out over the waters like it might be trying to get a look at its reflection. Its big, gnarled roots dug so deep in the ground, it dipped its toes in the flowing waters. It had a strong hold on the earth, had been there a long time, planning on being around a considerable while longer.

Pa liked that tree because long before the Cherokees were driven out, some unknown man named Williamson carved his name, and "1814," into its smooth white bark. This inspired Pa to cut his initials and "1880" into it too. Why he waited six years after purchasing the land to put his mark there, I can't say. Maybe he knew it wouldn't be his forever and wanted the land to remember him. Wouldn't surprise me if that beech tree was still there, preening out over Chickamauga's rolling waters.

Once Pa brought us a brand-new spring wagon he'd bought with profits from selling our crops, and we took much pride in it. It was such an improvement over our old hard-riding farm wagon that neighbors soon had it in use as a hearse to carry loved ones to their final resting places. Pa usually furnished the team, serving as driver. But he never took money for this.

If a nearby family was sick or in trouble, Pa often started an offering of food or help on their farm—whatever was needed. He had pretty good veterinary skill, too, sitting up with sick cows or horses that didn't belong to him. He wouldn't take money for this either, saying he considered it reasonable service.

Regardless of who did what, all profits went into one pot, and whatever we needed came from it. Once a year, Pa lined us all against the wall, cutting strings the same length as each child's foot. He took those strings and rode

William "Tom" Walker on Sharp.

into town on old Sharp, bringing back new brass-tipped boots and shoes for us. We'd go barefoot in summer, but when weather called for our feet to be covered, Pa made sure we didn't go without.

I reckon now our feet must've got pretty dirty, but Momma never let us in bed without washing them, no matter how cold. I recall cracking ice in the washbowl more than one winter night for water to wash my feet. Momma's rule was hard and fast. We were going to sleep on clean beds, and we did, though it was a tight squeeze to get a place in one. When my brothers had company, they'd stack crosswise in bed like cordwood. But all those extra bodies kept you warm.

After threshing, we'd drag out our mattress ticks and dump the old straw out. Pa and my brothers tossed that straw with a pitchfork into the log barn for animals to sleep on. Then we'd refill our ticks with fresh straw and drag them back into the cabin. I used to dread that work, but it did smell sweet to sleep on clean, fresh hay.

I shared a room upstairs with my sisters, not big for one, let alone three. The ceiling sloped, and you could only stand in the peak. At night, we'd lie awake if we weren't bone-tired, telling the most outlandish, frightful tales of ghosts and hobgoblins. I liked to land my half-open hand on Mary Agnes's leg and holler, "Look out for that big old spider!" She'd whoop and jump so, I wonder she didn't wake the entire household. As many times as ever I did that, she always jumped and hollered—tickled me to death.

My sisters were prettier, but Momma said I had a pleasant face, and being tall made me look healthy and strong. One thing none of us ever wanted to be was sickly. We kept the front door open nearly always, and the brick hearth fire never went out. The chimney had once been stick and mud, which Cherokees built, but had a bad habit of catching fire, so Pa replaced it with Graysville bricks.

Could be all that fresh air gave us strength to fight off fevers and sickness. We'd get ill from time to time, but it didn't stick. Except for the time Pa was overtaken with chills and fever so long that it brought him great despair—us too. It kept coming back, so he took drastic measures. There was an old Indian tale that a man suffering from fever could dip during the chills in our cold spring and be cured. The man was to wait for a fit of chills and fever to hit, then strip and plunge into the water, covering himself with it until the fit passed.

Our spring might've once been deep enough to cover an average man, but hardly one of Pa's stature. It had filled in since its curing powers were discovered, now being hardly waist-deep on Pa, sitting down. So he arranged with a neighbor, Sam Wofford, to follow him to the spring, where Pa removed his clothes and sat in its water. Sam poured ice-cold water over the rest of Pa with a gourd dipper while he sat shivering in the shallow pool.

We feared the remedy might finish him, but he said he'd just as soon meet his Maker in this fashion as be plagued by bouts of fever. We could hardly argue. From that day forward, he never suffered another chill. I reckon Indians don't make up tales the way some white folks do.

I told you my sisters were prettier. It's true, but I liked them anyway. They and Momma were my best friends. But my brother Bob liked being the baby so much that when Mary Agnes came along, he pitched a fit! He offered to help Pa take her to the Chickamauga and drown her, and he was "dead" serious! It was shocking awful how he carried on; he could see she would be his replacement in Momma's affections. Of course his fears were unfounded, and it didn't take him long to see that. He grew to love Mary as much as we did; she was so sweet.

My brothers! I loved every one of the dirty, rowdy rascals. They were always picking on each other, making some mess, pulling pranks—more often than not on me. I'll never forget putting on my shoe and finding a dead mouse in the toe. Bob said it crawled in to keep warm, and the smell killed him. Will and John pretended to know nothing, trying to act above such a trick, even suggesting the cat was the culprit. But if you live around folks long enough, you get to know their ways, how they think. I knew blamed well my brothers had done it, but they never 'fessed up!

They'd stage wars, heaving corncobs at each other till they were plumb exhausted. They'd also do it with rotten apples, peaches or anything they found as an effective missile. I don't think that speaks a whole lot for their creative thinking, and they might still do such things, for all I know.

My brothers could be wild but never destructive. Pa wouldn't let his boys turn out like that. The only reckless thing we knew of back then was Christmas Eve, when some neighbors would take our wagon apart and hide the pieces in different parts of the yard. I can't for the life of me understand what would compel grown men to do such a thing, and on the night of our Lord's birth! But they did! Pa and my brothers spent most of Christmas Day locating and reassembling our wagon. Once it was on the barn roof. I reckon it was a kind of tradition, not a very joyful one.

We hung our stockings the night before, examining them in early morning, enjoying nuts and oranges together. Then my brothers would go outside and set off firecrackers Pa gave them. That was our joyful tradition, and not even a dismantled wagon could spoil it.

Before Mackie School was built, we attended Mrs. Thornbury's subscription school, where I managed to learn reading and writing. It was not inspiring and, for Bob, was sheer torture. We met in a log house with one room, backless benches, no desks and no heat. Sometimes bench legs hit a tilt in the floor, sending whoever was on it over backward. We made ink from oak galls and pokeberries and studied our lessons out loud. That was the worst conglomeration of voices you ever heard, more raucous than a springtime frog pond. Bob was four when he started with the rest of us, and he hated it!

An old sow lived on the property, and at recess she'd slip in and help herself to our lunches. She was especially fond of fried chicken sandwiches and quince preserves, and I had to quiet Bob when she took his, though she'd gotten mine too. One day Will and his friend John Martin barred themselves and the sow in the room and took after her with brooms. Such a racket of squealing pig and broom handle strokes! John Martin got a V-shaped mark on his foot where the sow stepped on him, but she never troubled us again.

When Pa purchased the Thornburys' farm and home, it shut its doors as a learning institution. They moved to Gabriel Mills, Texas, asking Pa to follow. The idea of riding a horse while cultivating tempted him, but he chose to stay.

Two years later, we and sixty others were at Mackie School. Rules were strict; if a boy was caught chewing sweetgum wax, he had to drop the wad on the floor, roll it in dust, then chew it some more. It liked to have made me sick.

Twenty years had passed since the Great War, our community composed of veterans' families of both sides. Many fought in the Battle of Chickamauga, on Lookout Mountain and Missionary Ridge. When General Bragg retreated, his army followed the road by our home, and us kids used to hunt their cast-off ammunition.

Most folks had given up taking sides, but boy students organized themselves into Union and Confederate armies, battling over Mackie School grounds with popguns from hollowed bamboo growing along the creek. My brothers were among those gallant soldiers—wouldn't have missed it—Union, of course. They used dogwood berries and hog hawthorn fruit for bullets. I got hit with one, which stung like the mischief! When there weren't berries, they'd resort to nasty wads of chewed-up paper for bullets. I could hardly stand it! Handkerchiefs were flags, colored to represent whichever army they were leading. When not playing "hull-gull," "bull pen," "one-eyed cat" or "dare," they were in daily military conflict.

We picked pawpaws and muscadines along Tsula Creek, gathering hickory nuts with hulls so thin we cracked them with our teeth. Later, at Walnut Grove, we had modern desks with fold-down tops. Like squirrels, we'd store nuts in there.

Beechnuts were good too, but their shells were so tough, they went a-begging, but we collected persimmons, black haws and chestnuts. Later on we gathered black walnuts and butternuts, which we busted with rocks.

Some Mackie School students were as old as twenty. John, eight, accepted it as his lot in life, but Bob, two years younger, despised school so that one morning he took his speller behind Momma's cookstove, sat down and flipped through his entire book. Bob announced he'd completed it all, making it unnecessary to ever go back to school. Momma always did think Bob a little different, so she let him stay home a while.

Later she started for church, perching him behind on her sidesaddle. At Mackie School, Mollie Davidson and Josie Julian lifted him off her horse, and Bob suddenly found a new reason to go to school. I reckon things haven't much changed with him, even now.

When Bob was ten, Pa bought an old square piano, engaging a music teacher, Miss Sally Taylor, to live at our home while she taught us girls music. Bob decided he wanted to play too, so Pa offered him and the boys an opportunity for lessons. Bob was coming along pretty good, practicing mornings before he left for school. Our teacher took an interest in him until his only earthly possession, an old razorback sow, took to killing chickens.

Pa ordered Bob to pen her up, and the best that boy could do was chop down some little trees near our house and build a rough log pen. Soon that sow had scraped mud and manure all over, creating such a nuisance it got all over Bob when he fed her.

After this delightful addition, one morning I noticed Miss Taylor at our piano, using one hand to point the route for Bob's hands to tread the keys, closing up her nostrils with the other. Bob was further humiliated when she sent him a message by way of myself that she could not continue lessons until he disposed of his ill-smelling hog. Music prevailed over the razorback, and Bob got to where he could play pretty good.

Our closest neighbors, the Woods, had a very fine organ. Their log cabin was across the tracks, facing ours directly. They were a Negro family, and Pa thought highly of them. Sometimes my brothers, who fancied themselves singers, would join in a hymn singing with Mr. Woods's sons. Bob, who learned to knock out a tune on our piano without hitting too many sour notes, much admired Lindsey Woods, their oldest, who played the organ unusually well but all by ear.

Momma and I would hear their voices lifting those old hymns, and it would come carried by the wind, drifting back to us on our porch, and we thought that music as heavenly as any we could hear. I think about that now and then, and sometimes if I listen real close, I can still hear their strong, young voices all blending into sweet harmony, passing like a whispering breeze through the treetops of the land I loved so well.

Pa's family never kept slaves. He was proud of that, telling us how Tennessee was divided on that issue during the Great War. East Tennessee, particularly much of Hawkins County, hadn't held with Secession. Pa's older brothers John and Preston enlisted in the Federal army, leaving Pa and his younger brother, Gabriel, to run things at home. Lots of Hawkins County families had great- and great-great-grandfathers who'd fought in the Revolution, so they took a dim view of dividing the country their ancestors had maybe died trying to bring into being. Pa's family believed in a united country, and although Pa was conservative in many views, his beliefs were strong about this.

He had less than four months' schooling, the Civil War interrupting everything. But he took up studying law at night after we all came along. He gained the habit of reading and subscribed to a newspaper and two magazines, *Zion's Landmark*, a Primitive Baptist journal, and *The Independent*. He read the Bible and newspaper aloud so we could all benefit from it. In this manner, he eventually studied law at home between planting corn and digging potatoes.

Pa became so proficient, he was offered to practice law in Chattanooga, which he declined. He set us a good example about getting educated, and every last one of us finished school.

He trusted us too, and because of his confidence we told the truth. If any of us got a switching at school, we knew to expect another at home. Bob got one once, but that's the only time I recall him getting switched. Pa disciplined himself the same as us, and when he decided the tobacco habit was bad for his health, he quickly put it down.

He knew our beautiful woods along the creek were a hangout for fever at certain times and had his eye on nearby land with a bigger log house. Around 1884, he bought it but kept our creek farm for its good land. We moved into the new place a while, where he believed the air was healthier. It was a twin sort of structure, connected by a dogtrot. I'm not complaining, but that house was so cold, we could watch the wind whistle through the log chinking, and at night Bob stuffed his trousers in the cracks. Both chimneys were stick and mud, and I would dread to light them, for fear of burning down the place!

But in 1899 we moved into a new home, weather-boarded with tulip poplar and ceiled with yellow pine. By then, we were a family of nine, Chess being the first born in the new house. Two years later Charlie was born, so we made good use of our big house. Soon after we moved from our drafty double house, the county took it over as a workhouse for prison road crews.

Sometimes the county workhouse furnished lively amusement for my brothers. Bloodhounds were kept to discourage prisoners escaping, and sometimes trustees were sent out on make-believe escapes to train new dogs. Guards asked Bob and a friend, Frank Crabtree, to tramp on foot three miles one night to give the dogs practice. After they left my sight, I could hear one old hound baying in the distance. When Bob got home, he looked pale and bad, saying when he and Frank heard dogs coming, they dropped their lantern and scrambled up two saplings. Bob's was too slender for his weight, and it bent over twice and set him on the ground before they found a sturdier sweetgum tree. The dogs overtook them, leaping and barking like they wanted to gnaw it off at the ground.

We still worked our creek farm, but once we were gone, the old cabin began to look forlorn, like it missed our family. But leaving it was the right thing to do, for back in '72, Chattanooga was hit with yellow fever, killing many. Even so, part of me didn't want to leave—I'd been born in that cabin; it was hard to let go.

I haven't told how my brothers liked to have burned up our new wagon. It started when Pa sent John and Bob into town for a load of hogs. As they left, I handed them the coal oil can, which they took, promising to fill it, and off they went in our wagon with our feisty little dog, Huse, and a couple of smug grins. Big boys, off to the big city in a fancy new wagon—know what I mean?

I don't know when they got back, for it was dark and late. I heard a commotion but had been fast asleep, as were my sisters, and none of us cared enough to rise and say, "Well, I see you finally got home."

Next morning, their smug grins were nowhere to be found, and they seemed quite chastened. They'd gotten Pa's hogs, for we could hear them snuffling in the back lot. But my coal oil can was as empty as when I gave it to them. I was going to inquire about this when I caught sight of the wagon bed. Hogs will make a pretty big mess, but I've never known them to scorch something, for far as I know, hogs don't carry matches. But our wagon bed was smartly singed, smelling strong of smoke and fumes. Then I figured out what had become of my coal oil.

I reckon the boys told Pa soon as he was up, and it filtered down to me of how they'd spilled oil all over the wagon bed. Once they unloaded the hogs and saw the mess, one of them got the bright idea of burning off the oil. I've only got one brother whose mind stays on lofty things so much, he'd figure this for a good solution—but I'm not naming names. They actually lit it, but it didn't take long to realize they'd burn up the entire wagon, along with the problem, if they didn't do something fast. So like the big heroes my little brothers are, they stripped off their coats to beat out the flames, destroying their only coats in the process.

Sometimes I think young men just haven't got their thinking processes in order as well as women. Neither would admit whose idea burning off the spill was, but I know any boy who will break an arm falling out of a post oak tree to look at a bird nest will take other chances.

That's what Bob was famous for in our family. He loved anything that flew, hopped, creeped, crawled, swam, wiggled or grew out of the ground. Sometimes we wondered if he'd ever amount to much, and once or twice he was even accused of being lazy. But he couldn't help himself. He was just fascinated by living things, and I know how it sounds, to say I have a brother who loved plants, but it's true. I've even caught him talking to them, like they could hear and maybe was going to answer. It was kind of interesting, some of the things he would tell. But I never did see a lot of use coming from it.

Momma thought different. She knew he was not much like us and didn't seem to mind. I think she loved him all the more for it. Whatever she thought he was going to do, only she and God and maybe Pa knew, but she never discouraged him. I think deep down, she knew Bob would never make much of a farmer and hoped he'd find another direction to take off in.

It liked to have killed us when Momma died. Lizzie had recently got married to John Davidson. Momma was visiting them and took sick when she got home. For two weeks, she got worse and worse. One day we were told not to go to school.

All of us gathered to bid her goodbye. Pa was bent over her when we came into the room. He lifted Charlie, four, to kiss her; next came Chess, then Mary, John, me, Will and Lizzie. We had little to say to each other that day, except what was needful.

Neighbors arrived on foot, in buggies and others on horseback to do what they could. Around ten that morning, Mr. Lowe came in—walking three miles to get there. He said at breakfast he told his family something was wrong at the Walkers and he had to find out.

It hit Bob especially hard. He'd been messing with his string of tobacco tags from the workhouse prisoners. Mrs. Jasper Davidson had tended Momma, and she called us all in to see her at the last. Bob's face was the most sorrowful I ever saw. When he saw she was gone, he would not be comforted, though he was a big boy of twelve. He stayed by her side with his head down, not saying a word.

Pa crouched his tall self down to look into Bob's face and spoke something to him—I never did know what—then they left the room together, coming back with Momma's scissors. Pa snipped off a lock of her hair and handed it to Bob. He stuck it in his shirt pocket over his heart, and we managed to get through her sorrowful burial.

We weren't in our new home long when Momma died. With the log house on the property now housing prisoners, the county was converting the old corduroy road to town into a modern one. It was a community's duty to furnish a dwelling for working prisoners. Most had been arrested for trivial offenses like riding on freights or trespassing on railroad tracks. That seemed unfair, and I didn't care who knew it. Momma'd taken pity, baking cobblers and pies for them, knowing they were only furnished with fat meat, coffee, corn bread, cabbage, potatoes, canned tomatoes and tobacco.

They weren't bad neighbors. One of them, Frank Mundstalk, a German, was so gentlemanly that our neighbor Reverend Stephenson paid his fine and took him home to give him a second chance. The night of Momma's passing, while neighbors sat with her body and sang hymns over her, we could hear the voice of Frank Mundstalk singing in broken English "Jesus Will Give You Rest." Those prisoners grieved over her loss nearly as much as us.

It was a fever that took her, in spite of Pa's best efforts. But we believed the Lord knew best and had to trust Him to work things out. It would be hard with no Momma to care for these young'uns. Mary and me did our best to fill her shoes. With Lizzie married, I was now the oldest woman at home, so most of Momma's responsibilities fell to me. I tried to carry on in a way I hoped she'd approve.

Pa was lonesome. Sometimes I'd catch him gazing off in the distance, not fixed on anything, and I knew he was thinking of Momma. Shortly after she died, he left off farming a season or two, taking a job with a Mr. Johnson, buying and selling sheep. They had agents back in the northern Georgia mountains who bought sheep from farmers, rounded them up and met up with Pa and Mr. Johnson, who'd herd the sheep into Chattanooga. Pa had a faithful employee named Shep the dog who understood orders better than most humans.

This new occupation kept him away a lot, but he did not leave us alone. Will and I were ready to take charge, but Pa felt better with a grown woman caring for his children. He hired Mrs. Kitty Thompson to keep house. She held the place together, with Mary and me helping. She also had Lottie, a baby girl so tiny and doll-like, she hung the child on the wall by fastening her clothes with a nail. It kept her out of mischief, and she could see what was going on. My brothers found this living decoration fascinating.

A year after Momma passed, Pa quit sheep-herding and took a position as county road supervisor in 1893. This led him to oversee construction of the four-mile road up Walden's Ridge, terminating in the shape of a W at Fairmount. Even though the land was surveyed by Mark Long, Pa did his own survey, making improvements over the original. October 11, 1893, with work nearly done, Pa was honored with an inscribed gold watch at a ceremony. Fairmount folks planned to carve a bust of him at the top of the road, but this was never done.

Pa remained a widower for four years till one day, shortly after completing the W Road, he married again, a fine woman, Miss Annie Pickett. She might not have been our real Momma, but she filled a great empty space. We grew to think the world of her. She and Pa even had us a few more brothers and sisters, but I'm getting ahead of myself.

Bob grew to love our new Momma, though he never seemed to entirely get over losing his own. He wrote little verses to her and would talk about things she did, but never in a mean way to make Pa's new wife feel bad. Bob could appreciate everybody for who they were and didn't compare folks, which I guess is a real tribute to Pa's choice for a second wife. So Bob, like the rest of us, found room in his heart for both.

Folks say if you want something bad enough, you might get it, and there came a day I boarded that train that had so long teased me. Will married a nice girl, Hattie Dorsey, and they moved to Atlanta. When their son Avary was born, they wrote asking Pa to let me and my two brothers come down to the big exposition there. I liked to have died waiting for Pa's answer, but when he agreed, we were on our way!

If I hadn't gone, my brothers would have been out of luck, as Pa was unlikely to trust those two anywhere after their hogs-and-wagon caper. But I was keen to see a new place, so the idea of shepherding them didn't faze me. I would have consented to keep charge over a pair of live alligators to make the journey. Come to think of it, there wouldn't be much difference—'gators would likely have been less trouble.

I was seated at the window when the train shook and pulled away in a din of steam and rattle. As we passed through little towns and crossings, young children ran out to wave, and I saw myself in their curious, hopeful faces. Now I was riding a train to a big city, dressed in my best, seeing things I'd never seen—even the capers of my two companions could not spoil it!

We got to Atlanta around ten that morning, and such a great, bustling, noisy place I never saw! I was grateful for Will's face in the crowd. He took us to his home where we met our young nephew, Avary. Then Will took us to the great exposition, full of sights and smells and sounds I will never forget. After the first day, Will decided I could take my brothers without him. I think we plumb wore him out. So we returned, and Bob did look cute with a little basket on his arm, collecting literature and pretty cards they gave out.

Those boys were good as gold, and I got to thinking I'd been wrong about them. I no sooner thought that when Bob let out a whoop and jumped three feet, sending his papers flying. I finally got it out of him that as he signed his name on a register, a huge wolf spider landed on his hand. At that point, John, laughing so hard he couldn't speak, pointed overhead to a man standing on a second-floor walkway above. He had a big rubber spider dangling off a string, dropping the thing onto unsuspecting folks below.

Bob was real embarrassed—but then it was sort of funny, and maybe he'd earned the shock of it. (I had recently found another deceased mouse in my shoe, and as usual, nobody would own up.)

We stayed another night with Will and Hattie, and I never saw so much food. They had fish eggs, which Bob said were the best he'd ever eaten. We were proud of Will, but it was good to get home to the country after all that city racket.

Let me say Bob was a hard worker and didn't sit idle. But when Pa talked of crops, Bob's questions would be something like, "What kind of birds is that likely to draw?" Pa'd answer best he could, but he'd eye Bob like he was trying to figure how this boy's mind was working. Bob seemed less interested in the process and results of farming than what dwelt or traveled on its perimeters.

Pa kept books for us, but my other brothers were likely to spend free time hunting or fishing or tormenting each other. Bob did these things too, but he also read a lot.

We were fascinated by relics that turned up in what we called the "Indian Field," across the Chickamauga. We plowed up near-perfect bowls, beads and arrow points—some bones too, which we buried again with a reverence, for we didn't feel right disturbing the dead. But other objects were such wonders, some so beautiful, we kept them to admire. Shortly after buying the creek farm, Pa turned up a complete set of heavy shell beads with an unusual big carved shell, all engraved with a snake design we'd never seen the likes of. There was also a pair of thick shell ear-posts, and it puzzled me how anyone would wear those things, unless they stopped up their ears with them.

We finally realized the field had been a graveyard from hundreds of years past, and while we hadn't meant to disturb their rest, it was just that we farmed that field, and whatever the plow turned up, it turned up. Later on my brothers made a hobby of collecting axes and spear points, which they found washed up on top of the soil after a good rain.

It just made me remember all the more those Cherokee families who had gone before us and that we were, just as they had been, merely tenants on this land. None of us ever really owns anything. Sometimes I wonder if some farmer, hundreds of years from now, will plow up my bones and wonder who I was. Maybe he will keep my relics in a safe place and regard them with awe and respect. I don't know, but I think about that sometimes. Life is short, you know.

I used to want to marry as strong and wise a man as my pa. Momma said if I made good soap, lived by the Good Book, kept myself neat and clean and spoke quietly, I would find such a man, she was sure. She could have been right. I could see myself turning into a fine young woman. My skin was smooth, of a healthy, rosy hue. Momma called it my best feature. I washed my hair often in rainwater, sewed well and all my clothes fitted neatly. I stood straight and didn't slouch to hide the fact that I was tall. Momma said I must never do that, as it would make me look cowardly. In summer heat, I carried a turkey wing fan to stir up a breeze. When all us womenfolk got to flapping those things, it sounded like a woods full of wild turkeys. Momma made us all bonnets, teaching me to make them too. The church was full of women wearing bonnets of all different colors, and when Bob was little, he paid unusual attention to them. We tried to keep him from staring at folks.

Momma made it a point to stick Bob next to her in church, like he was an extra arm or leg. One of our neighbors was preaching once, got "happy" and went shaking hands with everyone, most of who started to cry. The look on Bob's face plainly told that he could not fathom any of this. He whispered that the reverend was pinching hands hard enough to make them cry! As the preacher passed in front of him, Bob jumped straight up, shoved both hands under himself and sat on them until the man was a safe distance away. I liked to have strangled trying not to laugh. Momma just yanked him closer and tugged his hands back onto his lap.

Once or twice in church I noticed a few young men looking at me. I even held conversation with a few, and they were most pleasant. They were nothing like my brothers, who, even long after they were old enough to know better, left things like old cheese under my pillow and hid my combs where the Almighty himself could hardly find them.

I was happy then. I could see everything Momma told me was going to be true. I worked hard but saw myself moving in another direction. I was going to be a teacher at Morris Hill. That was a good profession for a young woman, and it interested me.

I can't say why I went out riding the day after Christmas toward Morris Hill with friends, Mr. and Mrs. James Burns. He was in charge of the school. It was a crisp, cold afternoon, but a winter sun was shining in a white sky overhead. I heard birds crying in the trees above and thought about Bob—likely he could've told what each one was. I had a jacket over my plaid shirtwaist, but I was shivering, and when Mr. Burns climbed into the buggy seat and got his old horse moving, I was wishing for a wool blanket.

We weren't talking a lot that afternoon. Mrs. Burns said she thought it might rain, but I didn't think so, the sky was too white. Maybe it would snow. I was leaning back, studying those clouds, wondering was she right.

Mr. Burns hied Old Moe into a frisky pace, almost a gallop. I leaned back a bit more, holding on with both hands to the board seat, watching thin white puffs of low clouds drifting like solitary bolls of cotton. They were so transparent against the cream-colored heavens I could nearly see through them. The air was blowing against me, fragrant and sweet, cooling me more, then all of a sudden I couldn't feel the cold, and I didn't mind. I was just studying those clouds, thinking how soft they would feel against my skin. We traveled down the road a while—maybe ten minutes or more without talking, Mr. Burns driving his crazy old horse with Mrs. Burns next to him, me behind them, leaning back against nothing at all, drawing in the sky with my eyes.

It didn't take a second. I never did know what spooked Old Moe so bad he took off like he did, but he no sooner lit out like our buggy was on fire than it hit a deep pothole and flipped. I flew out backward, and Mr. and Mrs. Burns fell off too, though they weren't much hurt. Somewhere down the road they caught up to that fool Moe, still hauling the empty buggy on its side like he had somewhere to go.

It happened quick. One minute I was speeding down the road and the next I was flying through the air—then everything was absolutely still. Nothing was moving—not the sky, or the branches, or me. If anybody said anything, I don't recall it. They might have.

I reckon I knew then that was all there was going to be, maybe in the way a candle knows it's going out just before the light in it dies. It didn't hurt. I did think for one quick moment about my family, how I wouldn't see them again—not until that Great Day when we're all reunited. I wasn't scared.

Goodnight, folks. I love you all. See you in the morning. That was what I thought. That's about it. Now it's still and quiet, like it is up on the hill where our old cabin still stands. It's quiet and peaceful, and Momma and me are getting a good rest. It never occurred to us back then how hard we all worked just to stay alive. I reckon being alive will always be hard work, but it's good to rest now. I know we'll get together again one of these days and have us a big family reunion, one to last forever.

DBW, 1902

Chapter 2

ROBERT SPARKS WALKER, 1899–1903

CHICKAMAUGA, TENNESSEE, JANUARY 1, 1899

This year, Bob Walker began a journal recording his social activities and farm work. He complained of struggling with geometry, though he would soon receive his diploma from Walnut Grove School.

His father, by studying later in life, had shown that a man should never stop learning. Yet Bob nurtured a private dream, encouraged by his late mother, to write books that would benefit mankind. In pursuing success, Bob hoped to honor her faith in him. He was, he reminded himself, a good farmer's son who knew to wait patiently for a good crop. Work often interrupted Bob's education. For income, he taught school at Morris Hill, James County, from July through October 1898 before resuming duties at home.

Bob's family still farmed the Chickamauga land and fished the creek, hunting small game—squirrels, 'possums, birds—to supply meat for the table. He celebrated his twenty-first birthday on February 4, 1899, parching corn around the hearth at his father's home, where he lived.

Even in the severely cold winter, Bob was incurably optimistic. He constructed puzzles, which he sold to the *Toledo Blade*, paying for his subscription and leaving a little extra. He had been selling his writing to *Home and Farm* and the *Toledo Blade* since he was twelve, both he and his brother John saving to buy land on Missionary Ridge.

Walnut Grove School graduates, with Walker in the center, 1899.

Bob frequently rode their old mule or a horse to the store in Whorley to visit and learn the latest news. He described hauling firewood with his younger brother Chester (Chess), who suffered from diabetes.

March produced heavy rains, worse than the 1886 flooding, with waters up to the wagon beds. The Walkers blockaded roads to prevent accidents.

Bob and R.G. Davidson celebrated his graduation by driving to Varnell, Georgia, where Bob visited Miss Annie Bare. His labors for his father prevented any more immediate visits, as he was locally engaged in plowing, planting corn with a drill and making hills of cucumbers, squash and watermelons, all before procuring fertilizer in Chattanooga, splitting firewood and hauling loads of tombstone—an exhausting schedule.

Rains washed out many crops that had to be replanted, further curtailing Bob's social life. He stated that April had flown by as if it had wings, though he felt more that it had sore feet from all the plowing. He finally attended a few ice cream socials as breaks from his labors, escorting local young ladies. Then he joined brothers and friends in a fishing expedition at the Chickamauga but afterward spent a day at

Thomasson's blacksmith shop and bound wheat, which he described as "mighty warm business."

Bob's active social life was taking second place to his need for an occupation. He had graduated but hoped for higher education. To fund his aspirations, he again taught at Morris Hill and accepted a temporary job as a census taker. When both jobs ended, Bob was again seeking work.

He was the fifth child born to William Thomas and Mary Elizabeth Moore Walker. His siblings were Sarah Elizabeth (Lizzie), born 1868; William, born 1870; Dona Bell, born 1874; John Samuel, born 1875; Mary Agnes, born 1881; and Thomas Chester (Chess), born 1884. Following Tom Walker's second marriage to Annie Pickett, Bob would gain four half siblings: Martha, born 1895; Theodore, born 1901; Wilder, born 1903; and Marion Gabriel, born 1905. Thus, Bob was seldom at the mercy of solitude.

The Walker family frequently assisted burials at Concord Church. It had long been the custom to toll the church bell at the death of a member. Bob's father would dispatch two of his sons, armed with pick and shovel, to Concord cemetery to assist in digging the grave, Bob and his brother John having dug more than one. If the death was in a poor family, church men made a heart-pine, walnut or cedar coffin, while another family would furnish a wagon and team of horses. Tom Walker often offered his wagon as a hearse.

In June, Bob took a trip with friends to Asheville, North Carolina, via Southern Railway. He returned with a souvenir tintype to commemorate the journey, but a wreck on the tracks at Hot Springs stranded them for several hours.

His interest in Annie Bare continued, and he made occasional journeys to Varnell via bicycle. They corresponded and attended numerous "sings" together at churches in northern Georgia and the Chattanooga area. Bob enjoyed the company of other young ladies, though he seemed for a time to prefer Annie Bare.

He constantly worked his father's farm, plowing corn, threshing wheat and whitewashing a well-house with lime from Graysville, which he described as "very corrosive work."

In August, he again taught at Morris Hill, bringing a big brass hand bell, which John once used in teaching there; several of the Walker siblings had held this position. One night Bob was awakened by a neighbor, Ira Denton, who told Bob he had just shot a burglar—but the burglar turned out to be Frank Denton, so Bob went back to sleep.

Letters between Bob and Miss Bare became more serious, the young woman's mother suggesting Annie might be "lovesick." Bob sent her a poem but "encumbered himself" registering legal voters at Chickamauga, where he slept in the Whorley store and clerked a few hours to pay for board. Mission accomplished, he returned to teaching at Morris Hill.

He reflected on his 1897 visit to Hawkins County. At seventeen, with Tom's consent, he had taken the Southern Railway's vestibule train to Otes, bringing a new hat to his grandfather, Edward Walker, purchased by his father. Bob found the old man lonely, though he was living with his son Preston and wife, Ellen.

Bob's secret intentions were to see a young lady there, but he found she had been called away. Undaunted, he spent time with his uncle, Lieutenant John Walker, and Grigsby cousins. (Both Preston and John were Union veterans.) He described an uneasy night with Joe and Laura Julian Grigsby, who owned a store in White Horn.

The Grigsbys had another guest that night, Methodist circuit rider Brother Bandy. For some reason, preachers scared Bob then, and this one was unique in that he had a perfectly round nose, "prominent as a shucked ear of corn," unfortunately drawing everyone's attention to it. Bob was later told that while Bandy was once a guest in another family's home, the housewife unconsciously inquired as she poured coffee, "Brother Bandy, will you have cream and sugar in your nose?"

To Bob's horror, Laura informed him he would share the bed with the preacher. Bob felt like Daniel in the lions' den, though both slept soundly, side by side. He returned home on the train route through Nashville, the fare being cheaper than direct fare to Chattanooga, though both cities were quarantined against yellow fever in Louisiana and Mississippi, requiring a health certificate to get through.

Bob's schoolmaster career ended in November. He began studying for the Civil Service Examination by mail but had to take on a more immediate line of work: transporting prisoners. He spent Thanksgiving escorting them from the county jail to Mill City. His father, chairman of the workhouse commission, helped secure his position, but Bob referred to the job with distaste, even years later.

He spent the night in the workhouse but had never carried or fired a pistol and now "toted several pairs of handcuffs and a big revolver by my side." A Negro drove the wagon team of handsome gray horses. In making sure no one escaped, Bob sometimes put handcuffs on too tight and had to unlock and loosen them.

He recalled his father telling of a time when he was guarding a man arrested for murdering another on a ship at the docks. The miscreant offered

Tom forty dollars to let him go but had chosen the wrong man to bribe and remained in custody.

(In several instances, fine details of events described in Walker's early journals reappear in later ones, with incidents reported in considerably more detail.)

He spent Christmas Eve in the workhouse, attending an early fireworks display before dawn with a friend. He described driving to and from jails and reformatories all month with his charges in cold and miserable weather.

Bob escorted several ladies to more parties, but having earned enough for a semester at Maryville College, he set off to follow his dream of higher education.

1900

On January 1, Bob took his trunk to the depot and boarded the "hoodoo" for Chattanooga. Then he collected his pay at the jail and went directly to the Central Depot, bid friends goodbye and left for college in Maryville, Tennessee.

Maryville was a new world for Bob. He met new friends, giving his new address as 38 Memorial Hall. He reported twelve Negro students in his Latin class and no one objecting to their presence.

He studied in Laurar Library and attended YMCA meetings in the gymnasium. He met a Mr. Wright, a professional boxer preparing for the ministry. Bob challenged him to a wrestling match, and the fellow readily accepted, inviting ten boys and girls to attend. The match took place in Bob's room, where Bob accidentally hit Wright with such a forceful blow that he almost knocked him out a window. In the end, Wright gave him a thorough walloping, and Bob vowed never to challenge another professional boxer to a contest.

He began to use his full middle name after a bookkeeper at a horse stable named Robert S. Walker received Bob's private love letters, read them and shared them with his Latin teacher. So "Sparks" it was from that day forward.

Bob was a good student, enjoying the camaraderie of friends, but he ran out of funds, requiring him once again to find work. He regretted leaving school but applied for the position of mail weigher with the Railway Mail, which was to begin in spring. Once he was hired, he learned the job would begin in mid-February. Walker hated leaving school, always fondly describing his time at Maryville College.

Bob tackled his new career with zeal. The train ran to Atlanta, where he attended church at Second Baptist, though he did not like working on Sundays.

He still corresponded with Annie Bare, who addressed her letters "Mail Weigher, on Trains #70 and #71." It amused him to receive her letters so shortly after she posted them. But Annie began needling him about another young woman who had been introduced to her as a "loved one" of his.

Bob earned three dollars per day, all profit, since he lived on the car, keeping his trunk of clothes there and borrowing blankets and pillows from the crew. Wednesday nights, passing through Worley, he threw his old clothes to John, who took them home for washing. John then took Bob's clean clothes in a tow sack to the mail catcher, and the engineer would blow a short whistle blast to let Bob know his things were hanging so he could grab them.

But the job lasted less than two months. Later journals recount several amusing incidents that precipitated his decision to end this career.

The engineer, John Welch, liked to race the long passenger trains to Cincinnati. His first day of work, Bob was obliged to reach across the rails while both trains were moving at more than a mile a minute and, as a show of sportsmanship, shake hands with the other engineer and crew. Such excitement! Walker congratulated Welch for running a splendid race without jumping the tracks. But he never forgot the thrill when Welch permitted the fireman and Bob to pull the train a few miles up to a siding for an approaching train to pass. These races out of Chattanooga continued until railroad officials, recognizing they could not change human nature, instead changed train schedules, putting an end to this dangerous sport.

In pitching out mail, Bob was not always a dead shot. One small depot below Kingston had a post office known as Cave. The train never checked its speed when passing it, and after throwing out the mail pouch high in the air as they flew past, Bob often saw it lodge on the depot roof. It was a predictable, comical spectacle to witness the postmaster dragging a ladder to climb atop the depot and get his morning mail. While Bob had fun sending him to the depot roof, the postmaster schemed to get even.

One dark evening, Bob's train headed north, with Cave the last postal station where pouches were exchanged by use of mail grabs. There were so many whistles blown for so many crossings and flag stations that Bob became hopelessly confused as to their whereabouts, though instinct said they were somewhere near Cave. In the dark, smoke obscuring everything, he lifted the mail grab, felt his cap blow off and heard a tremendous crash. Bob caught the pouch, but the handle of the catcher broke off like a broom straw. The mail bag should have been thrown out when he brought in the pouch, a hundred yards before this spot, but he had let it go the moment of the crash. As the train rumbled over the bridge, Bob realized he had tossed the mail pouch into the creek below.

The next morning, he was relieved to see the pouch hanging on the crane, but pulling it into the train, he found it completely water-soaked. The Cave postmaster described seeing a bareheaded clerk throw something into the air but found no pouch. So late that night, the postmaster took a lantern and rowed a canoe down the creek, where he found the pouch containing mail for postal patrons of Cave lodged on a log. After drying letters before the fire, he made out addresses. Bob's reply was to suggest the mail crane be moved one hundred yards away from the creek bank.

Once, a plowboy astride a mule pulled an envelope from his pocket and sailed it into the open door of the mail car as it sped past. "This spirit of determination makes great men," said Walker.

He was equally determined not to be run over by the heavy mail scales mounted on four wheels kept in the car, a menace to all in their vicinity. The curves and grades on Western and Atlantic tracks shook it loose, so it would run wild in the car. Bob often caught the thing as it neared the open car door, about to leap the embankment below. On one raging rampage, it rammed its strong arm through the car's glass door and strewed broken pieces along the tracks as the train sped through a farm.

One mail clerk came on duty under the influence of intoxicants. Every time he stooped to place a label on a mail pouch, he pitched headlong into the sack. Ultimately, he crawled on all fours to the back of the car, disappearing among the hanging sacks of mail. After an hour in obscurity, he emerged, grabbed a wooden stool and threatened to kill everyone on the car except Bob, whom he declared was his only friend. But then he decided he might as well make a complete job of it and kill Bob too. A muscular clerk wrestled the stool away, and when the train reached Atlanta, he was docile as a lamb.

One evening, Bob was tossing heavy bundles at long range, practicing direct hits in open pouches, and was acquiring considerable skill. A surly mail inspector was sitting on a stool in the section where Bob was tossing trans-Pacific mail into a box directly above his head. An ugly frown enveloped the face of another clerk working with Bob, and he beckoned him aside.

"If you throw anymore heavy packages into that box, we'll both be fired, because I've got a quart of whiskey hidden there, and if you break it, the inspector will get soaked," he hissed. Bob was thereafter more gentle with mail for residents of India, China and Japan.

April 23 marked his last trip on the Railway Mail, and if his experience with the mail pouch at Cave had anything to do with his resignation, nothing was ever recorded. He afterward resumed his city workhouse job, was back at work on Tom's farm and again registered voters in Chickamauga.

In May, Annie Bare came to town, and Bob escorted her to the Flower Parade and Dewey Park. Bob's friend H.H. Brown wrote to him from Maryville. Bob was never short on friends but always short of funds, signing on to take the census again. His cousin Albert Walker, son of Tom's youngest brother Gabriel, moved to MacGregor, Texas. Gabriel had recently moved his family there to raise cotton. This would not end favorably, as letters revealed, and they eventually returned to Chattanooga. A letter to Bob from his cousin Lula reveals their despair.

> *McGregor, Texas, October 8, 1900*
> *I have been very busy the past four or five weeks helping Pa pick cotton. We picked five bales then Pa sold the remainder of his crop in the field. We could not get help—and Pa, Vannie and I could not do so very much good picking. So we thought it best to sell it rather than let it waste. You may believe I am not sorry either for I just fairly <u>hate</u> cotton picking.*

Bob voted for the first time on May 29, then spent June filling census books. He was glad to complete them and return to work his father's farm. A letter from Annie Bare said she had fallen down the basement steps. She further declined to write her ideas regarding their future, saying it would be too lengthy, then referred to a button of hers that she had given Bob. He decided to send it back. The old custom of trading buttons or favors between sweethearts may have been what was going on here. Bob apparently remained undaunted by what appears to be a breakup. He could not know he was on the brink of two life-changing encounters.

In July, he spent time with his sister Mary's friend Bert (Elberta) Clark, taking her on an evening boat ride on the Chickamauga. Later, he escorted Mollie Wofford to Crawfish Springs, but before leaving for Canada, he again called on Bert Clark in Highland Park.

He spent Election Day watching the returns elect his father to the court again by seventy-four votes. He then prepared to leave for Toronto and Niagara with friends Haden Scott and R.S. Mulkey.

On returning home, a dramatic encounter with publisher Elwood Mattson stabilized Bob's wanderings, settling him in the field to which he had always aspired. He would become a newspaper editor and hold this position for nineteen years.

On August 25, Bob wrote in his journal:

> *Eureka! Today, I am a newspaperman! Elwood Mattson and I have gone into business, he supplying most of the capital. We are partners in an agricultural publication, the* Southern Fruit and Truck Grower. *To raise revenue, we sell advertising, and I am elected business manager... When Mattson first proposed buying half-interest in his paper for $250 last spring, I was immediately interested. He took this publication in trade for an unpaid debt. The* Grower *was begun in 1896 by Hannibal Lightfoot, but changed hands and is now a second-rate paper.*
>
> *I mentioned to Mattson that I had been writing for newspapers since I was twelve...We discussed the proposition...I said I would answer after talking with my father, who is Mattson's friend. Pa knows nothing about publishing, but reasoned that Hannibal Lightfoot had no success with this paper, others having failed also.*
>
> *"Here you are," he counseled, "with no money and no experience, so I cannot approve of you taking it up. I would let it alone."*

Thoroughly disappointed, Bob heard of the round-trip excursion to Niagara Falls, costing $25. Having saved $275 from the mail service, he felt he could afford it. This journey was primarily to overcome disappointment over not becoming a newspaper publisher.

But ultimately, he had a desk on the second floor of 102 East Eighth Street, his Columbia typewriter loaned by the Press Publishing Company. Bob had again encountered Mattson, who told him to bring his father to his office. Mattson worked his magic, and Tom Walker consented to Bob's purchasing the paper. Bob signed a note for $250, Tom signing as surety.

Unlike in today's families, parental permission was important in the Walker household. If Tom Walker signed a loan for Bob, he had to approve its use.

In September, Bob brought Elberta and his sister Mary to the Ridge, showing them a lot he was buying. In the midst of landing advertisers for his paper, Bob continued to see Elberta throughout the rest of the year. But for income, he had to work a second job at Red Plunder.

1901

Most of 1901 was spent pursuing advertisers and working on his publication. In September, he took in a two-day meeting of the East Tennessee Horticultural Society in Knoxville with Hannibal Lightfoot. Bob was to help prepare exhibits but also intended to promote his paper.

From Knoxville, Bob went to Greeneville, staying with cousin James E. Walker, assistant principal of Greeneville schools. Finding James not at home, Bob lay down on his bed. When James came in at eleven o'clock, he was much surprised to find an occupant.

Next day, Bob headed for Johnson City, attempting to locate the "guiltevious" Mr. Austin, whose poultry plant owed him for back-due advertising. He started on foot to the poultry plant, only to discover the culprit had moved. Not to be outdone, he set out to find Austin's present location, getting as far as Carnegie, Tennessee, before deciding he had no more time to pursue the scoundrel.

He again visited the Grigsbys in White Horn and many Walkers. At his Great-Uncle Will Walker's, he again found cousin James ("Ira" to the family), and they headed out to see Tom's oldest brother, Lieutenant John, about an hour away. There, they were asked by Lieutenant John to locate his old blind mare that had wandered away. They found her trapped in a deep ravine on a steep hillside above the house. All efforts at rescue failing, they felt the best policy was to kill her, as she was trapped in the ditch in great distress. After receiving authority to use the axe, they knocked her once in the head, ending her sufferings.

On the train home, Bob suffered a severe headache. It turned out to be chickenpox.

He and brother John now paid elder brother Will six dollars monthly to board in town with him, which must have been interesting. Returning from Georgia one night, the two sheltered under a coal chute, waiting for a train. It was raining. "The night was black, wind screamed, and water from the coal shute trickled down our faces," requiring them to wash thoroughly before "flying up to roost" at Will's.

On November 22, Mattson approved Walker's suggestion to drop the word "Truck" from his paper. Bob felt *Southern Fruit Grower* sounded more professional and began referring to it as the *SFG*. He spent many evenings in Highland Park; for Bert Clark's twenty-first birthday, he gave her a gold ring with pearls and an opal, her birthstone. He was seriously courting her.

Traveling again, he arrived in Indianapolis as Queen Victoria was dying and was in the railway station when they announced her death. From there he went to Chicago, calling on advertisers for the *SFG*.

He visited the produce house of John Scales, who invited Bob to dinner with his family despite Bob's cheap suit, which looked like he had been sleeping in it—because he had. Bob folded and slipped it under the mattress to press it, realizing, after meeting Scales's family, that they would have treated him like a prince even if he wore rags.

Scales, a Civil War veteran, met Bob at Lincoln Park, there reciting the Gettysburg Address from memory. He had been present to hear Lincoln deliver it and considered him the finest man who ever lived. He warned Bob not to go to Lake Michigan, as gangsters were killing people daily, dumping bodies into the lake. Nevertheless, Bob toured it, keeping an eye out for gangsters.

In Chicago, he found one block on Water Street stacked

Sarah Elberta Clark, circa 1902.

with jackrabbits piled like cordwood, high as his head. These were shipped in by hunters in North and South Dakota. He got one merchant to cut off four ears and send them to his "sweetheart" Elberta for powder puffs.

1902

In January, he traded partners, William Cooke now sharing space at 717 Cherry Street. Cooke was president of McGowan-Cooke Printing Company and an excellent printer. Bob hoped to turn out a better publication with Cooke, moving to the office vacated by Cooke's deceased partner, Frank McGowan. Walker had his own roll-top desk, typewriter and an office to himself.

He tirelessly sought revenue for his paper, traveling to Philadelphia, New York, Washington and Baltimore to stir interest in it. The banter to his cousin in the following letter is a tip of the Walker humor's iceberg, coloring generations of family lore and sinking the dignity of many a family occasion. From Washington, he dashed off this ridiculous note to cousin Dewey Walker, replying to Dewey's recent reference to Annie Bare as "Miss Annie Naked":

> *Gentlemen:*
>
> *Regarding your letter, in reply will say I cannot use your 'possums, or 'possum hides. The market is off, and as I know you are on sufferance, I will allow you to draw from my bank the amount of $10. This is only an act of charity...Dewey, I saw your cousin today. He came into Philadelphia with a load of tripe, and I certainly felt sorry for him. I spent two nights in NYC and everybody that is anyone there came to the train when I left...J.E. Walker and I have returned from calling on four ladies from Virginia. All are fond of me, and fine as silk. J.E. is giving me his pass, and I will take a special seat in Congress before I leave.*
>
> *Goodbye, R.S. Walker*

He traveled up the Hudson River by steamer and learned in Atlantic City that a punch he had enjoyed the night before was spiked with liquor. Because he did not drink alcohol, he was much chagrined.

James joined him in Washington, where they toured government buildings and the White House, viewing one of Roosevelt's children on the veranda and three riding bicycles in the backyard.

February brought eight inches of snow to Chattanooga, with businesses suspended. He was still pursuing Elberta Clark.

In April, he visited family in Chickamauga, Chess meeting him and friends, as usual, at the Ridge with the buggy. For dinner, Lizzie served April Fool pie, made of cotton and cottonseed. The end of April saw Bob and John boarding with Mrs. Burk on East Seventh Street, their erratic late hours too "inconvenient" for brother Will's wife.

In June, he and John moved in with Mrs. Parsons on West Sixth Street, Cameron Hill. John eventually married her daughter, Ida. Bob took a Saturday job, working with Will at Miller Brothers. He and John spent another evening in Highland Park with Frank Clark, Elberta's brother, a few years her senior. Her youngest brothers, Henry and Bailey, still lived at home.

The Walkers took the train to Chickamauga to visit family and swim in the creek in the unbearable city heat. They afterward returned to Highland Park for more phonographic entertainments at the Clarks', where Elberta was present.

Bob and John often caught a moving train to Worley—but their financially advantageous means of travel had risks. Walker once miscalculated in leaping from a speeding train and landed in a pile of cinders. For the rest of his life, he carried a stain the color of India ink behind one ear as a souvenir.

Bob complained of advertisers bartering goods for services. His preference was legal tender, but he was being paid in tins of peaches and live chickens. The shipment of coffee (which he could not abide) he gave away, but for the fifteen-acre tract of land in Texas near the Gulf, he sought expert advice from his cousin Albert, the former Texan, who assured him it was acceptable.

He also received shares in gold and silver mines and was offered the opportunity to invest in real estate in the wilds of Miami Beach. Walker saw little excuse for investing in it, saying it was useless and too far from other cities.

He was very much drawn to the interesting Miss Clark. She loved hiking, which they did together. She collected wildflowers, knowing all their names and pressing them in books. Her years in rural Athens had created her love of nature, and he recognized in her the same love of country life. Elberta also had a keen interest in literature and was an excellent Latin scholar. Walker was indeed smitten.

But he determined to see the West, in August traveling with the Tennessee Press Association—one hundred newspapermen heading for Salt Lake City. Their train arrived late in St. Louis, but hearing of their delay, the World's Fair people met them at the depot, chartering two electric cars for viewing the Botanical Gardens, park, zoo and proposed midway for the 1904 World's Fair. Then the pressmen headed for Denver.

Bob awoke in the grazing prairies bordering Kansas and Colorado. They passed hundreds of miles without one human being, only towns of prairie dogs. He admired their vigilance, running to stand on their mounds at the train's approach. He described owls roosting on these mounds, presumably for company. They saw no one except cowboys in this dry country.

Denver had fine streets, splendid stone buildings and a five-dollar fine for spitting on sidewalks. The pressmen headed for Colorado Springs and Pike's Peak. The sky was storming above, but the determined party headed for Manitou, seven miles away, at the peak's base. They took the Cog Wheel Route to the summit, one mile by rail, 14,147 feet above sea level. Several became nauseous, Bob (who soon recovered) among them. The car's continual jogging and scarcity of air contributed to this.

Lakes on the mountain were covered with ice, which had not thawed since winter. The thermometer registered seven above, and before they left, it began to snow and sleet. The railroad's only competitors were burros, small donkeys that were hired for three dollars but took a whole day to make the trip.

At Garden of the Gods, Bob had his photo taken beside its massive gate, a red sandstone monolith. From Colorado Springs to Salt Lake, the train passed through the Royal Gorge, Bob stationing himself at the head of the Pullman to enjoy the scenery. Traveling through Leadville and Tennessee Pass, ten thousand feet above sea level, required two engines.

By morning, they were in the Grand Canyon and, by afternoon, Utah, described by Walker as undoubtedly the most desolate state that can possibly exist, "with no beneficiary foliage other than sagebrush and cactus." Half the houses were "dug outs," literally dug out of the ground. Others were covered with dirt or straw. At Salt Lake, Bob procured a bath ticket and went into the water. The water was so salty he could float like a log, making it impossible to sink, the bottom being nothing but salt. Walker called it the most enjoyable bath he had ever taken. He spent the night at the Castel Hotel, choosing to sleep rather than attend the world championship prize fight in town.

He left the Tennessee Press Association behind for San Francisco, passing through the great American desert. To go through the Sierra Madres, it took two to three engines, the railroad crossing the mountains by a series of loops. Snow sheds over the tracks protected the most dangerous places where the train could become snowbound.

In the fruit belt below the mountains, the train stopped in Sacramento, running on the largest ferry in the world to the river's other shore at Oakland. More ferries took the train to San Francisco, four miles across the bay. Bob toured Golden Gate Park, City Hall and Cliff House, completing his journey from Atlantic to Pacific and hoping to see China Town.

The desert soil contained so much alkaline that he lost the warts on his hand. On this account, he felt it good for something. In the Grand Canyon, the train's axle twisted in two, tearing up ties for half a mile, causing a six-hour delay.

Back in Chattanooga, President Roosevelt was in town on September 8. Two thousand people packed in to see him at First Baptist, Walker among them. Walker then attended services at First Methodist Episcopal with Miss Clark and her mother before viewing the presidential parade, consisting of the cavalry and Chickamauga Park veterans. Bob greatly admired Roosevelt.

Gabriel Walker and family all returned to Chattanooga after their failed attempt at Texas cotton farming.

Thanksgiving Day saw Walker thankful to be alive, having battled a severe case of typhoid for two months. He credited the loving kindness of family for his recovery. Dr. Blockford saw him daily. Walker was able to receive sassafras and honey and small amounts of food, had lost much weight and was at times delirious. Blockford, a renowned surgeon who had done graduate work in Heidelberg, Germany, had been a surgeon in Bragg's army and was in the siege of Vicksburg.

Walker hoped for a visit from Elberta, who was unable to come but sent flowers. His sister Lizzie's boy, Grady Davidson, fourteen, brought the buggy a few times weekly to take Bob on outings. When a friend encountered them driving down the Graysville Road, he stopped his horse, lifted both hands and exclaimed, "Bob, what is wrong? You look like a haint!"

Walker and Mary were invited to take Thanksgiving dinner with the Worleys, but Tom feared he might eat the wrong food. Mary returned with a box of sugared orange peel from Mabel Worley. Despite being warned not to eat it, Walker stood by the fire, nibbling a piece as his family had dinner. He then heard what he thought was a strange noise in his stomach. As he leaned on the mantel, the noise again set up. He felt sure it meant certain death until he realized the sound was not coming from himself but from a mouse behind the fireboard gnawing a hickory nut. He got well immediately.

But Grady came down with typhoid. Bob feared the boy might have caught it from him, though Grady was careful not to eat or drink anything at the Walkers' house. Mary then caught it, and Charlie was unwell. Bob worried that somewhere between Chattanooga and California he had picked up typhoid germs and brought them to his family.

1903

February 4 marked Walker's twenty-fourth birthday, but he did not celebrate. Grady had died the day before. Still recovering from the disease, Bob watched with heavy heart from the front yard as the funeral procession passed.

By late June, he was traveling again with the Tennessee Press Association to Jacksonville and Miami. At Atlantic Beach, Walker and a friend foolishly went out too far and got caught in the current and carried into the ocean. There were no lifeguards, and they seemed doomed in the fierce undertow. They miraculously survived, but Walker swallowed much salt water and was sick all night. It did not keep him from leaving the following day for St. Augustine via the East Coast Railway.

In St. Augustine, the odor of sulphur water plagued their noses. His associate, Charles Turner, and he rented bicycles at fifteen cents an hour each and rode into the country. It was hot, and they learned everybody went to bed at 11:00 a.m. and slept through the heat until 3:00 p.m. All the stores sold gopher turtles, more highly esteemed for their meat than chicken or turkey.

When they found it was Election Day in Duval County, for a joke, Walker suggested they try to vote. Before they could mark ballots, one of the judges asked where they lived. When Walker replied, "Chattanooga," they were told to scram and hurriedly biked back to town.

They visited the oldest church in America, respectful of those praying on the kneeling board. But as one man knelt, he inadvertently pinned Walker's foot beneath the board, and he yelped in surprise. A dog lying nearby did not like Walker's looks and growled. The clumsy tourists quickly left.

They hired a one-horse wagon to drive across the river to the Anastasia Island lighthouse, walking to its top. Then they visited the turtle and alligator farm, where Walker posed for a picture holding fast to a rope tied around the throat of a stuffed alligator.

On the train for Miami, they stopped near Fort Pierce in the middle of a pineapple farm, where Walker got off to cut pineapples. In West Palm Beach, a man took them across the bay to the Breakers, a hotel so big it took twenty minutes to walk around it, though they took a room in a modest hotel.

Next morning, they learned that one of their company, a Nashville editor, had been disturbed by a big beetle buzzing his room. The editor pulled out his pistol, shot the beetle, then calmly went back to sleep. They were also plagued by mosquitoes, but flocks of dragonflies (called mosquito hawks by Floridians) would pick them off their faces. On the train, dogflies gathered on their ankles, but newsboys came through the train, stood passengers in the aisle and sprayed them for fifteen cents.

Food and rooms in Miami were good and cheap. Several pressmen hired buggies to Coconut Grove, where land was about fifty dollars an acre and there were few homes. For fun, Walker sent their drivers on a fool's errand, hiding the horse and wagon while they were gone. It was hot, the joke

Walker at the Alligator Farm, St. Augustine, Florida, 1903.

resulting in irritated drivers, but Bob called them good sports. Walker humor struck again.

Bob booked a trip on the Peninsula and Occidental Shore Ship for Havana, Cuba. He was hoping for the company of a young Jewish man, Mark Seinfield, whom he had met, but the man's elder brother intervened, accusing Walker of kidnapping Mark, who was twenty-one. So Walker spent three days on his own in Cuba, enjoying the culture, though he spoke no Spanish. Their foods interested him: he mistook plantain for banana, having to be told it must be cooked before eaten—embarrassing for a fruit-growing publication editor! He bought a dozen bananas for five cents and tried to give them away, but nobody wanted them. He learned that one favorite Cuban food is green coconut, slashed in two, the pulp stirred and mixed with the milk, salted and eaten with a spoon.

In Havana, while writing to Elberta, he was approached by a young Cuban lady. The girl spoke no English but pulled up a chair and sat beside him. The surprise came when an austere-looking Cuban gentleman entered, and she hastily shoved her rocker back. The man was her father, a doctor who spoke English fluently.

He invited Walker to see an area of wealthy Cubans' homes. However, his daughter, eighteen, was not included in the excursion. The doctor said he had lost all but one of five brothers in the war with Spain, his one remaining brother now living in Brussels.

Walker toured the fort before departing, observing a regiment of soldiers whose drill abruptly turned into a fistfight as they began beating each other up. One picked up a crosstie and threw it at another, which, had it struck, would have killed him. Walker was glad to leave the fort and Morro Castle.

In Miami, he told a local reporter that Miami was too far away to ever amount to much. Heading back through Jacksonville, he stopped at the ostrich farm, purchasing an ostrich egg and black ostrich feather fan for a dollar each for Elberta's twenty-second birthday.

On October 1, Elberta accepted his proposal of marriage. They planned to wait a year to marry. Bob presented to her an engraved gold watch and neck chain inscribed "Robert to Elberta." He now had reason for working even harder on the *SFG*.

Three days before Christmas, Bob's brother Chess was discovered ill at the old cabin by his sisters. He died at their father's house. He had been unable to stay away from sweets and had moved into the cabin to avoid temptation at the family table. But despite his best efforts to avoid sugar, he would walk the tracks to the Varnells' store and buy all the jellies he could carry. Insulin was not available then, and despite his body's inability to process sugar, he continued to crave it, inadvertently poisoning himself.

In moving to the cabin, Chess had also made room for Tom and Annie's new youngsters. Theodore, now two, was replaced as baby of the family by Wilder, born three months before.

Walker reflected that it was Chess who had met him in Chickamauga with the buggy, regretting that he had not seen as much of him recently and calling him a faithful brother, too young to die at only nineteen. Chess was buried by his mother and sister at Concord. It was some comfort that Mary and Charlie were recovering.

Chapter 3
1904–1915

1904

On August 16, Walker took supper at the Clark home. At nine o'clock, he and Sarah Elberta spoke their vows in the front parlor, departing at eleven on the Southern Railway for Asheville and spending three nights at the Battery Park Hotel.

Elberta and her mother belonged to Highland Park Methodist Episcopal Church, so Reverend Van Tassen arrived by landau from Harry Chapman's Livery to perform the ceremony. Her sisters Ida and Nora attended, along with Mrs. Clark, Miss Bessie Wood, Mrs. J.W. Fowler, Mrs. Van Tassen, Walker's brother John and his new wife, Ida. Bob and John maintained a lifelong friendly competition, Walker joking that he couldn't let John outdo him by taking a wife, so he got one too. Walker stated that the joyful occasion was not spoiled by Nora's presence, even though Nora's "unholy temper" was detested by most of her family.

In Asheville, the newlyweds attended a conference of the Southern Nurserymen's Association and saw the Vanderbilt Estate. The hotel gave the Walkers a free stay, claiming Bob was responsible for the Nurserymen's convention there. The newlyweds then left for Washington, D.C.

The elevator at the Washington Monument was out of service, so Elberta suggested they climb all 555 feet of it, which they accomplished in twenty minutes. On descending, Walker made a list of all memorial stones, noting one from Hawkins County. He also found another from the Cherokee

Indians. Walker considered life experiences fodder for writing. Years later, he turned this visit into an article, "Turning the Washington Monument Inside Out."

Elberta began a collection of silver coffee spoons from places visited on their honeymoon, continuing her hobby in later travels.

They took a boat down the Potomac to Mount Vernon. Seated on its lawn, they took time to smooth out some misunderstandings, discussing adjustments necessary in being man and wife. Walker stated it was now his greatest pleasure to introduce Elberta as "Mrs. Walker, my wife."

They had saved $400.00 to begin life together. Back home, they stayed briefly with Elberta's mother, insisting on paying her. But they soon rented three rooms in the home of Mr. and Mrs. C.W. Beise at 403 East Fourth Street for $12.50 monthly.

The Walkers acquired furniture, and Elberta chose a grape silver pattern. When she admired a rose-painted Prussian chocolate pot and cups in Fisher Evans's window, Bob paid four dollars for it and presented it for no special occasion.

1905

In June, Walker received his graduate diploma from Grant University's Law School in Chattanooga after fulfilling his degree's requirements at night. He later recalled an incident at graduation. Dressed in caps and gowns, the graduates were waiting outside City Auditorium when a fellow student "wobbled up and approached me," asking for Walker's help. He had met friends, taken one drink too many and now could hardly stand. "Let me hold the tail of your coat till I can reach the platform and be seated," he pleaded.

Walker, a teetotaler, had little sympathy, but "here was a fellow classmate who wished to use me as a telephone pole, so I yielded. But what a conspicuous pair we were, striding down the aisle...my inebriated friend twisting my coattail into a rope. Even so, it would have been all right, had he not blurted out loud as we reached the stage, 'Slow down, damn it, or you'll stand me on my head!'" The ceremony proceeded without further incident; Elberta began wearing her gold locket containing a picture of her husband in cap and gown.

He invested in law books and paid five dollars for the bar exam but had little interest in pursuing law. Instead, the couple hoped to add an upright piano to their household.

In October, the Walkers went to Savannah and Tybee Island, Georgia, Bob returning with the story of a caged alligator just outside the old cemetery. On bending down for a better look, he found the 'gator "not in his office." Getting up, he discovered the alligator had crawled out of his wire enclosure and that, while crouched, Walker had been straddling him. Due to perfect camouflage, he had not noticed the lizard's presence beneath his hindquarters and was "thankful he had been so kind as to not take a bite out of my rump."

On the train to Tybee Beach, the couple encountered a Reverend Clark and family, who had been conducting revivals. Elberta's father being a Methodist circuit rider, they thought this an interesting coincidence but could not determine if they were related.

It was a trip of multiple coincidences. In Augusta, Georgia, heading home, Walker briefly left Elberta at the hotel. On his return, she introduced him to a man there named Robert Walker, editor of *Walker's Magazine*, a dignified ladies' publication. Later, en route to the depot, a woman recognized them as having stayed in the D.C. boardinghouse where she was employed while they were on their honeymoon.

Walker was amused by stern warnings Elberta received about Mrs. Beise, their landlady. Elberta was told she was a wildcat and no one got along with her. They found this completely untrue, she and Elberta becoming bosom friends.

But in September they moved in with Mrs. Walline and her son at 107 Battery Place, having the whole downstairs (four rooms) of a brick house for fifteen dollars per month. They acquired a new sideboard matching their dining furniture, enjoying their dining room for its panoramic view of the Tennessee River. The house was conveniently located close to Telfair Brooks on East Fourth Street.

Walker had a Stevens shotgun for hunting with his brothers in the country. Shooting geese, he broke a spring and took it to the umbrella shop for repair. He picked up the repaired gun, shouldered it and, walking home in the dark, stopped by the jail to say hello to someone he knew there. Walker's home was about four blocks from the Walnut Street Bridge, and he was stunned next morning to see on the *Times*' front page the horrible story of the lynching of Ed Johnson, a Negro. A mob had forced the jailer to unlock Johnson's cell, then took him to the bridge and hanged him. He was accused of raping a white St. Elmo woman in Forest Hills Cemetery. Besides the violent crimes involved here, Walker was horrified that he could have been arrested on circumstantial evidence as taking part, since anyone seeing him could testify he was at the jail carrying a shotgun on his shoulder.

The Walkers'
Christmas portrait,
1905.

By December, the Walkers fulfilled their desire for an upright piano shipped from Forbes Piano Company. Bob remembered old hymns he once played at Concord. Elberta also played but, according to her husband, employed a finer hand. They gave each other the mutual gift of a piano bench and had a portrait made together at Hajos studio, Walker claiming most of the good looks came from Elberta's side of the photograph.

On December 11, Walker had a dream he felt obliged to relate to Elberta. He dreamed her mother came to visit a few days, took sick and died in their room. Although it was disturbing, the couple decided not to give it credence. At the same time, Walker's father and wife, Annie, had a new son named Gabriel for Bob's uncle.

Walker experienced another embarrassing incident. He had been dictating letters all day, including in each a Christmas card on which he had written— he thought—"Merry Christmas and Happy New Year." Soon after, some of Elberta's friends asked her to explain what was meant by "Merry Christmas and Happy New York."

1906

In January, Walker paid Lizzie's husband, John Davidson, $436 for a piece of his father's old farm. He was not sure what to do with it but was glad to have secured it. He and Elberta hoped to buy their own home, preferring somewhere in town. Elberta loved their vista of the river, but the Walline house was not for sale.

For extra income, Walker began taking written orders at Telfair Brooks, delivering groceries while maintaining duties at *SFG*. Then, on April 15, Walker's prophetic dream came true. Elberta's mother passed away in their bedroom, as his dream foretold. She had come to spend a few days but, as she was readying to leave, was taken ill. The couple gave her their room. Mrs. Clark had suffered previously from gallbladder trouble but this time did not recover. Walker was the only person in the room when she passed, holding her hand as she died in his arms. He later felt it would have been too much for Elberta and was glad for advance preparation, since the sad experience fell to him.

All of Mrs. Clark's children attended the funeral except Frank and Henry Clark, who lived in Waco, Texas, and Nashville, Tennessee. Elberta's older brothers Joe and George did come from Texas. Mrs. Clark was interred beside her husband, Reverend Elbert Clark, and several of his children in Wesleyanna churchyard, six miles east of Athens. Elberta did not attend the interment. (Bailey, Elberta's youngest brother, soon to graduate high school, likely moved in with one of his older brothers.)

Walker hired a wagon from Chattanooga Transit Company to take Joe to the depot. Joe had traveled over twenty years as a salesman for a Chattanooga-based medicine company. He and George, a druggist in Tyler, Texas, invited them to visit. In June, Bob and Elberta took the train for Memphis heading to Texas. Walker watched a tenacious katydid clinging to the train window, refusing to be dislodged.

In Dallas, he attended a Nurserymen's convention. Mayor Holland, publisher of *Farm and Ranch* newspaper, invited Walker to see the town, but as there were no automobiles anywhere, they walked. Bob wanted to stay at the convention a few days, but with little to interest Elberta, she went on to Weatherford. Walker was later met by Joe Clark and his wife, the former Minnie Owens of Athens; their daughter, Bertie, eleven (Elberta's namesake); and son, Joe Jr., six.

Joe Clark came from a strong East Tennessee Republican family but told Walker a Republican had no chance in Texas so he had turned Democrat. The Texas governor was a neighbor, and Joe was a partner in the Kindel-Clark Drug Company, though he acted as its traveling salesman.

Walker drove a buggy with Elberta and her niece to the Fain ranch, the home of Joe's friends. Joe drove the surrey carrying his wife and son. Walker noted an abundance of wildflowers, jackrabbits and large spiders. Joe encountered a tarantula as big as a fist in the road and killed it with his buggy whip. From the Fains' porch, they could see distant lights of other farms and the faraway lights of the village of Aledo. Walker called the night heavens indescribably clear and vast, filled with myriad stars.

They bid Joe goodbye for Tyler, Texas. George Clark had a drugstore at the corner of South Broadway and Square, several acres nearby and a house in town. He sent his wife and son to meet them, and they visited briefly before leaving for Galveston.

One local fellow informed Walker that the boll weevil turned out to be a godsend to Texans. Once farmers discontinued growing cotton, they began planting vegetables and tomatoes, worth twice as much, and were glad the boll weevil had gotten them off cotton.

In Houston, they stayed at the Rice Hotel but discovered that after checking their bags for Galveston, someone had broken into their luggage and stolen things, among them a beautiful white dress Elberta prized. Both were left with barely enough clothes to return home and expected the railroad to reimburse the loss.

At Galveston, they rented bathing suits to bathe in the Gulf but were stung by jellyfish, and finding no breakers, they enjoyed it little. A year before, the Galveston flood had submerged the city in ten feet of water. The city was finishing the big stone wall along the Gulf, filling behind it with sand pumped in from the ocean.

Elberta bought another spoon for her collection.

Heading for Laredo, they missed a train to San Antonio and had to spend a night in "a desolate place near Hearn, Texas, in a cheap frame building run by a widow and her son. These two lonely souls who spent their lives on the prairie…could not conceive of a hill or mountain so large that a wagon could not run over it."

It was a long wait for the next train. Boxcars clustered on the rails housed Mexican section hands, which was the town's population. Passenger trains stopped long enough for travelers to eat and depart. Walker said he felt like hugging two Chattanooga Southern Railroad cars on a passing freight, had they not been moving.

Finally, they arrived in Austin, where they toured the capitol and met its custodian, John L. Sullivan, an author and old newspaperman. He had an apartment there festooned with letters and things of testimonial note.

Although the Walkers were exhausted, he kept them talking until midnight before walking them partway to the depot.

They arrived in San Antonio the next morning and visited the Alamo, and Elberta got another spoon. From there, they headed to Laredo through a forest of giant cacti, some ten feet high. Boys selling cactus candy met the train; local farmers burned off spines with a torch, let the milk run in, then fed their cows with it, as cactus seemed to improve the milk supply.

The couple was so thirsty on arriving in Laredo that they drank three pitchers of water. It was the sweetest, purest water Walker ever had, and he was told it was rainwater.

Before dark, Bob and Elberta crossed the Rio Grande bridge into old Mexico. "The water below was dark and muddy, full of sand, and the poor Mexicans were busy hauling drinking water in casks from it because they were not able to buy better drinking water. We were deeply touched…and wished we could do something about it."

They purchased a few artifacts from vendors before crossing back to American Laredo. Both were eager for home and weary from the trip.

Back in Chattanooga, Walker organized notes on western flora and fauna for articles in *SFG*. He found that his salary, around $120, had more than doubled from the previous month, advertising revenue making the difference.

He was alarmed by the San Francisco earthquake, noting, "We sent $5 to a relief fund…Such destruction is incomprehensible…to think I was there only four years ago! Many sights I viewed no longer exist. This tragedy with much human suffering reminds us our days on the earth are brief and fleeting."

In December, George Clark sold them the Clarks' old home in Highland Park for $2,000, on payments. Walker calculated that with repairs and improvements, they could live there.

Elberta was less enthusiastic about the old house, missing the river. But Walker thought fixing the roof and porches and adding nice mantels would make the old house pleasant. To be supportive, Elberta chose two glass chandeliers with beaded fringe for the parlor and dining room.

1907

In May, Walker agreed to be baptized, as Elberta had been after him for some time to do this, for though a Christian, he had not taken that step. He was baptized at First Baptist Church, their friend Reverend Luther Freeman from

The old baptizing ground in the Chickamauga, circa 1910.

Nora, Elberta and baby Robert, 1907.

First Methodist performing the baptism. Walker said he and Bert were now confident of permanent union through all eternity. But they had another reason for joy, as doctors confirmed that they were expecting their firstborn.

September 21 brought them a son. Miss Daisy Wagner, the nurse who had been with Elberta for two weeks prior to delivery, attended. Elberta had become terribly swollen with what doctors then called a kidney ailment. (This was likely preeclampsia, characterized by swelling and often stillbirth. A risk factor of preeclampsia is weakening of the kidneys. Elberta's final illness may have had its roots in this unfortunate condition.) Walker wrote:

> *That Robert was born at all is miraculous, for two weeks before his birth…the doctor pronounced him dead. When he was born alive, the doctor only charged fifteen dollars.*
>
> *I cannot describe my feelings on first holding him. We named him Robert Sparks Walker, Jr., that name selected before his arrival…He came in the morning, Dr. Woolford bounding upstairs to tell me I had a son. Nothing compares with holding the little fellow, although I am not yet sure what to do with him. He is fat and pink and has a fine pair of lungs. Elberta has declared him worth all her sufferings and cannot see enough of him.*

In November, Walker became sole owner of the *Southern Fruit Grower*. His partner, Cooke, accepted Walker's property in the country as payment for his share of the publication.

Elberta had not been well, and her recovery from Robert's birth had been slow. She began spending time with her sister and brother-in-law, Ida and Ves Polk, in Menlo Springs, Georgia. Ves operated the Menlo Fruit Packaging Company, giving Elberta access to fresh fruits and vegetables, and Walker felt the Skybow Mineral Spring water and country air would do her good. It seemed to restore her for a time.

1908

This year Elberta spent much time away from Highland Park trying to recover her health. It seems possible she may have suffered postpartum depression, though she was also plagued with headaches and persistent pain "in her side." She traveled back and forth to Menlo Springs, Walker visiting her when time and money allowed.

ME TOO

Yes, I am interested in that order too, which the Boss wrote you about for_____. Look at my picture and you'll know why.

Let me have the order, if you don't care to send it to the dog, or the Boss. This lawn mower is sure hard to push and an order from you means a rest and some help for me.

Surely you'll let me have the order. If you like you may just address your letter to

"**Robert, Jr.,**" care of

Yours in haste,
R., Jr.

THE SOUTHERN FRUIT GROWER,

Chattanooga, Tennessee.

P. S.—We have one more card to send you. but it takes an order to get it. Why? Because its the kind the Boss is using to acknowledge orders with. I'll see that you get one too, if you'll send me the order the dog failed to get.—"R., Jr."

(The subscription price of The Southern Fruit Grower is 50c per year, three years for $1.00)

SFG advertising postcard of Robert Jr., 1908.

He never reproached her for the expense and inconvenience, being concerned solely for her welfare. When she did return, he was overjoyed to have her home and them a whole family again.

1909

On September 5, their second son was born.

Today, Labor Day, I have another fine son! We named him Wendell Clark Walker, and I believe he is bigger than his older brother was. Such strength! The nurse laid him on Elberta's cedar chest to fetch towels to wash him, but on returning, found him on the floor. He had slipped off the chest and rolled down between it and the wall! No damage was done, but we consider ourselves well warned to watch this one! Now Robert has a companion and Elberta has another little man to sew for.

Walker related a failed venture with cousin Albert, his partner in a poultry farm of ten thousand hens, which looked promising, as they were turning out twelve hundred hatchlings at a time. But chicks began to disappear, sometimes three hundred per night.

Ultimately, Bob discovered the whole area infested with rat runs stuffed with dead chicks. "At season's end, only sixteen chicks remained, so scrawny and bare of feathers they might have belonged to a nudist colony. Albert hauled them into town and disposed of the lot for two dollars and forty cents. Here endeth the poultry farm."

1910

In June, Elberta's health declined again, an "old trouble in her side returning." It was hot and noisy in Highland Park, and she had worsened since Wendell's birth. Walker again sent her to Menlo Springs. The climate and water had proved beneficial to her health following Robert's birth and helped her resume normal life for a time.

Walker suffered greatly from his family's absence but delved into work. He and Elberta often discussed his selling the *SFG* and resigning as editor, which he somewhat desired to do, as the publication hogtied him to one place, restricting opportunities. Also, many contrary things had happened recently due to his refusal to accept quack patent medicine ads in his paper, so to be rid of it seemed welcome. But there was no buyer.

Their house in Highland Park had become an albatross. It was unbearably hot in summer, damp and drafty in winter and Elberta thought it contributed to her illness. Had he known she would grow to despise it, Walker would never have purchased it, though at the time, it seemed a good decision.

He, too, wished they were out of the city but was determined to be content in all circumstances. Still, he pursued every avenue of selling—and even renting—their house, stating that he pitied the poor bachelor who had no one to live for but himself.

He purchased Elberta a steamer trunk with drawers and compartments for children's clothes. The cost for Elberta's board at Menlo Springs left barely enough to cover Walker's expenses. The *SFG* was not generating enough cash, even from advertising. He was open to other ideas, becoming intrigued by a pump-spray to improve crop-spraying for growers. He sought investors to develop it.

Letters from Elberta were not encouraging, as she reported little improvement. For her eventual return, Walker installed a hedge between their yard and the Gilberts', next door. To give his boys a "country" place to play, he dug a trench by the hedge, lining it with sand and pebbles, and hid a garden hose in the ground to create a little stream where they would wade, float boats and make water wheels.

Thirty years earlier, his house had been considered a fine, modern home. George Clark had bought it for his widowed mother, baby sister and brothers. Sometime later, the water company turned off his mother's tap because George, on an extended business trip, let the bill become delinquent. Enraged, George had a seventy-five-foot well drilled, installing a hand pump on the back porch, where it remained. The well was deep, connecting to an underground source that filled the limestone quarries a few blocks away. Elberta and her mother never used the pump except for the garden or, if the pipes were frozen, subtly getting city water turned back on without telling George, who lived in Texas.

Bob asked cousin Albert about buying his Uncle Gabe's farm in Silverdale, but it was not for sale. But in typical Walker spirits, he first bought a piece of Limburger cheese, planning to put some in Albert's shoes and under his pillow when he stayed overnight. He then wrote to his wife, signing off, "Goodnight, my beloved Elberta, may He who rules the universe keep you."

A visit to the country resulted in viewing his father's new colt, which Walker described as black as a crow with hair like silk.

> *Pa has four colts large enough to break this fall… When broken, they will make excellent buggy horses. Even before the little scamp had his navel string cut, he was trying to get up, and once up, went to sucking. We led the old mare out, the colt following, appearing to have palsy at first, before gaining control of his equilibrium. Then the little scamp kicked at me, throwing both heels in the air before he was six hours old. I believe horses are born with all the knowledge they will ever know.*

He described his prank on Albert with the Limburger—keeping Albert up until midnight sniffing, fanning, raising windows, saying something was surely dead. He couldn't sleep and guessed he'd go home. When Albert decided to bathe, Walker admitted what he'd done.

He was wracking his mind to find a good place for his family and now considered placing them with his father's brother, his Uncle Pres at Otes. This did not work out either.

Instead, he mailed Elberta wallpaper samples, saying their place looked pretty forlorn. He wanted to make the house look better for selling—or staying. He hoped she might be content to stay if he found someone to cook and clean and suggested himself for the job. He promised she would do

The Walkers in the country, circa 1909.

nothing but tend the babies. "We need not have company, but if we do, we can lock them in one room and not let them out!" he offered. But Elberta's health was poor, and Walker hated being a bachelor.

One afternoon he and Albert, sitting on his swing, seriously discussing where to get something to eat, saw a big old chicken in Walker's yard, and they took it for supper.

A friend mailed a package of fireworks to Elberta for Robert, but Walker hastened to warn her not to let him have them, fearing he might eat them. He continued seeking a country place. "I have written Lizzie that you changed addresses, but did not know quite where you were going, that you were traveling—Robert looking after the monkey, Wendell blowing a French harp, and you playing an accordion."

Walker placed his house with several real estate men to sell it, to no avail.

He bombarded Elberta with uplifting letters, receiving in return little encouraging news. He searched his daily life for amusing anecdotes to relate. "Tell Robert old Maltese [Emily Gilbert's kitten] stole into my house last night, and I was awakened by something stealing my breath. I found the cat sleeping at my nose and had to throw him to the floor three times before he would obey. Later I heard Emily calling him, and when I went back inside, found the little scamp asleep on your bed!"

He took frequent trips to Georgia to visit his absent family, more recently to Summerville, where Elberta had begun lodging with the Gamble family.

71

He wrote, "My cousin Albert goes to a Prayer Meeting one night, then comes home with me and kills one of my neighbor's chickens. What do you think of that? Is that consistency?"

My Dearest Elberta,
July 10, 1910
    Where is my mousetrap? Kindly ask Robert. The mice are abundant.
One slept on my pillow and snored so loudly I could not stand it. My
biscuits this morning had tails as long as Halley's Comet.

He then enclosed a piece torn off the hem of his new shirt for Elberta's approval.

In 1899, while sitting astride a mule, Walker had witnessed the passing of an odd-looking wood-burning engine. Its smokestack was big as a barrel, and certain parts of it were so polished that they glistened like gold. It bore the name *The General.* This was the first of several times the Civil War engine traveled through the creek farm to various exhibitions. Members of Union spy James Andrews's raiding party, who died stealing the locomotive, were buried in the nearby National Cemetery. Walker believed its tale would make an exciting moving picture. He sent off his story, "Andrews' Raid," to the International Moving Picture Company in August 1910. It was not accepted. (Yet in 1956, Disney made a film on the subject, *The Great Locomotive Chase,* starring Fess Parker.)

Jury duty kept Walker tied down. One case involved a railroad, the defendants having seventy-five witnesses. Another case received a record amount of personal damages: $19,000.

A disconcerting letter arrived from Elberta, describing no fewer than three places where she wished to reside, none of them Highland Park. Walker had a large extended family. He sought to work out something with one of them or perhaps build on Missionary Ridge, if Elberta were content with that.

At last he visited her in Summerville, returning home with two hundred chigger bites. He expressed to Elberta a growing desire for an auto, but in the next sentence, dinner was obviously on his mind. "Somebody around here has four old chickens, and they are not reticent at all about what they want. They stay in our yard and scratch up everything. I think they have killed your parsley. They belong to the same family as the one Albert and I killed and ate. I hate to repeat the same course, but necessity may compel me. If I get in trouble, will you come to my rescue?"

Elberta's reply was that she wished to stay longer in Summerville. Walker agreed. When someone bought out former partner Cooke's stock in the *SFG,* Walker wished he were buying his share as well. Yet to cheer Elberta, he wrote:

Walker and Elberta with sons Robert and Wendell, 1910.

I left my shaving brush at your place, so had to use the paint brush. Could not find a single undershirt, so am not wearing any...I have worked it out, and here is what a trip to Summerville cost me:

Railroad fare.	*$2.32*
Livery.	*$1.00*
Board.	*$1.80*
Lard and salt for choegers..	*$1.50*
Lost undershirt.	*$.50*
Value of sores caused by choegers.	*$2.00*
Nails worn off by scratching.	*$1.00*
Blood lost from ticks.	*$1.00*
Time lost fishing for minnows.	*$2.00*
Total.	*$13.42*

Will try to eliminate some of these on my next trip! I miss you and the babies, but I'll fight to the finish! Laugh it off, romp it off, and the world will grow brighter!... Think how you can make each present moment happiest for yourself and others. You have no mortgage on the future and it's important to make the best of the present. I will send Riley's Love Lyrics *to you.*
Your loving husband, Robt. S. Walker

Still Elberta's health did not improve. Walker patiently stressed that he would provide anything to help her, regardless of cost.

His neighbor, schoolteacher Bonnie Gilbert, invited Walker over to view a set of plates she had hand-painted for her mother. A gifted artist, she later painted a set of berry bowls for Elberta.

A man from Summerville approached Walker about trading for the mineral springs there, offering to meet in Summerville to discuss it. Walker also met a Mr. Watson who expressed interest in funding the pump spray but wanted first to sell the old hotel at Kensington. Built during the boom, it cost reportedly $60,000, and he wanted $6,000.

Walker hoped Elberta's latest relapse would not last:

> *It is hard for me to see my once strong and brave little partner, who loved hiking and exploring better than life itself, become reduced to an invalid's existence. I cannot comprehend how such a thing could befall her.*
>
> *She is still young, and should have most of her life ahead. Yet I see in her eyes a silent, dark despair, as if she knew some terrible thing and were keeping it from me.*
>
> *Even more difficult to explain is her restlessness, her need to be in constant motion, always changing location. I sometimes fear she might never be content to stand still again. I am utterly baffled, yet I know she is only desperately seeking relief from discomfort and unhappiness. If love would heal her, she would be whole as instantaneously as the woman who touched the hem of the Master's robe, for she is everything to me. But this is not enough, or she would be with me, not far away battling illness again.*

By early August, she seemed on the mend. Walker was trying to wear smiles but feared the neighbors might think he was delighted to have his family away. He said, "If you laugh, the world laughs with you; carry your head around in a sling, people will go seven miles out of the way to avoid you."

Elberta's letters began to sound promising, encouraging Walker to hope for his family's return. He ordered a set of Hugo's works, since he and Elberta enjoyed reading. Winter would soon come, and it was time to lay in coal. Then taxes were due. Just living was costly, he acknowledged, but he believed in deriving pleasure from even these things. He would not put things off, believing the future too uncertain. Only the present was sure.

He amused himself with nature, finding an old toad on his walk, feeding him grapes by letting them roll down the walk one at a time. The toad took after and swallowed them. Walker discovered that toads never swallowed anything until it showed signs of life.

He wrote Elberta:

> *In mid-August, a one-man jury returned a verdict on the chickens that had been trespassing on the Walker property. After much debate and deliberation over guilt or innocence regarding the vandalizing of Walker's garden, the chickens were ruled guilty. Their crime carried a sentence of death by asphyxiation, based on the laws of Tennessee which allow a man the right to justice when wronged by a neighbor. The verdict was further supported by the Sovereign decree of man's dominion over winged fowl, reference Genesis 1:29 and 30.*

Walker said he felt completely justified in this decision but confessed that hunger of a man on his own, without benefit of wife or cook, might influence judgment regarding a public nuisance that was far more useful fried than ambulatory.

To depict his lone condition, Walker confessed he had used one of Elberta's good tablecloths for a sheet and had been snoozing on it for a week, explaining he must have put it on in the dark of night.

A friend recommended he buy land on Lookout Mountain, since better transportation up there was soon coming. Walker considered the idea. A California friend sent an article on apple growing, and he also thought he might like living out there. He was hoping to hear from extended family about a comfortable place for Elberta and the boys. Still, he hoped she would like it at home once it was cooler. Their living situation confused him as badly as Elberta.

Understanding his loneliness, Bonnie Gilbert invited him over to meet two of her mother's brothers. Walker feared they thought it odd Elberta was gone so long, especially when his suitcases came in from his Summerville visit, deposited on the Gilberts' porch. They were sewed up in tow sacking, and Walker told Phillip, Bonnie's brother, that if he heard a sewing machine running, he'd know Walker was making underclothes from it.

Walker could sit for hours gazing into the skies, longing to get there. He felt that studying the heavens was ennobling work. He told Elberta that misfortune polished us like rough stones; that discouragements and temptations were the Creator's tools for refining us to make us fit for a better world. It would soon be hard for him to remember this.

He offered to buy new rugs, a self-heating iron and several ferns to entice Elberta home. He sent the ill-fated tablecloth to the wash, promising to never treat it so rudely again. He promised to drive her out west if he were to get an automobile. But he had decided not to purchase the mineral springs at Menlo at any price, believing their operation was barely paying expenses.

He discussed purchasing a place on Lookout Mountain for a summer home, if only to spend weekends. In the next sentence, he considered sending Elberta to a restful place in Florida for the winter.

Clearly, separation was causing confusion. He dreamed of walking with her to the old mill in Menlo, picturing the large spring and the sand dancing incessantly before the emerging water. He pondered how long it had been going on, how long it might yet continue and man's short years on earth. He signed a letter to Elberta: "I bid you fond goodnight, and should I never wake to see you again, I hope we shall in some happier clime bid each other a sweet good morning."

Walker thought that if he could rent their house, he would borrow and build on his Ridge lot, adding that if

Dr. George Walker, circa 1905.

he lived there, he would want an automobile. Hearing that his neighbor had gotten about $5,000 for his house further fueled Walker's desire to sell. Yet the real estate market was poor. His brother John was planning to build. But Elberta charged Bob not to. So he decided to find a farm for his boys.

In September, he added Balzac, Shakespeare and Hugo to his library. He encouraged Elberta to stay where she was, saying the neighbors did not blame her for her absence.

She was depressed, and Walker did his best to support her. His youngest son had a first birthday; his family had been away from home three months. He began again looking for farms in Tyner. His Aunt Mary Walker and cousin Dr. George Walker lived nearby. George encouraged surgery for gallstones, since Elberta's pain was below the lower rib on the right side and on the back under her shoulder and seemed to be worsening.

Walker wrote: "If I could shoulder her affliction, I would be glad. If she must stay away all winter, I am prepared, for I would die for her comfort and happiness, having been blessed with the art of concealing a bleeding heart beneath a smile."

City plans were to pave many streets in Highland Park. Walker was glad, as passing autos stirred much dust—one of Elberta's complaints against their home. When Elberta's ailing sister Ida regained health, Elberta returned to the Polk household. Ida's husband Ves apparently named a new dog for Bob—a family tradition of sorts.

Walker read a book discussing absentmindedness. Its author described a college professor ringing his own doorbell and asking a newly hired maid if he was in. When she said no, the man left, disappointed. Elberta often suggested that Bob was absentminded.

She was also fearful of surgery, ruling it out. Her recovery would restore their living situation, but Walker stated he would rather live separated forever than talk her into something that might kill her. "The decision must rest solely in her hands, where it clearly belongs."

The rest of September, Elberta vacillated between despair and seeming improvement, affecting not only her frame of mind but his as well. Noting that his house was "simply a sight," he pondered papering a few rooms. He continued writing hopeful letters, joking, "Did I leave my shaving brush with you? Have you been using it? I am using a big paint brush for shaving, and it is awkward!"

He again expressed interest in owning an auto, noting that neighbors Berger and Meyer both had them now.

Elberta returned home before Christmas, staying for Christmas Day but shortly afterward making a two-week visit to Chicago with her best friend from school, Mamie Harver. One wonders why she would return home only to strike out again for another two weeks to such a cold place, but in her defense, perhaps the constant company of two small boys had exhausted her in her weakened state. The company of an adult friend must have been appealing.

Walker's sister Mary stayed at their home to care for the boys while he took his father by train to Hawkins County to spend Christmas with relatives. They ran into Dr. Henry Van Deman, horticulturist, bringing home a dressed 'possum in a tow sack for Christmas dinner. Because Van Deman's wife refused to eat 'possum, Van Deman planned to tell her it was pork (a pig possum). Walker's father showed him the red and gold watch presented to him on October 11, 1893, when he finished the W Road up Walden's Ridge. Van Deman's cousin had made the presentation speech.

Walker and his father, Tom, walked over a mile from the depot to the Walker homestead, where Preston and Ellen lived. The next day, they visited the family cemetery to see his grandfather's grave. But the living were in Walker's mind, and he had the Memphis Special flagged down to return home and "play Santa" for his boys. Elberta sent a New Year's Day telegram, Bob and the boys wiring her a similar message.

1911–1912

September 16, 1911, was Robert's fifth birthday, Wendell turning three on the fifth. The two were inseparable.

An adult Wendell recalled a reprehensible act he and Robert participated in sometime during this period involving the family graphophone. Its flaring horn protruded above the desk-like cabinet, tempting both to use it as a chamber pot—little boys marking territory. On another occasion, while parents entertained guests elsewhere, Robert climbed onto the dining table with a visiting boy and, with Elberta's shears, snipped off bead fringe from the chandelier. There is no record of the discipline for these transgressions.

Walker had recently purchased, for $1,000, twelve forested acres near Tyner, which he called Helvellyn, and considered building on it. He began his first venture into fiction writing, "A Bearskin for a Sheepskin," which he hoped to sell.

1913

In June, more than ten thousand Confederate veterans encamped in Jackson Park within sight of Walker's house. He brought his boys, spending hours conversing with the soldiers and making photographs, including one of Robert and Wendell with the oldest soldiers.

Mid-October saw Walker's harrowing visit with his cousin George in Daisy. They were playing checkers when a man rode up after midnight, yelling that someone had been shot three miles away. Leaving Elberta and the boys with cousin Albert, the two grabbed a lantern and headed out. The crunching of discarded crockery underfoot told them they were passing the Herty turpentine cup factory. They trekked into dark, wild country before reaching a deserted log hut, its door ajar.

Fifteen feet from it, in total darkness, they tripped over a lifeless man, gun still clamped in his hands. They did not see the dog guarding him. When George picked up his arm to seek a pulse, the dog jumped him. George removed him with his boot. Shouting for help, they headed toward a creek running over the road and then heard, "We're up here!" followed by agonized groans.

There they encountered a man, five barefoot children, a wild-eyed woman with a loaded shotgun and a wounded woman wrapped in a quilt, a load of buckshot in her thigh. A teenage girl held a lantern. George and the man

Robert and Wendell with Confederate veterans, 1913.

carried the injured woman to the hut. The children lit a fire while George and Walker moved the dead man to the chimney corner, covering him. The dead man was married to the dark-skinned woman with the gun, who had shot him; they were estranged, and he had come to take her back. She was staying with her sister, mother of the half-clad children, who begged not to be left alone.

The dead man had shot at his wife but hit her sister, and now this woman was in great misery from bits of her dress ground into the ugly wound by buckshot. George and Walker picked out garment particles but could do nothing for her pain. At this point, the man left. Meanwhile, the woman with the gun slid on her knees and hid behind a table near the open door, constantly eyeing outside and cocking the gun at intervals. She was expecting her husband's relatives to arrive and open fire on them.

Wrote Walker, "I was not glad to receive this news," telling his cousin they had undertaken hazardous work. George finished dressing the sister's wounds, leaving to locate a neighbor to stay with the family. The hut was eerie, and specters were easily seen in the woods on all sides of that mountain. Walker stayed at the open door, listening for crunching gravel under human feet, and when he heard George returning, "the sound was sweet as angels' voices." George had with him "a tall rail-splitter," to whom they turned over the women and children. On the walk back, they stopped to report the murder to Squire Poe, who said he would call the county coroner.

1914

Walker and Elberta resumed a fairly normal life, despite frequent illness. He did indeed buy an auto—a Ford. In August, he was returning from a church concert with a carful of people. Passing Chickamauga Battlefield, his car was struck by a bus and knocked down an embankment near the Georgia Monument. When the bus driver climbed out, he was clearly drunk. A passenger, "Pup" McWhorter, climbed the bank and hailed a ride to town, returning with a rental car. Walker got home near dawn, relieved to find his car not seriously damaged. Years later, "Pup" would be shot in the heart by an officer arresting him for reckless driving. Another drunk driver would do far worse damage in the year ahead.

It saddened Walker that Elberta never regained the vitality of their early days together. But, he wrote, "I love her more than the day we married." He regretted that finances tethered them to Highland Park, despite wishes to go elsewhere.

Walkers at Chickamauga Battlefield (in the first car), 1914.

Nevertheless, they spent happy hours rambling through town and country. Robert was becoming a naturalist, and Wendell would not be outdone. Walker stated, "We may not travel the world in luxury, but are rich indeed... Riding in my auto, surveying the countryside, we feel like kings of the earth! I never experienced such an exalted feeling riding Pa's old mule."

Young Robert may have been a gifted nature student, but anyone witnessing his less-than-scholarly arrival on his first day of school would never have imagined him a star pupil. Elberta brought him to Bob scrubbed, pressed, combed and armed with pencils, pencil box and tablets. One might have thought him the most eager young man in all first grade. Such was not the case.

As it became apparent to Robert that public school was the unavoidable consequence of reaching the age of seven, he began to protest. He determined he was not going to school, the matter settled so far as he was concerned. It simply remained for his parents to understand.

Walker saw words of reproof were useless, so he took the dilemma by the horns, Robert by the thoracic region and carried him out the door. The boy's sustained bellowing brought out most of the neighbors, most of whom they had not seen in years. Bob thought this act of authority would snap Robert back to his senses, but he had grossly misgauged the depths of his son's contempt for higher education.

He carried Robert eight city blocks from Greenwood Avenue to Highland Park Grammar School, every step punctuated by Robert's howls of protest.

Walker and sons: "the happiest man on Earth," 1914.

Yet once at school, he became meek as a lamb and went in by himself, becoming a model student, according to teachers.

Walker was selling articles and poems to other publications to augment his *SFG* salary. Elberta took interest in his work, helping edit manuscripts. They were working together on stories for young people. She began collecting Bob's ground-down pencils and worn-out pens, securing them in a drawer like a squirrel's cache of nuts. She labeled some to indicate what he had written with them. When asked why she was saving them, she replied he would be a famous writer one day, making these pencils valuable.

A New York publisher sought to buy Walker's *SFG*, and he was eager to sell. The proposed sale caused him to delay a trip to Nova Scotia orchards, but the sale was eventually thwarted by the outbreak of World War I. Instead, he visited Waynesville, North Carolina, spending two weeks tramping through its orchards with his cousin. Walker wrote, "I lay plans, but always things conspire to anchor me in Tennessee."

For several years, beginning in 1908, Walker was involved in a dispute involving his *SFG*, the assistant postmaster general and a patent medicine company because the *SFG* would not accept patent medicine ads. Although the conflict had died down, it would surface again in the coming year. Yet it would be eclipsed by a far more tragic event.

1915

On September 23, Walker and his family were waiting in their car by the entrance to Warner Park. Robert was returning with a pack of gum from the store across the street. Suddenly, a car driven by a drunk Frank Fairweather careened around the corner and struck Robert in the middle of McCallie Avenue, dragging him half a block. Walker and his family witnessed everything.

He and Elberta tore from their Ford and ran to their son, collecting his nearly lifeless body, badly torn and shattered. Frantically, they sought help to take him to Woolford's sanitarium, several blocks away. Fairweather, driver of the other car, insisted on taking them. They seized his offer. Cradling his damaged boy, Walker climbed in, Elberta joining him, desperate parents seeking to save their son by any means. They rode together in that car, a curious quartet—the murderer, the murdered, the victim's mother and father—all holding one silent, fading hope that life might be sustained in the face of certain death. In their frantic state, Walker and Elberta left Wendell,

McCallie Avenue, 1915. The site of Robert's accident is marked with an X.

five, in the back seat of their parked auto. Mercifully, his only memory of the tragedy would be of a kind, unknown black woman comforting him, telling him everything would be all right. If only that had been true.

Only that morning, Robert, "looking like a little man in the white linen suit his mother made for him," had delivered a poem for the Pilgrim Church Sunday school.

Hours later, he died at Woolford's hospital less than thirty minutes after he was carried through its door. He had turned eight only eight days before. Elberta collapsed, requiring a sedative, which she violently resisted. Once Robert was declared beyond help, Walker, covered in Robert's blood, suddenly remembered his other boy, fearing for one awful moment that he might lose him too. Suppose he were stolen? Suppose he were injured? Would God take all his children in one blow, as Job's were taken?

He stayed with his wife until the sedative took effect. Only then did he dash back to retrieve Wendell, finding him in the safekeeping of the older woman, who wept when Walker told her Robert was dead. He could not remember who drove his car home. But he would never forget the images of that day—Robert smiling as he dashed across the street; screaming in terror with the car bearing down as he ran for safety; the merciless sounds and sights of the auto striking him, Robert disappearing under the car as it dragged him over the brick pavement, crushing him. Walker would remember these things as long as he lived.

He moved a cot into Elberta and Wendell's room to keep close, "like a family of quail." That night, Robert's silhouette eerily appeared on the window screen, lasting for weeks, and was seen by the family and close friends.

Walker struggled to resist the unspeakable grief that crushed Elberta, knowing if he succumbed he could not help her or raise his remaining son. He referred to "this devouring grief whose appetite knows no satisfying," believing this was a test of faith and God's goodness. Yet Christianity reminded him that without the promise of Resurrection, there was no hope at all. He believed, as King David did, that "we will see our boy again. He will not return to us. We must wait to go to him."

Soon after the accident, Sherman Sanders, son of Senator Newell Sanders, arrived to console them. Sanders spoke, especially to Wendell, about losing his own older brother, who drowned in the Chickamauga. But even the best intentions cannot restore what tragedy has taken.

Services for Robert were held in the Walker front parlor, where his parents had become man and wife. Walker bought a four-person burial plot in Forest Hills, and the devastated parents laid their son to rest. A photograph made on that day by Walker with Elberta seated by the grave reveals the depth of her stunned suffering. She would never fully recover.

Elberta and Wendell at the grave after Robert's funeral, 1915.

November found her and Wendell wintering in Fruitland Park, Florida, with a college friend, Mamie Casson. The coming Christmas holidays would be a torment for both parents.

The grand jury returned an indictment against Fairweather, charging him with manslaughter in Robert's death. Though Walker was suing him for $25,000, he questioned the point of pursuing it when nothing would bring back Robert.

> *I have gone over Fairweather's tearful testimony a hundred times and believe him when he says he would prefer to have killed himself than run over Robert. What man would choose to live with such knowledge? He stated he was traveling ten or twelve miles an hour, and did not see Robert until he was but a few feet away. He pulled the wheel violently and grabbed the emergency brake to avoid hitting him. Clearly, he wished to avert the tragedy as much as I, for we were both in tears. I have lost much sleep going over that awful afternoon. I expect to lose more.*

Walker spent the holidays working, knowing that if Elberta were in their dark, grim home without Robert, it would be her undoing. He feared losing her. He stayed temporarily with his brother John on the Ridge.

He described the completion of Riverside Drive along the Tennessee River, a pleasant route past the waterworks, but he bemoaned the obliteration of Citico Mound in its construction—a landmark that was ancient long before Europeans arrived—which he called a shortsighted decision that would be viewed as progress.

He wanted to visit Elberta but did not have money for the trip. But he determined to be cheerful, though "I am sorrowing inwardly," hoping he might make the day happier for someone whose sorrows were worse than his own. He picked up two Negro boys and gave them a ride. They were freezing, and he was deeply touched when one offered to share Christmas nuts with him. Walker exchanged little gifts with John and Ida, and Bonnie Gilbert accompanied him in the cold to Forest Hills Cemetery, where they placed two holly wreaths on Robert's grave. Bonnie set crocus bulbs around it.

Walker continued living at his brother's, pressing his own pants. "I spread a newspaper on the bathroom floor and it doesn't take long to mash them out."

His chimney blew down while he was away, and his car broke again. He was still writing "The Beechblock Circus," which he had begun for Robert and Wendell.

Chapter 4

1916–1924

1916

In February, Walker told Fairweather's attorney that although Fairweather was guilty, he was withdrawing prosecution. The man had a wife and children and would likely go to prison. Two witnesses had observed the accident: the motorman operating a streetcar and Detective Payne, on the car's platform, who arrested Fairweather for reckless driving. Ironically, Bob's call to Fairweather's attorney was made just before he received Elberta's letter in which she vehemently opposed such action. Walker regretted deciding without her but demanded all bills incurred from the accident be paid by Fairweather.

Suffering a "crick" in his neck, Walker wrote about his visit to a chiropractor. "My first treatment from a 'Backboneologist'…He threw me down, took off my clothes, sat on me, and spit in my face. That being the first of the series, I wonder what he will do next time."

In his next letter, he continued:

> *The "Criminologist" gave my spine a rub with perfumed oil, which terminated in a tempest. He used 110 volts of electricity, claiming to have a high voltage of human electricity. When he put one hand on my back and another underneath, I felt electricity jumping from his fingers. Then he kicked me in the back, cropped off my right ear, knocked my front teeth out, and loosened my jawbone. I should be getting along fine by next week.*

He and cousin Albert went to hear Helen Keller, describing her as a modern miracle. He was still wrestling with future plans—whether to build on his lot, sell his *SFG* or move to Florida. He sent Elberta instructions for teaching Wendell about planets by watching the night skies.

He reported making it up the Ridge in his Ford after a blizzard, first getting the car to its base by wearing a pair of overshoes and using twenty feet of grass roping. At his last chiropractic session, he was told to eat potato chips and praised for his growing literary success. He was unaware of having achieved any.

In March, Elberta returned to Highland Park, Walker expressing mixed feelings about living there again. It was their longest separation since their marriage. He had adjusted to the comforts of John's home on the Ridge and still considered building there.

He wrote to the paper explaining his reasons for withdrawing the case against Fairweather:

> *The penalty for involuntary manslaughter is imprisonment in the Penitentiary for one to five years. I believe Fairweather deserves punishment...but sending a man to prison would not likely result in a better man returning... Meantime, his family would suffer and this would hardly comfort the bereaved family of the dead child...For the sake of mercy, this suit was not prosecuted by me.*
>
> *Autos in the hands of careless drivers are a public menace...We should have perpetual revocation of the license when a driver is incompetent...But now [Fairweather] may continue to drive, and who knows who will be next? It may be you, or your child.*

He stated that they must somehow leave the past in peace and move on with their lives, which they tried to do. They painted their house (Elberta pronouncing it a public disgrace) but didn't like the tan color. World War I had broken out, leaving few choices. The Walkers raised produce in the backyard and bought war bonds. They resumed hiking, cooking outdoors on country rambles and even lighting fires in the backyard and having supper outside.

Elberta's health was delicate, but she soldiered on. Walker had not sold either house or the *SFG*. He had begun construction of a house on Missionary Ridge, on South Seminole, which was now finished. Though Elberta helped plan it, she expressed little interest in moving there. So Walker rented the new house to Lura Lane and her mother. Lane, an aspiring poet, had two volumes edited by Walker.

Wendell plows the "back forty," 1917.

1917–1918

Walker now considered selling the Ridge house, as well as the "albatross" in Highland Park.

There was a report of his demise in May 1918. He boarded a loaded streetcar, but though his name was now known as a writer, his face was mostly unknown. He stood listening to their comments.

Many said he would be "greatly missed," a meaningless phrase people usually say when someone dies. He was trying to learn his cause of death and went to eavesdrop behind two men he knew farther up the aisle. He learned he was well remembered since he had gone to the Great Beyond and was no longer a pest in the neighborhood. Hearing enough, he tapped one's shoulder.

The man's face paled the color of flour. Walker feared he might be discussing the event in this man's life that everyone thought had come to him. Apparently, the *Times* had posted a glaring news bulletin in its window that Walker had perished in the sinking of the steamship *President Lincoln*.

He got off the car, reassured that he had taken no fateful cruise without telling himself. Returning home, he found that Elberta and Wendell knew nothing of the alarming report. That night, his pastor drove him downtown to the *Times* in front of the sheet reporting his passing. For weeks, people hailed him on the street to ask if the report of his drowning was true.

Mrs. Martin and Elberta with a shotgun, 1915.

Walker's letter of inquiry to the navy resulted in information that the *President Lincoln* had been converted to a troop transport, was sunk and among those lost was one Robert Sparks Walker— from New York.

Walker wrote to Robert every year on his birthday, filing the letters away. "Those who believe time erases such memories will find their confidence shaken when called to endure a loss such as ours. Life will go on, but Robert took so much…I fear Elberta will never be the same."

Elberta, always ready to depart Chattanooga, returned to Menlo Springs. As much as she desired to be free of the house on Greenwood Avenue, she seemed unable to extricate herself, having no strength for uprooting. Relocating a whole household was overwhelming, and in leaving their home, they would leave behind what little of Robert was left.

1919

Elberta consented to a gallbladder operation in September at Woolford and Johnson's sanitarium, where Robert had died. After long resisting, believing she would never survive it, she was now some better, but recovery was slow. To cheer her, her brother Joe came to visit, bringing his wife and

Clarks on Umbrella Rock, 1919. Elberta is second from right.

daughter Bertie. Henry and Norah Clark joined them in touring Point Park and Rock City.

Ever restless, Walker and Elberta spoke frequently of moving west, possibly to Florida or one of the northeast cities, like New York. Northern publishers were good markets. He and Elberta often spent afternoons in Jackson Park seated on swings, working on nature articles while she edited and recopied manuscripts.

One of Pilgrim Church's founding families, they attended services, which met in the Bijou Theatre for three years. But enough money was raised to build a new church. A marble baptismal font and kneeling board were purchased for it with Robert's savings account as a memorial.

1920

Thanksgiving Day saw a great celebration at Gabriel Walker's in the country, which Elberta attended, despite not feeling well. Walker was grateful to have her present and grateful to have overcome stomach trouble plaguing him since his bout of typhoid. He sold their Missionary Ridge house and became active in Scouting. Wendell motivated him to take groups hiking at Camp Raccoon in Pan Gap and teach nature, helping them earn badges. Working with the Scouts would become one of Walker's greatest contributions.

Scout Camp Raccoon, Pan Gap, 1920.

1921

At last, for $6,000, he sold his interest in the *SFG* to Alex Labon, a "peculiar" bachelor accountant. Labon paid $500 down, with a six-year note. Walker agreed to edit the paper for free for six months, finishing in July. Going to his old office, he found the place stripped of all furnishings and hired an attorney, who went after Labon's bank accounts and netted Walker $2,000. When the lawyer attached Labon's household goods and netted another $500, Labon's bank said he had closed all his accounts and left for Ocean Beach, California, to reside with his aunt—but that he had another $10,000 hidden somewhere.

Walker sued and received a judgment in his favor, but Labon died of stomach cancer before anything could be collected. Walker considered it the price for freedom, as he could now write more inspiring work. "Gone is one less link in the chain that binds us to this location indefinitely." He now hoped for sale of their house, which would enable them to move north, "most likely New York." Elberta expressed a strong desire to see the Hudson River. She was able to join him on short hikes and attended Tom Walker's seventy-fourth birthday celebration at the creek farm, where she said the blessing. Walker viewed the future with guarded hope.

At thirteen, Wendell had set his sights on becoming an Eagle Scout. He acquired a new pet for $3.50, a raccoon named Raccy, which he and Walker brought home on the streetcar.

HAMILTON COUNTY, TENN.

This is to Certify That _____, is a

Legal Voter having duly registered on the _____ day of _____, 192__.

His Her Registration No. is _____ Color ____ Age ____ Avocation _____

Residence _____

(Here give Name of Street or Road, Number of House or Owner thereof)

and is entitled to vote in *N I N T H W A R D* (Second Precinct), in all elections held in Hamilton County, in said Ward, within two years from the second Monday, being the 8th day of August, 1921, twenty (20) days after the issuance of this Certificate provided he she otherwise qualifies _____ self as an elector.

_____

_____ } Registrars

Above: Elberta's voting certificate, 1921.

Right: Walker teaching nature to Elberta and Wendell, 1921.

93

In 1920, Tennessee became the thirty-sixth state to ratify the Nineteenth Amendment, giving women voting rights. Walker, no strong supporter of women's suffrage, accepted the law of the land. Elberta exercised her new privilege for the first time in August 1921.

Since his "release from prison at the *SFG*," Walker had time to hike trails on Lookout and Signal Mountains and his father's old farm. He was restless to accomplish more. He often took Elberta to her favorite nature spot, woods off Bennett Road, bringing a folding chair, as she tired easily.

The cornerstone for the new Pilgrim Congregational Church at Lindsey and Oak Streets was laid on December 21. Preparing the copper box to be placed in it, Walker included a recent magazine article and a stone staurolite cross from Patrick County, Virginia, which had been in his pocket the day Robert was killed. These were called "lucky stones," although legend said they brought bad luck.

1922–1923

April found Elberta back in Menlo with her sister, leaving Wendell with his father. Two months before, she had suffered a severe kidney attack, placing her in the hospital for a month. The kidney was abscessed. Walker began writing newsy, amusing letters to cheer her. "My dear Elbertee, The 'coon bit Wendell while he was putting a collar on her. Then she escaped into the house and is now slumbering somewhere between the walls. I know she thinks she has found the largest hollow tree that ever grew." Walker bragged that Wendell had sold two stories and was "flying in the writing game."

He mentioned the George Miltons bringing a manuscript for him to review. Although he was good friends with both, after George Milton's death, he would become even better friends with Abby Milton—for a time.

Then, in a peculiar postscript, he added: "Elbertee is Cherokee. I like it better, don't you?" The significance of this may be the fact that Elberta had hidden her Cherokee heritage, which the Clark family took great pains to conceal. This was discovered after her death, and although the information was never passed to their sons, it seems certain that Walker knew of it, this simple postscript revealing much. In those times, Native American heritage was not desirable in white culture. Although Walker admired "educated Cherokees" in white society, he respected her wishes and kept it secret. But he continued to address her, and she signed her future letters, as "Elbertee."

He revealed frustration at being unable to pack up and head east. "The way I feel now, I do not think I would even want to visit Tennessee again." He decided not to write anymore until his family was resettled. He was still examining Mrs. Milton's manuscript, which she wanted to take to New York publishers.

Elberta was still able to sew. Walker closed one letter describing a pattern he was sending for Wendell's shirt, saying, "I will measure his throat with a string and enclose it, since I have broken three rulers trying to bend them around his neck."

If writing was momentarily declining, his speaking engagements were popular. He gave an address to the Scoutmasters and was asked to speak at the Jewish Men's Club, which he readily accepted.

Raccy with Wendell, 1921.

With Elberta away, housekeeping was also declining. Walker was building fires from cast-off tennis shoes, a bicycle pump and linoleum for heat. The raccoon got trapped in the ceiling, so Walker and Wendell prized up a floorboard to let her out. When they took her to the sink to wash her off, she rubbed soap all over and then washed her bread and banana. After eating, she took their hands and pulled them to the sink, as if to say thanks.

Walker encouraged Elberta to ask for anything she needed. "Home is little above a felon's cell without you. I went to Kress's to get things you asked for. When I asked for four sets of bustles, the girl liked to have died laughing. Then I re-read your letter and found it was dress shields."

Still he was hardly writing, stirred by nothing but Elberta. "When you are away, I feel an inward power draw me in your direction, as if my soul had strayed from me. Half of me lies buried until you are home. You have been my closest companion for so long, I will never be happy until you are with me every day. Beethoven could not write unless he could smell rotting apples, but Walker cannot write unless his wife is near."

In July, Elberta came home but had a relapse and returned to Menlo. Her kidney problem was much worse than the gallbladder trouble, and doctors were at a loss. Dr. Abernathy prescribed one-thirtieth grain of strychnine three times a day for her heart, thinking her trouble was caused by "nervousness."

Walker began writing again, despite himself, because he loved to write—and he wrote voluminously. "If I am able to reach people by every true thing I write, I am doing the world a little good." Then he recorded having ninety-four manuscripts returned, "enough to dishearten a new writer so, he would never venture out again."

He was looking into goat's milk to help Elberta while working on his "State Flowers" manuscript. Wendell built a wagon with a 'coon cage on top for the "circus" he and friends were performing. He painted a sign and toured the neighborhood, charging one-cent admission.

Walker wrote declaring his faithfulness, asking Elberta to do the same, hoping if either were to die, he would go first. Then he reminded her if she recovered, it would be the mercy of God, not the skill of man. Considering the medical practices of that day, he couldn't have been more right.

Despite their best efforts and hopes, things did not improve for long. She returned home in October, becoming almost bedridden, scarcely venturing from her room. She sat with the family at Christmas dinner but could eat little.

1924

By January, Elberta was an invalid, yet she appreciated the antics of Raccy, who came into the bedroom, removed hairpins from her hair while she slept and hid them on the mantel.

Walker was trying to work on a fiction romance, but concerns for Elberta consumed him. She went to Erlanger Hospital and had a "very disagreeable kidney treatment," undergoing an operation to wash out her kidney.

February found Walker escaping his overwhelming anxiety by focusing on the raccoon's comic relief. "Raccy woke Wendell and me this morning, jumping on the bed, trying to pull him from it by his arm…She began searching for a dark nook, examining the fireplace, which she likely took for a hollow tree, but

Above: Raccy washing her food.

Right: Raccy exploring a cereal box, 1924.

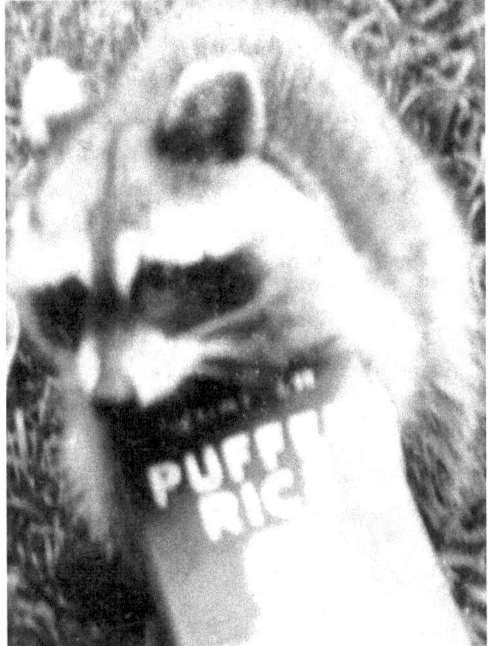

the fire prevented her entering. She worked her way between mine and the chair's back and began removing things from my pockets...We let her out and she found her usual retreat between the floor and ceiling."

Elberta came home by taxi in agonizing pain, for which she required a hypodermic for relief. Walker "sat by her side until midnight, then lay down beside her."

The next day she woke with a severe headache and a temperature of 104. Nurses and doctors tended her round the clock, without improvement. She still recognized her husband and son, but as her fever climbed to 106, hopes of recovery fled. "It is punishment of the soul to watch her suffering while unable to do anything." On February 21, he wrote: "Our hearts, our affections, our prayers have one center, saving the life of my companion... How I pray God will spare her life!"

On February 23, doctors diagnosed her condition as pernicious anemia. Her fever subsided, but she was going into a "deep stupor," or coma. Doctors said she would not recover. Walker wrote:

With our hearts ripped open, it is so hard for the pen to write. So often recently my companion has asked if I thought we had taken our last hike together...I have remained hopeful. But how crushing is this blow!... When she was at her worst with fever a few nights ago, she came to me in my sleep and asked if we should not bear this cross.

This is the second such ordeal—and the one who shared the first, in leaving, is causing the second. When we lost Robert, I thought it would have been easier had he died of sickness, to prepare us for the loss. But Elberta's long illness has shown shock and sorrow is not lessened in the least by the event's foretelling.

Wendell and I are close by her side. I hold her beautiful, soft hands, thinking of the sweet caresses bestowed on her family during the last twenty years. I hold her long, braided hair, and wish I might transmit some power through it to awaken her from this deep sleep. Surely our twenty years together have been heaven and our honeymoon never ended. If she must leave, I know we will continue our sweet relationship in the world to come.

We have often talked over the strange event we call death. She asked me ten days ago, if she died, would I remarry. I answered that I would, only if I found a woman with all her beautiful, noble traits; whose disposition was precisely like hers; or if, in fact, I could find her again...But I believe there will never be a woman of as sweet character as Elberta. Another day of unrelenting suffering passed.

After kissing her goodnight—a kiss that might be the last this side of eternity—I lay down. Wendell is so anxious. He shook me from sleep, saying, "Daddy, how will you pay all the expenses? Let me take all I have in the bank and help pay for it."

Elberta and Walker had promised to hold each other's hands in the event of either's death. On February 26, Walker and his son were awakened early by Mrs. Henry Clark, Elberta's sister-in-law, telling them to go to her.

Walker and Wendell, and others who saw, were deeply impressed that despite her long year of terrible suffering, a remarkable transformation had taken place. Elberta's features inexplicably changed, appearing young and beautiful again. Bob lay down beside his beloved wife, pressing his cheek to hers, holding the wedding ring on her hand. It was too much for Wendell, who whispered he would wait outside the door. Walker wrote:

> *Her breathing was slow, broken…and while my cheek was pressed to hers, her hand in mine, she breathed her last. It was five forty-five in the morning.*
>
> *How unreal, how dreadful it is. The person who boasts of his faith in God and eternal life will awaken to have it severely tested under such circumstances…I realized what a pleasure it is to have our loved ones with us, even as invalids….Nothing can prepare the human heart for such a loss. I would give all to have her back.*
>
> *My manuscripts are filled with her little notes, and it chokes me that she will never come into my office again. How happy Elberta must be to have her arms around Robert. I move about my house as in a dream.*

A postmortem exam revealed multiple abscesses on her right kidney, where no treatment could reach. Elberta had approved the autopsy, hoping it might help others, and Bob was comforted that his cousin Dr. George Walker had been present for it. Walker and his sister-in-law Ida chose a white dress and coffin, but Elberta had not wanted a vault, saying it would cheat nature.

Her body was returned to the front room of her childhood home, where she and Walker were wed twenty years before.

> *How taciturn is death…she appears to be sleeping. If not for Wendell, it would be sweet to…go with her…Here I am peering into the depths of eternity. This is a nightmare from which there is no waking.*
>
> *As I gaze across the horizon marking the veil between life and death, it occurs to me that we are the poor souls who deserve pity. I believe she is still alive; what we see is her cast-off garment….She told me shortly before her death that she wanted to come back to help us, if possible…My prayer is God will help me finish my life in the same pure spirit that was her ideal, that whatever I do reflects the good influence she had over me.*

*She hated pomp, conceit, and vanity, but delighted in making her home
the most cheerful, pure and holy place on earth. She was braver than I, her
nobility of character enabling her to withstand this ordeal far better than I.*

She was only forty-two.

Elberta was buried beside Robert in Forest Hills. The family plot was in
"the most beautiful place in the cemetery, but really, is anything beautiful
about a place where the dead are interred?...Our dead are not here...How
hard it is for my pen to write these lines. What a terrible subject fate has
compelled me to discuss on paper."

Elberta had asked for no flowers. Though friends wished to ignore the
request, Walker would not break his pledge to her. Strength to go on came
from his very large family. He entrusted Wendell to Mary and her family for
the time being while he stayed with his father, Tom. He remembered first
meeting Elberta there twenty-five years earlier.

The night of her funeral, he prayed God would let her come back, if only
for a day. That night she came to him in a dream, and they walked together
on the crest of a beautiful mountain. She told him he must take the road
leading into the dark valley below, traveling to its end, which ended at the top
of another mountain. When he asked if he must travel alone, she said it was
ordained that he must, but she would be waiting for him at the end. The next
morning he felt certain it was more than a dream. A walk to the old cabin
and creek farm, where he sensed her presence, cheered him. Elberta always
loved hiking the place. Every inch of it was holy ground to him.

He and Wendell planned to get away when school ended. Too much
reminded them of their loss, and both were grieving. Elberta had been
helping him with a story, left uncompleted now. "How I am to finish it, I do
not know. My pen won't write."

Lizzie's daughter, Nina, twenty-five, began spending time at their home,
Walker calling his nieces angels of mercy. Wendell received a cornet and joined
the school marching band, but Raccy had grown vicious. They chained her to
the porch. Walker lost interest in nature, which he had shared with Elberta. He
wondered if the indifference was permanent. He ceased attending church, he
and Wendell playing hymns at home on piano and cornet.

He wrote, "Long walks no longer comfort me; the silence of Elberta's
absence is as awful as if I were in the ocean all alone. I am so ashamed of
my lack of faith!"

Wendell and friend Bob Talley put on a vaudeville show at the Tivoli
Theatre. Walker acquired a billy goat named Dr. Hunt, tethering him

in the yard so they didn't have to mow grass. They were trying to tame Raccy again.

He took Wendell to give out candy to children in a poor section of town, teaching by example the importance of sharing. He went hiking with Wendell and friends, his spirits lifting some. "Morning burst in like a sapphire…I dwell in the shadow of what was once the light of a perfect love. It seems the earthly reward for perfect love is a hell of loneliness…still I continue to write—I scarcely know what."

He spoke a few times to schools, teaching nature, and began venturing out with friends. Elberta's brother Henry took him to visit old residents who had lived on Chickamauga Battlefield during the Civil War. He would eventually interview them for an article.

When they stopped on the Ridge to see the Corblys' new electric clothes washer, he looked down on his father's old farm. "How I longed to walk every foot of ground, listen to the birds, see every flower and hear the rippling Chickamauga." New homes were going up, civilization was pressing in and Walker confessed his desire for the farm of his boyhood to be spared for a nature spot.

Wendell accidentally invented a "Ghost Machine" by tying a white handkerchief to a small wire hoop. When it rolled across the yard in the dark, only the handkerchief was visible, which amused his father.

Walker described his strong kinship with wildflowers in the ways both struggled against the odds. "But I do not feel such a bond with cultivated flowers, for no one has ever done for me the favors that are bestowed on them. They are out of my class."

He declined a ride through Missionary Ridge Tunnel from an elderly Negro man driving a mule team hitched to a wagon. When he explained that he was walking for exercise but once drove a team like this, the man pulled his wagon to one side so they could converse while passing through the tunnel together. Walker claimed to have never met anyone who was not able to tell him something he had not known, adding, "People who restrict themselves socially are the poorer for it."

In May he took his son and two nieces to Menlo Springs to visit Elberta's sister Ida and husband Ves. "We all took buckets and walked to the spring. We drew our shadows' outline in the dust, drinking the cool mineral water, telling ghost stories."

The next day they hiked across Shinbone Ridge, tramping over the site at the springs of the old hotel that had burned. Walker's first trip here had been as a reporter in 1901. The Chattanooga Southern, which became the

TAG Railway, once ran a train to Menlo to sell lots. By 1924, the venture had failed and nearly vanished.

He and Reverend Freeman visited Brainerd Cemetery, despairing at its neglected graves, which included Cherokees, Negroes, whites, Dr. Samuel Worcester and John Arch, the Cherokee who first translated the Bible into that language. Pilgrim Church was interested in purchasing the mission site. (The Brainerd Cemetery and mission site are now under the protection of the DAR, Daughters of the American Revolution.) Walker sold another Missionary Ridge lot to finance a trip he was planning with Wendell to Massachusetts.

They gave their billy goat to Tom Walker, who pastured the goat with his hogs. At home, the coon was incorrigible, Walker admitting she was too smart for an animal—he had been outfoxed by a 'coon. She went on another rampage, pried through the screen door and disappeared for weeks.

By June, the Walkers had accepted the solemn duty of ending Raccy's life. She was terrorizing neighbors, entering coops and killing chickens but was too shrewd to be trapped. Brother John volunteered to shoot her in the basement, her favorite hangout. He descended the stairs, but the coon charged twice. Startled, John fired the shotgun, blowing a hole in the kitchen floor. They decided to solve the problem another way, later baiting her into a portable trap, driving her out into unsettled land and turning her loose.

Wendell by a lifeboat on *City of Savannah*, 1924.

On June 18, Walker and son went by train to Savannah, boarding the steamship *City of Savannah* for Boston. The purpose was to research material in museums and libraries, in particular Dr. Worcester's records. They spent time in the Library of Congress, Walker reading correspondence and journals of early Brainerd missionaries, saying their beautiful letters made him feel they were still alive and working there.

They visited historic churches and buildings and publishers before returning to Chattanooga on July 4. From this journey, a book was born in Walker's creative mind.

Walker and son stopped in Johnson City to see his brother Charlie, and they all went to Big Stone Gap, Virginia, to visit Uncle Nelse Moore, a former Union soldier and their mother's brother. Near Abingdon, they passed a prison gang doing road work. A sign painted on a boulder warned, "This is Camp 5. Be good or you will be sorry," reminding Walker of his old transfer job.

Walker's cousin Lula showed him the Moore family Bible, revealing that his mother and siblings were born near White Horn and the Moore ancestors came from Botetourt County, Virginia. This information apparently was previously unknown to Walker.

Because Walker did not drive now, he frequently accompanied friends who did, being particularly interested in places related to Moravian missions and the Cherokees.

In August, he and nieces Hallye and Dona hiked over his childhood "stomping grounds," visiting Hattie Lowe, who was celebrating her seventy-fifth birthday. Walker reflected how he and his friends would throw a ball across her roof, playing their game "Aunty-Over." Hattie's father, Thomas Sparks Lowe, who supervised the Western and Atlantic Railway's construction, had given newborn Robert Walker his middle name, Sparks.

Hiking around the old farm, Walker visited the "Beech Bottoms," where he traced names carved in beech trees years before, coming across his own several times. "With what tenacity does the past cling to the bark of these trees! Nature was doing her best to eradicate the old road, but these trees were still filled with memories."

In Forest Hills, Elberta's gravestone was placed identical to one marking Robert's grave. Walker had ordered it before leaving for Boston. He rode to Concord Churchyard, where lay many friends: R.S. and L.G. Martin, T.S. Matson and R.G. Davidson, brother of John Davidson, his brother-in-law. "Then I came to the graves of my sister, brother and mother. I found it hard to breathe, let alone speak here."

Riding past Mackie Schoolhouse, he was overcome with memories.

I saw an apparition of two horses stalking along, carrying two women on side-saddles. A boy of eight—myself—was behind one of them, my sister Dona. The other was my mother. A sweet-faced girl name Josie Julian lifted me from the horse. I loved her then because she treated me so kindly.

Elberta in Jackson Park, 1922.

Children never forget kindness…My mother has been traveling that mystic journey which we imagine we see through a dim twilight of faith. But here I sit a hermit…in the House of Silence…watching the procession go in, as I wait my turn.

Excitement stirred Walker's neighborhood when the city raided a nearby house, arrested two bootleggers and found seventeen gallons of corn whiskey, which Walker abhorred.

The Wheeler Syndicate in New York proposed that he bring his nature columns to their daily newspapers, resulting from his recent call on their New York affiliate. The *Boston Transcript*, previously a closed market, also bought a story, and *Christian Science Monitor*'s Children's Page accepted his bird poems. He called this windfall "the best tonic for a struggling author."

He was now "mothering, fathering and brothering a boy all on my own," but writing was never neglected. He and five o'clock formed a loyal partnership, he said—when he did his best work. He still avoided church services, finding Elberta's absence too burdensome.

He began revising "Nature Study on a City Lot," which he and Elberta had edited together, sitting on Jackson Park swings following her gallbladder surgery. He let the dedication to her stand, acknowledging it could not have been done without her.

In September, Elberta's brother Joe Clark died in Baylor Hospital in Dallas. Walker called him such a positive man that, given opportunity, Joe would have taken the "mist" out of "optimist."

Walker was seeking to publish "The Beechblock Circus." Despite loneliness, he began appreciating his solitude. With Wendell at school, he could write uninterrupted.

In December, he and Wendell spent a short time at Sutherland's Madison Rural Sanitarium outside Nashville for a supervised rest. Walker was concerned about his son's stomach complaint, which turned out to be an ulcer.

On Christmas morning, Walker presented his son with a gold-filled watch. His old habit of writing had returned, and he admitted being never so happy as when writing. He was sleeping better too. Even the whistles and cannons of New Year's Eve failed to rouse him.

Chapter 5
1925–1928

1925

Walker's agent, Robert Thomas Hardy, was trying to place some of his rewritten manuscripts. Walker still rose early to write, claiming he could do more in two morning hours than in five the rest of the day. On his forty-seventh birthday, his son gave him as many boxes decorated with his trademark: a raccoon's paw print. Walker spent the day hiking with a friend, claiming, "An excursion outdoors makes me feel young again."

On the first anniversary of Elberta's death, he reflected on her appearance during her last week of life. Because her face had become beautiful again, Walker had hoped for recovery, not realizing it was the final stage of her illness.

He would often examine manuscripts for friends and was approached by Mother Reed from the Orphans' Home, who had published a book by her late niece, Myrtle Reed, a successful author from Chicago. He was surprised by a letter from Annie Bare, now Puryear, wondering if she wrote because she had heard of Elberta's death.

He believed a person's life was never a failure if he could do one thing to benefit humanity. "I write, speak, and lecture, but whether I do these well, someone else must judge. But friends have told me I make good bread."

A recent picnic with friends was somewhat spoiled by moonshiners watching as they hiked up Lookout Mountain. "If there is one thing in America that should be free for all to enjoy, it is the mountains."

In March, he declined an offer of editor of a paper proposed by the *Arkansas Gazette*. Having extricated himself from the *SFG*, he felt better off on his own. He was working on *Anchor Poems*, which would be his first published book. He commented, "Settled another wild swarm of thoughts into the poem hive."

He and Wendell spent time at his sister Lizzie's, her family becoming their surrogate family following Elberta's passing. Walker often sat by their fireplace, "reading" the fire: "How cheerful and warm is a big wood fire—a real live companion, as interesting as a book." He did not care for hot water or steam heat, preferring instead open hearth fires.

On Easter, he took his "tribe" to the Chickamauga creek bed, preparing breakfast by burying potatoes, building a fire over them and frying bacon on sassafras skewers. Previously boiled eggs completed the feast.

He saw resurrection in white violets and shooting stars, trout lilies and jack-in-the-pulpit springing from dead leaves and decay. All impressed him as most holy but not solemn. He lay on the fallen log in the creek, reflecting on his failed efforts to portray its beauty to those who had never seen it. He apologized to the creek and promised Creator that given time, words and strength, he would continue until he succeeded.

It was a happy day, Walker more at home there than in his own house. "The woods and fields were to me more holy than any church. How sacred and comforting are the sights and sounds of nature. My soul has surely been resurrected today!"

By April, he had set aside $500 in trust, the interest for prize money for the annual Elberta Clark Walker Poetry Contest. He hoped Chattanooga Writers' Club would conduct it.

On May 31, three dozen Walkers gathered to celebrate Tom Walker's seventy-eighth birthday, including Miss Hattie Lowe, also seventy-eight. A bad drought reduced to one foot the depth of Walker's favorite fishing hole in the Chickamauga. The bank had eroded, with tree roots sticking out "like snaggle teeth in an old man's mouth."

In June, Professor Bentley of the University of Tennessee asked Walker to go to Memphis to study the Argentine ant, which had infiltrated that city. He and Wendell hired on for a monthlong hunt, traveling by train to Memphis. Walker enlisted the aid of newspapers and civic organizations to explain his quest.

He was shocked to run across a jewelry store bearing the name Marcus Seinfield, the Jewish man he had invited to Cuba back in 1903. Seinfield had then hidden in Walker's room to avoid his older brother, who showed up and accused Walker of kidnapping. They talked over that misadventure, Seinfield saying his stern brother was now deceased.

Back on the swarming Argentine ant's trail, Walker found the health department's city physician unconcerned, taking a diametrically opposing view and leading the uninformed to believe ants were good citizens, harboring no danger. He had dismissed cutting weeds as a means of controlling insects, including the malaria mosquito. With that piece of news, and a visit to the mayor, Walker and son were eager to head home to a cooler clime. "Give me the dear old mountains; I shall never forsake them! After a month of collecting, boiling and processing ants in merciless heat, even our unkempt yard is a welcome sight." Ironically, on the train

Walker "gone fishing," 1922.

home, when Walker hoped to sleep, he met a man "very much interested in ants," who pumped him for information for three hours.

He began grinding wheat for whole wheat breakfast muffins. "White bread will kill a dog in a month if fed that exclusively, and it has surely poisoned me."

The old Read House was demolished for construction of a "modern" hotel, which stands today on the site. He described seeing *Quo Vadis* with Wendell at the Tivoli, calling it a "great contrast to the rotten movie we saw last week, which should have been destroyed by fire before it ever got on the screen."

Cousin Albert told him of a mother cat bringing fresh meat to her kittens in their barn. She preferred snakes, one of which was poisonous. She dragged in the trophy by the tail, and when it licked out its tongue, she slapped it across the head, chewed that off, then paid her respects to its tail by chewing off six inches of that before turning it over to her kittens. She was also seen bringing lizards, one of them wrapped in grass—a feline tamale, with grass instead of corn husks.

Walker, an astute observer, called himself a voyeur of the insect world. He watched a brown arboreal spider in his persimmon tree, camouflaged by her choice of both brown and green leaves. He fed her beetles, which had "done nothing to discourage her appetite for cannibalizing her mate."

He watched her flirting and retreating with a small male several times before "literally kicking him off her web with two feet, reconsidering, then drawing him again towards her…This scene re-enacted many times until passion was too great and she held him tightly with her feet locked. When I touched him with a straw, he was dead. She then devoured him! What a suitor! What a spectacle! Thus I may be first to observe this drama of the spider's life."

He billed a publisher who had kept an accepted manuscript for two and a half years without payment or publishing. The publisher returned it with apologies and a check for Walker's bill, which he had sent "to do justice to myself and compel him to deal honorably with his fellow man. I returned the manuscript to him, feeling I have done him, myself, and my brothers in the writing game, a favor."

In August, Walker traveled with Wendell and nephew Perry Davidson to Chipley, Florida, to visit Charles and Lilly Pleas, old friends he had never met. Pleas, a naturalist and nurseryman, had advertised in the *SFG* twenty years before. The trio passed through Georgia during a drought. Water was rationed, one druggist saying he was saving his supply for his soda fountain.

The Pleases' farm, Glen Arden, was a mile east of Chipley, far from the road. Mrs. Pleas was an artist who had kept an art store in town until illness impaired her eyesight. Now she helped with her husband's farm and nursery. Pleas kept one thousand chickens, and she milked one cow. Walker said her excellent landscape paintings were hung about the house. He also reported she could handle a shotgun as deftly as a paintbrush, bemoaning her killing of a rabbit breakfasting in her garden.

They drove through the Pleases' pecan groves and were shown waterfalls that dropped eighty feet into a hole in the earth before they left the next day for Panama City and Hurricane Island in the Gulf of Mexico. Panama City was only ten years old, making it hard to secure a pilot to take them into the Gulf. A youngster, eleven, who had been to Hurricane Island, took the job, bringing a teenage friend. The island, nine miles into the Gulf, was three miles long and half a mile wide, with a central dune like a backbone. They gave up swimming after being chased to shore three times by sharks.

Once he learned to run the engine, Wendell steered the boat back to Panama City, but the abundance of tourists made finding a room difficult. Walker noted many old *SFG* advertisers along their route, feeling his paper had contributed to developing the pecan industry. Stopping in Butler, Georgia, to repair a tire, Walker called it "a real old-time country town of the best kind. The newspaper boasts of being established in 1876, and the bank and court house appear not to have been painted since. Both black and white country folk were in town, telephone poles threatened with uprooting, by citizens reclining against them."

Heading to Hurricane Island, Florida, 1925.
Wendell and Walker are second and third from left.

They crossed the Etowah River on a covered bridge, spent a night at the Cartersville Hotel and headed to New Echota, last capital of the Cherokee Nation. A multitude of touring autos stirred clouds of dust on the dangerous Dixie Highway. New Echota he described as "sacred soil."

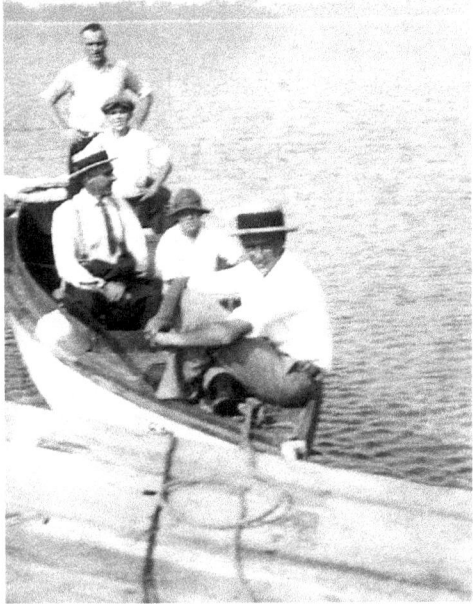

Here once stood the first and only Indian Newspaper, the Cherokee Phoenix, *edited by Cherokee Elias Boudinot. A clump of trees in a cotton field above the spring holds the grave of Mrs. Boudinot, a white woman from Connecticut who died here in 1836, two years before the Cherokees were driven out. Above the spring was the site where the spurious Schemmerhorn Treaty was signed, sending the Indians west. Such dreadful history for one spot! I could fill volumes, writing of it. I have often thought that nation worthy of a better fate, and hope to yet devote books to the subject.*

On Wendell's sixteenth birthday, his cat, Felix, presented him five kittens. Walker's gift was a three-day camping trip. Black ants discovered their

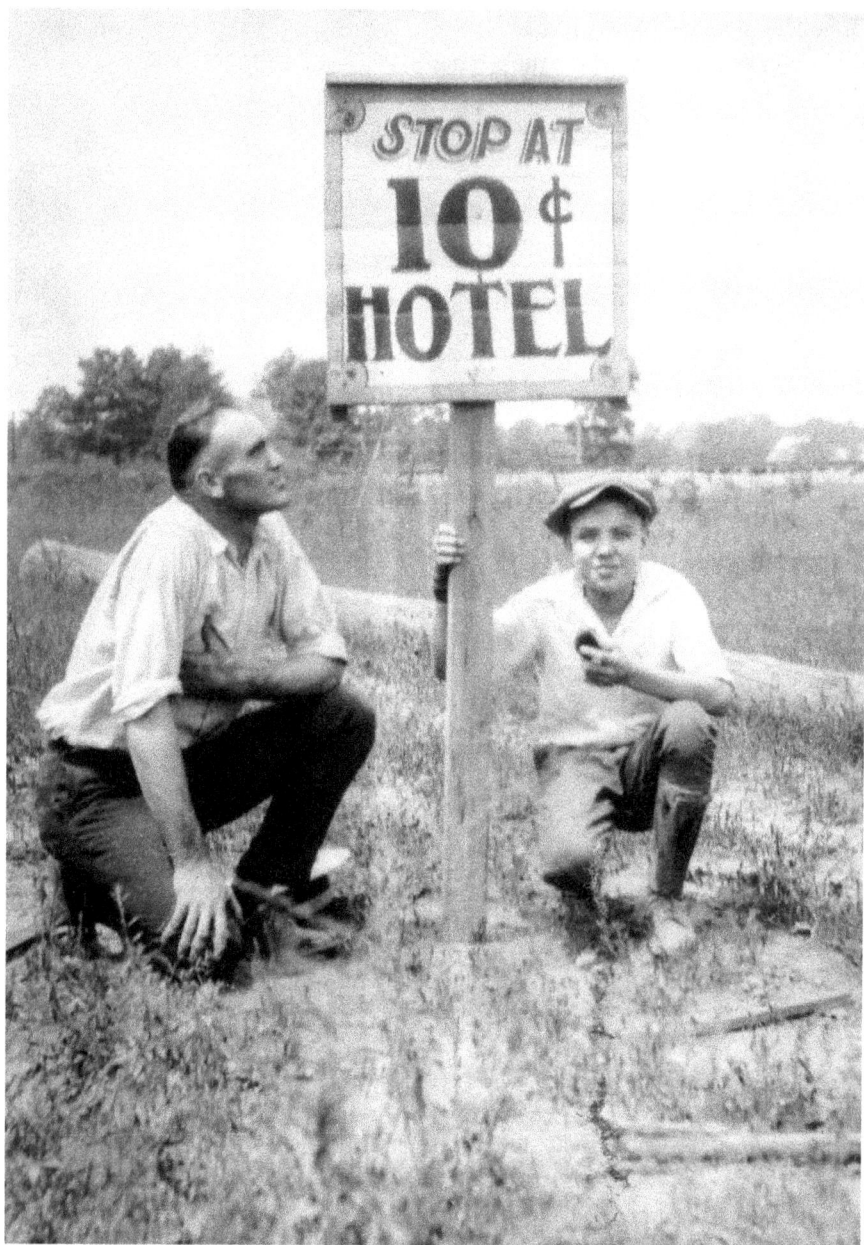

Cousin Perry Davidson and Wendell leaving Florida, 1925.

"pantry," tied in a tree, and his nieces' "fragrant" dog Nick joined their party, breathing in Walker's face while he tried to sleep. But the intrepid campers stuck it out three days and, once home, retired to a great ovation given by a host of mosquitoes.

Although the damp ground gave Walker back pain, he was inspired by spending days with the boys. He not only derived pleasure from their adventures but also discovered new material for writing. "When a man keeps an open heart...God speaks to him in the woods."

Yet he recopied older manuscripts. "I have washed their faces, counseling them not to divulge their ages to any editor. A clean manuscript keeps its age a secret, but one with dirty face and hands, and comments, tells about its experience and travels. So I have dressed them in new clothes and sent them out again."

Felix the cat was more appropriately renamed Felicia. "I was much impressed by the wisdom she exhibited opening a screen door with a kitten in her mouth. She laid it on the floor, pushed open the door with her nose, slipped inside, turned and re-opened the door, holding it open while she picked up the kitten and brought it inside. This proved to me that even a cat can reason."

On Robert's birthday, he reflected that Wendell would have had an eighteen-year-old brother. "What a joy he would have been for him!" The grisly accident replayed over and over, as it always did and would, on these dark days of remembering. He calculated its impact on Elberta, how she had never recovered from the shock.

"I wanted to curse the man who invented automobiles, but now realize the State who licenses fools and incompetents is really to blame." But from this darkness, he always emerged to face the future with hope and a smiling face.

He was working on his article "Turning the Washington Monument Inside Out," with material from his wedding trip. Among the monument's stones was one from Tennessee, declaring "The Union Must Be Preserved," and another from Hawkins County—the only U.S. county to have a stone. Walker was proud that his family had come from Hawkins, as no other people "strove more desperately to hold the Union together than those from Hawkins." There was also a stone from the Cherokee Nation, placed by them in 1850—the only stone from the American Indians.

Walker was sleeping under mosquito nets Elberta had purchased seventeen years before. "I retire, amidst a serenade by a mosquito band and a quartet of crickets."

His first book, *Anchor Poems*, was being published by Fleming H. Revell Company. Success as a writer was slowly coming. Even when he received a final meager check from the estate of Alex Labon for the 1921 sale of his *SFG*, reflecting a loss of $6,000, he quit worrying over it. He was "giving thoughts to purposeful and forward movement."

In October, the long drought gave way to rain, flooding streets and giving weeds in Walker's lawn "more promising careers." This was perhaps symbolic for Walker, who had a publisher request his manuscript *My Father's Farm*. The *Dearborn Independent* published two of his articles in one issue, crediting one to S.W. Roberts, presumably to keep its readers from knowing that one author had two stories in the same edition.

He was becoming more involved in Scouting, giving nature lectures to the Boy Scout Master Training School and visiting Scout Camp Tsuatanugi, the Cherokee name for Chattanooga. In November, his Uncle Gabriel's wife, Mat, died and was buried in Concord churchyard. Walker felt great empathy, knowing what lay ahead for his uncle.

December brought Walker good news that Payne's bookstore had ordered two hundred copies of *Anchor Poems* and hoped to sell many more. They promised a full window display of it.

Walker was now subsisting on malted milk, shredded wheat and rice biscuits, attempting to improve his health. He often experimented with diet, seeking a cure from illness. His back and legs troubled him so that he declined an invitation to dine at the Hotel Patten with the *Chattanooga News*'s editorial staff. Their guest was Will Rogers.

The winter was cold, but Walker and Wendell enjoyed Christmas at home in Highland Park. A horde of friends and family stopped in, and it seemed their life was becoming a "new" normal.

Winners were selected in the Elberta Walker Poetry Contest and published in the *Chattanooga Times*. Walker concluded that the two winners alone, from 350 entries, were worth all he had invested.

When Wendell purchased a spring gun, Walker sent him out to bag game. An hour later he returned, disheveled and sooty, with three pigeons, putting two in the fireless cooker for dinner. Walker calculated he had shot some hundred times to get them.

T.H. Payne had Walker's books in its front window. It was his first bound book, and he was very pleased.

1926

An older friend passed away, so Walker decided to visit eighty-year-old Mr. Bannons, who was "in charge" at Orchard Knob. He had been in Civil War battles around Chattanooga and was with Grant at Orchard Knob and Missionary Ridge and at Chickamauga during the worst of the conflict.

Walker and Wendell drove to Helvellyn, his acreage on Milliken Hill, paying a visit to the colored neighbor there, Gus Goree. Walker had no plans to build on the property but loved it as a beautiful piece of land.

The pain in his back and legs was diagnosed as severe rheumatism. His father was suffering the same complaint. Walker sought help from an osteopath. Cold weather provoked his condition, making it all but impossible to get out of bed. His neighbor, Dr. Gilbert, had begun treating him, but Walker could put no weight on his right leg.

By late April, he was mobile again, if not cured. Another old friend, T.P. Jarnigan, was hospitalized with a broken hip, resulting from a car striking him in front of his home. Walker went to see him. Seven years earlier Walker had suggested Jarnigan buy three hundred acres on Pigeon Mountain in Georgia. Jarnigan bought it, and another five hundred acres, transferring it all to a school. Said Walker, "One never knows what may become of a suggestion dropped into the well of a human heart."

He was teaching Wendell botany, finding him an eager pupil. When his son was away from home, Walker let the cat and her kittens lie by the hearth for company. By mid-May, he was again suffering sciatic rheumatism, barely

Orchard Knob, circa 1916.

able to leave his bed. Wendell and Dona waited on him, but little helped. He planned to get his tonsils removed as soon as he felt better.

His father, almost seventy-nine, came to visit. Tom read the newspaper without glasses and then apologized for his early departure to oversee the building of a rental storehouse on his property.

Walker's pain persisted. "What a tyrant pain is! Dona has applied hot cloths soaked in turpentine to my hip, my neighbor Mrs. Brockhaus has brought unexpected, delicious dinners, and my sister and nieces send pies. You can count on women being among the saints, but woe to the scarcity of men with wings!"

His nephew Perry took a position with the Farm Bureau in Jonesborough, Tennessee, and Walker would miss him. One evening, his brother John and several friends dropped by, which resulted in the telling of many tales.

In one long-ago incident, John and Bob were plowing the Sandy Bottom on the creek farm. John had a team of horses and Bob had mules, both covering a ten-acre tract. John realized he had lost his watch, a prize purchased from selling cucumbers. He lay down on the plowed-up ground, sliding his ear along the moist earth—worse than hunting a needle in a haystack. "Round and round he slid, but what rewards persistence brings! He found it by its tell-tale ticking! What a plot for a story—what a brother!"

Walker's extreme pain continued into the next month, and he found it hard to sleep. He even missed his father's annual birthday gathering and lost count of the many cures he had tried. His sister Mary Scott and husband Seth brought in a shovel and foul-smelling tin bucket. She made a large sock out of bed ticking, into which they shoveled cow dung, applied it to his right foot and slipped a large sock over that. Walker said it stunk so that he expected a visiting delegation of tumble bugs, noting, "But desperate people will try desperate measures."

In mid-July, Walker had his tonsils removed and "would not have them back for ten thousand dollars." His friend Dr. Willard Steele operated in his office and took him home. Within a week, Walker was walking without a cane or crutches, happy to be alive and ambitious to write again.

While Wendell was away with cousins, Walker amused himself with Felix/Felicia. He captured a June bug and tied a silk string to it, which she found entertaining until she decided to feast on it. Experiment over.

He was still recopying old manuscripts: "I have discovered they will sell when properly presented at the proper season." He had just sold "A Bearskin for a Sheepskin," written in 1912—his first fiction story. "It's had a checkered career, been out about fifty times at least, and twice to some publishers."

He got his first pair of reading glasses, which he claimed he had not needed in the beech grove where he found his name inscribed, dated 1890. He could almost hear the Barlow knife cutting into bark. "I am convinced everything we do is inscribed somewhere, and one day we shall come face to face with our deeds."

On July 18, Walker's father presented Wendell with his old long rifle, shot pouch, powder horn and bullet mold. It had been a flintlock, converted to percussion, the same gun Tom had used to hunt fox-squirrel when Bob was four. Bob had accompanied Tom to the woods then, thrilled by his father's good aim. Now Wendell was also thrilled, adding the rifle to his "museum," which he had established behind the house.

Walker liked studying nature at dawn from his front porch. "Nothing compares with the hour of dawning daylight; it is particularly beautiful and holy." He and

Wendell with his grandfather's long rifle, 1926.

Wendell were refurbishing their house, removing wallpaper, varnishing and painting. By accident, they discovered an unconventional means to protect their grapes. When Wendell spread a raincoat on the arbor to dry, Felix/Felicia seized it for a bed, spending hours there, a living cat scarecrow.

Describing a Rudolph Valentino movie at the Tivoli, Walker said the scenery was grand but the plot reminded him of a jellyfish—no shape. He sent copies of *Anchor Poems* to a Protestant library in Beirut, commenting that it cost three times the postage to send one to California. The practice of sending his books to libraries was one he often repeated.

He took numerous trips with his friend Dr. Freeman, whom he described as "eighty-six, and can drive nearer another car or pedestrian without hitting them, than all the people I have ever ridden with."

He received a note from Mrs. Luther Burbank, whose naturalist husband had died the previous spring. She said her husband had wept at the news of Robert's death, and Walker held Burbank's memory all the more dear for knowing this. They had been friends for twenty years. Burbank had planned to visit Walker someday to study the wild pea-potato together. Burbank had wanted to improve on it as a cultivated flower and edible root.

Walker declined an invitation to the opera, as he was studying a band of spiders that had invaded his dining room. He complained of the steady interruptions that disturbed his writing, remembering the unbroken time afforded by Elberta's former intervention in household matters.

In September, he drove with his friend Judge Lusk to Flint Springs Presbyterian Church, which Lusk had attended as a boy. Walker described Flint Springs as a "thing of beauty, surrounded by a concrete wall with a walk. Water bubbles up through a bowl of hewn granite, placed seventy years ago."

Older locals declared Sequoyah invented his alphabet in a clearing near the woods east from the spring. Lusk told Walker that F.M. Rice, an old resident, had confirmed this at this very place twenty-five years before. Rice

Flint Springs Schoolhouse, Tennessee, 1926.

was an army private who helped remove the Cherokees and was later an engineer on the East Tennessee, Virginia and Georgia Railway. Rice died around 1906 at the age of ninety-five. The federal government honored Sequoyah by naming the great trees of California for him, but when the Cherokee Nation voted him a pension, he became the only literary person in the United States to receive a pension for his work.

They traveled to Red Clay, Georgia, site of the former Indian Council Grounds, which had been a subject of Walker's writing. Blue Spring was located there in a cotton field, surrounded by majestic fruit trees. He described the spring as twenty-odd feet across and blue as indigo in its depths, which was a crevice between large stone ledges. Reportedly, a sinker tied to a line dropped down as far as three hundred feet without striking bottom. A plank spanning the little creek, formed by water leaving the spring, led to its rim. "This must have been a great treasure for the Cherokees, for a large spring was a special abode of the Great Spirit."

Debates were held here over the removal in the early part of the nineteenth century. When the Cherokees were forced to leave, traditional stories state they tossed their valuables into this spring to place them beyond the reach of the whites who had treated them so shamefully.

Walker and Lusk drove on to Ryall Springs, "joining the radiator in a drink of cool water." He recalled spending the summers of 1879 and 1880 with his family here, camping with the Julian family, to avoid chills and fever on the Chickamauga. They had to drive back and forth to work their farms.

Picking berries at Ryall's Springs, 1912. Elberta and her sons are at far left.

In October, Wendell's scoutmaster, Charles Peacock, opened the Indian Mound at Springfield farm near Daisy for the State Archaeological Society. It was Wendell's first major opportunity to work in that field.

Walker still owned a V-shaped lot on Missionary Ridge—or so he believed—at the intersection of five roads below it but was surprised to find another man had claimed it. He attended church for the first time in a year but continued to find God's presence in the beauty of nature. "God was not overhead, but by my side as He and I strolled together, discussing beauty, love and righteousness."

Walker was invited to a dinner given by Abby Milton (widow of publisher George Fort Milton) honoring New York writer Royal Dixon. Although Dixon volunteered to help Walker's career, Walker felt Dixon was more a lecturer than an outright naturalist.

Leaving "upper society," he recorded a humorous encounter on Market Street with struggling friend, H.D. McBroom, who sold newspapers. McBroom asked him to hear a poem he had written to welcome to Chattanooga a Romanian poet—who had, unfortunately, left Chattanooga out of his itinerary. "McBroom is a good poet who got into the clutches of dope a few years ago… and is trying hard to get out from under it." As McBroom finished his poem, a strong gust of wind carried Walker's hat into the middle of Market Street. He and McBroom took after it, racing neck and neck until they overtook it and "got it back on its bald throne. What a spectacle a—dope user and a bald man holding a footrace down the middle of a busy street."

Finances were problematic, with many manuscripts recently returned, so he declined an invitation to a dinner honoring winners of the poetry contest he had founded. "The person who writes must be willing to sacrifice every other pleasure."

Walker's Uncle Gabriel passed away on December 12 and was buried at Concord Church. He called his uncle a hero who brought sunshine wherever he went.

Paul Severance of *New South Magazine* offered Walker a nature department, and he accepted. The publisher of *Anchor Poems* declined to print a second edition, as sales were too low. Merit Newspaper Service was considering syndicating his nature articles, but previous experience with syndication had brought little success.

He and Wendell celebrated their first treeless and sockless Christmas at home instead of joining cousins in the country. They piled gifts on chairs, ignoring the temptation to feel lonely. Then they spent New Year's with the Davidsons, Walker noting that Wendell wished they could move to the country.

1927

Walker was seeking someone to lend McBroom $450 to put out an edition of his poems. McBroom had told him it was the dream of his life. Someone suggested that members of the Billy Sunday Club might lend the paper-seller money.

Walker visited the office of Provence and Hemphill, who had sold him his Ridge lot in 1919. The deed was worded so as to allow misinterpretation, allowing the abstract company to "steal" the lot through skewed description. "I have run across so many dishonest people...I wonder if there are any honest ones left at all."

In February, the Four Seas Company sent him a contract for *My Father's Farm*, his second book of poetry. He also signed a contract with Merit Newspaper Service for four-hundred-word articles and agreed to give an introduction to Royal Dixon, who was again in town for a speaking engagement.

Walker and niece Dona went to the Tivoli on his birthday to see Harold Lloyd's *Andrews' Raid Story*. Walker called it good, but "the real story of Andrews stealing the *General* came in for only a slight acquaintance, much disguised and hacked up." He would keep this topic in mind.

Wendell expressed interest in going west, which Walker attributed to a recent appearance in town by "some sort of wild westerner—a Wild Bill Something—who claimed to have been raised by the Sioux. We found him on the third floor of the Yellow Cab Company building on Carter Street. He had a 700-pound lion caged in a Dodge auto, which he claimed to have captured out west, and is still looking for someone to identify it. I believe it escaped from a circus, and this man caught it, supposing he had found it in its native haunts."

Walker was wrestling again with too little time for work. He had to refuse speaking requests to hold onto time, getting so many calls for lectures and questions that "some days my soul cries out for a minute of peace." He wanted his nature books published to be of benefit to mankind.

In April, a kidnapping occurred in Walker's neighborhood, but the two-year old was ransomed and returned a few days later; the culprits were caught with marked ransom money. Walker was "sickened by humanity's silliness, reflected by the steady stream of cars and pedestrians on Greenwood," all looking for the house where the child was abducted.

Bonnie Gilbert was helping with proofs for *My Father's Farm*. She was constant as the North Star, never interfering, always ready to do

Surviving Chickamauga Battlefield residents: McDonald, Poe and Julia Reed, with W.T. Walker and Wendell, 1928.

a kindness, and so she would remain throughout Walker's life—a truly good neighbor.

In May, Walker gathered a small interested party to visit Chickamauga Battlefield with some of its surviving residents. He interviewed Larkin Poe, Julia Snodgrass Reed, Mrs. Alva Red Ray and William MacDonald, who recounted eyewitness memories of the battle fought there. Poe, ninety-four, invited Walker to come, saying, "Do it soon, or it will be too late." Walker called the survivors "genuine treasures, living history, all the more so for their short time here with us."

Walker was processing wheat again to make bread. He washed a half bushel and spread it on a newspaper on the garage roof with a window screen over it to keep sparrows at bay. Then he ground it, baking it into tasty loaves.

He recorded the terrible Mississippi Valley flood, in which thousands were made homeless. Snakes climbed trees to keep from drowning and leapt into boats ("even a snake exercises judgment in times of disaster"), bears were seen in Arkansas begging food and people were sharing what little they had with them, "adversity making brothers of all higher animal life."

At last his house was repainted a dark chocolate, which he claimed had a greenish tint from powdered lampblack mixed in the paint. It was the first paint job since 1919.

Walker mourned the passing of old friend George Varnell. He and his brother had kept the store and post office in Chickamauga (Worley).

Walker washing wheat, 1927.

He visited the Georgia Talc Works, watching them grind soapstone into flour, which was made into talcum powder. This was only a sideline of their main business, manufacturing soapstone crayons, which he called very beautiful.

Wendell was given a 'possum. Walker described, "Mrs. Possum lying on her back with her pouch spread open, sunning eight or nine naked children… They were bald, no more than an inch long." In the next breath he went on to say, "The earth is so beautiful it is almost a punishment to stay indoors."

On a drive to the high ridge between Chickamauga and the Tennessee River, he observed Dallas Island (now under water). Northwest, across from it on a red, bare hill, was the site of Dallas, once the seat of Hamilton County, "before I was ever a native of this earth. Everywhere around is something that speaks of history or natural beauty, and I am glad to call this place my home."

Fifteen years earlier, Walker had purchased another lot on Crest Road from an old friend, John Lightfoot. He described it as hard to find, rocky and somewhat steep but with houses near and a road ending on it. He thought he might sell it one day but next time would go over the abstract with a magnifying glass.

The family held its annual party for Tom Walker's birthday, nieces Dona, Hallye and her friend Sue Morrison driving Walker, Wendell and Mrs. Possum and her children to the country. Walker began to interpret the 'possum's conversation, which amounted to the 'possum naming three of her children for the three women in thanks for the ride to the country. At the Brainerd Bridge, they released the 'possums at the creek as Walker continued translating the 'possum's thoughts.

"Mrs. Possum now says that after getting a good look at all of you, she asks to be excused from fulfilling her pledge to name her children for you. She wishes to make something of them, and cannot cripple them as namesakes for anything so ugly." Walker added a disclaimer that his knowledge of Possumese might be a little rough around the edges.

His book *My Father's Farm*, dedicated to Tom Walker, was published in time for his father's eightieth birthday. Walker privately wondered if his son would dedicate a book to him when he turned eighty. Tom Walker, a lifelong farmer, was not expected to put much stock in his son's book. When nephew Perry asked if Walker thought Tom would read it, he replied that his father would rather open the mouth of a good horse to tell its age than open a book of poetry, even though it was dedicated to him. But a number of times, to Walker's surprise, his father took down the book and read a poem or two from it, "which was gratitude enough for me!"

Sixty-five people attended the celebration, including Hawkins County Walkers. Walker declared it a grand success, despite being awakened in the night by a lighted match against his bare foot from cousin Ross Walker, whom he had not met before. They shook hands before Bob went back to sleep.

Uncle Bill Moore, his mother's half brother, brought his little grandson Lloyd, who was interested in wildflowers. When Walker suggested the boy might become a naturalist, his uncle stated, "That's just what I don't want him to do. I want him to amount to something!" Perry and others, overhearing this, howled with laughter. The Walker humor was in full bloom.

That same month, Walker's brother-in-law Henry Clark drove him and Wendell to Athens, Tennessee, former home of the Clark family. Along the way, people everywhere were excited over Lindbergh's flight from New York to Paris.

Henry took them to U.S. Grant University, which had become Tennessee Wesleyan College, where Elberta had gone to school. The grounds were shaded by maples, the main building shaky and braced up by a dense growth of English ivy. He found her old residence, Ritter House, still standing, "clean and neat, its entrance apparently trying to swallow a host of ferns and potted flowers." Elberta had boarded here and become popular for her sweet disposition. Walker wished he had brought her here while she was living.

Henry, too, had gone to school here, pointing out the site of an old home of his father, Reverend Clark. They then traveled three miles to Wesleyanna, a rural church and schoolhouse. Henry took them to six graves side by side in the cemetery, west of the church, about one hundred feet from the entrance. The first grave was an infant of Callie Clark Melton's, Elberta's older half sister living in Texas.

The second grave was Reverend Clark, Elberta's father, and the third his wife, Sarah Morrison Clark. Walker said he never knew a more noble woman. The fourth grave was Emma Clark, the fifth Charlie Clark and last Lilly Clark, none of whom Walker had ever met. The graves were all unmarked, but Walker made a picture of Wendell and Henry near the graves to mark them. The Clark family had been gone from the area over thirty years.

Henry drove west over the old road until they came to a small spring by the roadside. To the right in a small field was an unpainted two-story house hidden by a clump of cedars. It faced south and had once been a respectable residence but was now tottering—windows broken, brick chimneys leaning, sills rotting. A long porch extended across its back north side; two large rooms were downstairs, and the west room of hewn logs had been weatherboarded. Henry told them the house had been white. Walker observed a fertile garden north of the house with many peaches, despite the freeze.

A small fire burned in the east room, where Reverend Clark had died on April 3, 1891. He had purchased the sixty-five-acre farm when he was "superannuated" for age and ill health. The house was now owned and occupied by the Bryant family, who were poor but hospitable. Bryant, his wife, Nancy, and their three children had owned the farm about sixteen years. It was about a mile west of Wesleyanna and four miles east of Athens. The Clarks sold the farm around 1892 when Reverend Clark died.

Walker thought how Elberta had spoken of catching minnows with a dipper at the spring, the stream from it flowing through a nature spot full of birds and flowers. Small wonder she had become a naturalist—and the most perfect mate Walker could have found. He felt remorse for not bringing her back to see her old home.

He began revising "The Beechblock Circus," first written in 1916. He had a speaking engagement at the Brainerd Mission site, which Pilgrim Church had done much to promote. Now the road leading to this site was known as Brainerd Road and the area known as East Brainerd.

His camping and nature trips were eating into his writing time, though he found them hard to decline. Judge Lusk took him and Wendell to the lock and dam at Hale's Bar, descending into the dam itself, where they had cheese sandwiches at the bottom of the Tennessee River.

Despite his local travels, he was writing often about his discoveries on such journeys. He sold to *Commonweal* magazine in New York a manuscript on ants written from his ant-detective work in Memphis. He was revising a third book of poetry, *When God Failed*, noting that his income was depleted, quoting, "Writing is an excellent walking stick, but a poor crutch."

He paid Larkin Poe another visit near Apison. Poe said Apison was first called O'Brien but was changed when they found another town by that name. Poe was five years older than Chattanooga and had been living in the area when the Cherokees were removed. He had been in his present home since 1871, before there was a Chickamauga, Tennessee. Back then it had been the largest shipping port between Chattanooga and Atlanta.

Walker recorded a ride he and Wendell took on two mules from Lizzie's to the creek farm. The mule Walker rode was twenty-two, bony and not very spry. "If I could have got rid of my contact with Nathan's razor back, it would have been an ideal ride." They hitched their mules to fence posts, cutting weeds and laying them before their steeds. On returning, Walker found his mule had ignored the tasty plants but had pitched into poison ivy growing on the post, which he stripped bare, devouring it all. The mule's health improved considerably afterward, leading Walker to theorize there must be a property in poison ivy that the mule recognized as beneficial. "Animals have innate wisdom in such matters, which humans ought to acquire."

Walker canceled some trips due to Wendell's poor health—another ulcer diagnosis—but went to Raccoon Mountain with Fred Cofer, who was hopeful of catching rattlesnakes. Walker did not fancy riding in a car with snakes swirling at his feet in a tow sack. But his friend did not find any and had to settle for salamanders.

Walker was always investigating, discovering a large spider web two feet in diameter beneath his porch. He showered a handful of flour over it and the spider to show the web's design, leaving "its tenant strangely dressed in a white linen suit." To appease the spider, he offered her a cockroach.

Lippincott's agreed to publish *Breakfast Stories* but hired another author to rewrite it as a children's reader. This would cost Walker half the royalties but, he hoped, would increase its sales as a schoolbook.

The anniversary of Robert's death found Walker plunged into darkness, reliving the horrific details. He considered his lost son; the loss of Elberta, killed by grief; the tragedy's impact on his and Wendell's health. That one event had begun a chain of sorrow, always lurking, even on his best days. His only solace was faith that his family would one day be reunited.

"I am so thankful God inhabits places besides church buildings. While I would not live in a community without churches, I thank God that he goes everywhere I go. I hear his footsteps in the woodlands and weedlands, see his face in every dewdrop and flower. I hear his voice in every rippling brook, and read his message in every tree and stone. I think he must spend a great deal of time outdoors."

On October 5, Lindbergh came to Chattanooga. Walker and Wendell watched his plane sail over north of town. They walked to McCallie Avenue to see his auto passing. Lindbergh was seated on a platform behind the back seat, "wearing a dark suit that looked much used. He is just a young, sunburnt man—almost a boy…Now and then he saluted the crowds in a very nonchalant manner…Wendell snapped his picture."

Wendell was not recuperating from his ulcer as rapidly as doctors expected and was again put on a diet of milk and raw egg every two hours. But he was keeping himself busy making and developing pictures.

Both Walker and son were touched by the unexpected death of Sherman Sanders, forty-six, who passed away after an emergency appendectomy. They remembered the man's consolation when Robert was killed.

Finances were again problematic. Later that month, Lippincott's, after sending a letter of acceptance, sent a letter of rejection. "I have the worst luck…My first such experience was in 1919, when a publisher accepted a manuscript, held it two years, then went bankrupt. Another manuscript suffered similar abuse, and last year another publisher accepted my book, *Eating Thunder*, only to send it back three months later." Syndicating his material had twice brought the same results.

New South Magazine, "belabored by dirty sparkplugs and missing a few cylinders," had cut his material, failing to pay him for published articles. Now he was borrowing money. "No author can count a manuscript sold, until he cashes the check…One ought never tell anyone he is having a book published until it is in distribution."

He complained of a luncheon he attended involving "wrestling a smothered chicken leg with knife and fork...Chicken ought not be served when employing table silver, since more than half goes to waste, the rest going down the esophagus with oaths on the swallower's lips."

Rascally brother John told a friend Walker was "sitting up nights watching spiders" so calling him at any hour would be no disturbance—thus explaining a 3:20 a.m. phone call he received. Walker pranks were perpetuated by another generation, as Wendell threw a garden hose over the porch roof, stretched it to a guest room on Halloween night and spoke eerily into it, terrifying Walker's two nieces who were staying over.

They spent Christmas at Lizzie's, Walker recording his first present: a neatly scraped hog's foot in a candy box, "which I prize highly."

He placed wreaths on Elberta's and Robert's graves, "reminders of an earlier life, in which fate and circumstances conspired to crush the life out of me...Part of me remains with them, but the man I am now will go on with the business of life until I have finished my race."

He was fiercely working on manuscripts, finding markets. "I had one chapter chopped and hacked up like I used to slash briars in a fence corner...I am getting to where I can carve up my stuff like a pumpkin." But he preferred writing new material.

1928

In January, former sweetheart Annie Bare Puryear called him. She was now a grandmother, causing Walker to reflect on their youth, "when music and laughter were the purpose for living...the years have shown this as a myth, life extracting from us things we could not have imagined back then."

He visited Pan Gap, the Boy Scout camp on Raccoon Mountain that was sold in 1924 and a new site purchased, Camp Tsautanugi, north of Hixson. He recalled a conversation with one Scout concerning a turkey buzzard soaring overhead. Someone compared it to Lindbergh, causing Walker to comment that even Lindbergh could not approach the buzzard's mastery of the air, adding, "If Lindbergh were here, that buzzard wouldn't pay him the least attention."

To which one saucy twelve-year-old replied, "But he would if Lindbergh were dead, wouldn't he?" Walker still laughed over it.

He became nostalgic over old landmarks. A home belonging to John Hohn reminded him of "that old Swede from Stockholm" who aroused much curiosity among Christians by working through the Sabbath. Hohn was "knocked to his death from a railroad trestle, by a train."

The baptizing ground on the Chickamauga had grown up considerably, and he recalled women fighting to keep their skirts from inflating in the water. He wished he had been baptized there.

Walker turned fifty, sharing February 4 with Lindbergh, "though I did not receive a card from him." He remembered a childhood trip with his father to Graysville, where he was frightened by white prisoners wearing balls and chains and striped clothing, guarded by men with guns. They were state prisoners working the quarry, which produced limestone for the brick furnace kilns.

Leaving for an engagement, both Walker and Wendell had watches in the repair shop and were concerned about being punctual. The sundial would not fit in a pocket, an alarm clock being their only portable solution. Walker knew Wendell did not like being thought eccentric (true of most sons of eccentric fathers), but Wendell surprised him, saying, "If Thoreau needed a timepiece, he would take whatever was on hand—even if it were a grandfather clock." That settled the matter, and Walker left home with Big Ben ticking away in a paper sack.

He awaited response from Thomas Edison regarding a question of his using lightning bugs in experiments. He eventually received a reply, saying that he had not. Walker sent him a copy of *My Father's Farm* and received a note of thanks. Twelve years earlier, he had written Edison asking for his advice to young people but had gotten a somewhat surly reply.

Walker wrote nature field notes on spread-open envelopes from his mail, a lifelong habit, as he preferred them over notebooks. "To use them is as pleasant as drinking water from a gourd."

In May, Walker experienced something that defied reason. He received a call requesting a speaking engagement, which he accepted, thinking the invitation was from a group he had promised earlier. A Mrs. Martin, whom he did not know, drove him to the meeting.

She belonged to the North Chattanooga Study Club, a literary club of which he had never heard. En route to the home of the club president, Mrs. Green, his driver explained that Mrs. Robert Sparks Walker had attended their last meeting and gave a talk about Walker's work in the field of nature. His "wife" said she was returning from a long journey and had so favorably impressed them that the club had called him.

Stunned, Walker argued that his wife had been dead four years, yet all twenty-five women corroborated the story, claiming to have met the charming

"Mrs. Walker," her physical description matching Elberta. Dismayed, Walker wondered if it were an impostor—or possibly an angel? He found it hard to believe anyone would pull such a hoax. The group was most interested in his material, but he was baffled. He did not believe Elberta's spirit was in her grave, nor did he imagine her wandering the earth like a restless "haint." But although she had told him in life that, if possible, she would return to help him, he resolved that God would have to sort this out.

At Burnt Cabin Springs on Signal Mountain, he met a Mrs. Riggs who was filling a pitcher. He realized he knew her from Highland Park, where she once lived. Her husband had been a railway postal clerk who perished in the same fiery 1904 train wreck near Meridian, Mississippi, in which Walker's old pal Robert G. Davidson died. Walker still regretted his part in helping R.G. obtain the job as mail weigher, which had cost his life.

For Tom Walker's eighty-first birthday, Walker brought as a gift an old friend, Dr. Holtzclaw, whom Tom had once asked to become surgeon at the Hamilton County Poor House. Holtzclaw accepted but changed its name to the County Infirmary.

On a June morning, Walker took brother John and Wendell to his father's wheat field. John cradled wheat while Walker bound it, piling fresh bundles of wheat under an apple tree for his father to lie on while supervising.

"How good it was to work together like this again!" Walker said. They drove to the old cabin, Tom saying it once had two chimneys but he had removed one in 1889 for constructing the chimney on his present home. These were made of Graysville brick, burned by the Grays. Tom had taken down the original stick and mud chimneys, trading his cow for three thousand bricks. Bill Dunn had built the two cabin chimneys for five dollars apiece.

"A doctor named Watkins once lived in the cabin, but it was bought at chancery court sale by the Ellis brothers, who wanted its cord wood for furnishing fuel to the Western and Atlantic Railway," Tom said. There had been no well, water being carried up from the creek or brought across the tracks from a neighbor's well two hundred yards away. Tom hand dug a well, finding a good stream of water, but poisonous gas gave trouble until he blew out a stone on the bottom, which burned up the gas. It still gave good water.

Walker was encouraging his son's interest in photography, proud that he was becoming quite good, though his health was still impaired. He observed, "Sometimes I wonder if doctors know what they are talking about. So many are so conceited!"

He now had over one hundred poems and ninety descriptive essays out to various publishers. Finances were still tight. He was pursuing Title

Guarantee's erroneous title to a second lot on Missionary Ridge, in which they bestowed his property on another two years earlier. They agreed to pay for the lot, if he would sell cheaply, but he did not name a price.

He was requested to draw up a will for his father, whose health was failing; elderly Tom had wept discussing the details. "I find the subject so hard I cannot discuss it," said Walker.

As Tom's health declined, Walker, John and Charlie took turns watching over him. Visitors were turned away. When asked if they could engage a nurse, Tom said no. When they tested his memory with questions, he recalled Marsena Julian trying to get Tom elected to court to stop appropriation for the Brainerd Mission Bridge (Old Bird's Mill). Julian had felt it would increase his taxes, not knowing that Tom favored building it.

Walker, a consummate writer, continued rescuing old work. "I was re-dressing old manuscripts which have worn their clothes out, traveling in paper suits far away. I once planned a magazine entitled, *Rejected Stories*, in which no article could be published until it had been rejected at least half a dozen times." *Life* magazine had just taken up his idea with a new magazine called *Rejections*.

His father was frail. To cheer him, Walker pointed to a scar between his eyes, asking if Tom remembered when he got it. When his father said yes, Walker continued: "Tell me if John is correct, that I was strolling among hogs being butchered, was mistaken for one, and knocked in the head." His father had laughed uproariously.

Walker then recounted the true event, in which Will was splitting kindling and accidentally hit him with the axe. He remembered his father carrying him, promising a red-handled knife if he stopped crying. Said Walker, "You never got me that knife!"

"No?" said his father. "Then I must get that yet."

In a library book, *The Life of the Bee*, one particular chapter had many thumbprints, while others seemed untouched, "indicating the book was picked up for the chapter on mating alone…How decidedly everything seems to revolve around sex!"

August found Walker on a ladder in his backyard, picking Keifer pears. "I was in league with birds…how I longed for an orchard again! I was rudely interrupted by a heavy pear thumping me on the head. A second in the eye awakened me to life's realities, and as I shook the tree, a shower of webworms eating foliage fell all over my body…The idyll was over, but such is life."

Walker joined family at his father's to thresh the wheat they had cradled. Younger brother Theodore, John's son, and John Davidson fed wheat to the machine, as did the elderly Tom. He was improving.

Walker discovered poetic justice for a worm destroying his tomato plants: bending its prickly leaves over the worm's body and thrusting the stickers through. "Putting the responsibility for killing caterpillars onto the plant, while giving it the pleasure of using the spines the Creator has given it."

In September, Wendell, now nineteen, was well enough to finish his last year of school. Walker visited the hotel in Cloudland, Georgia, before traveling to the long lake made by damming the Little River. He had fished here in 1915 before the dam, but there was now an uncompleted $230,000 hotel project, which had fallen flat two years earlier when the Florida real estate bubble burst. It needed another $100,000 to complete, and he regretted the pretty place going to waste.

He attended niece Nina's wedding to John Smith at the Davidson home. "A large family, once broken, keeps breaking rapidly and soon all are flown and gone." Old Nick had been incarcerated in the barn for the happy event.

He found a blue jay feather on Elberta's grave, arranging it with wildflowers he had brought, as she had been fond of them. He was glad to see jays still visited her. Noting a striped chipmunk running into a burrow, poking its head out until Walker passed, Walker hid behind a tombstone, peeping over its top to observe the chipmunk. On seeing him, it would duck into its hole as Walker jumped back behind the tombstone.

A young woman placing flowers on a nearby grave grabbed her hat from the ground and took off, glancing back to see if Walker followed. He realized she thought he was crazy, as she saw no chipmunk and thought he was jumping at imaginary spirits. He was disgusted with himself and left, unfortunately on the same route she had taken. Two blocks later, she looked back, saw him and sped out of sight. Walker was glad not to be arrested.

He also had his black eye, "bestowed by one of my Keifer pears wearing boxing gloves."

But even the humor of the situation was overshadowed by the thirteenth anniversary of Robert's passing. "It all comes back today. And he who declares that time heals such wounds…has never lost a child."

One day he received no mail at all, so he sent copies of *My Father's Farm* to President Coolidge and Henry Ford and felt better. He also sold a chipmunk essay to *Harper's*.

A fruit jar left on his porch contained a newt found in a well. This would not be a solitary event. His porch would become the leaving place for many such specimens, both flora and fauna, along with requests for identification and information.

A friend brought him a sack of green coconuts, reminding him of the coconut's life cycle, which always inspired him. He placed four in his bathtub with the water on to study their behavior at sea and another in a jardiniere full of salt water to germinate. "I shall keep it, to retain my faith in God, for as long as I have such a remarkable manifestation of his intelligence, I shall not doubt!"

He observed a man reading a newspaper, standing on top of a pole on the Tivoli roof, where he had been for twenty-four hours and was to remain another day. Walker observed, "I do not want his job, it seems a hard way to make money."

He voted for Hoover, describing the outcry of "wets" against prohibition, which Walker supported, as he did not drink. He visited his intrepid father and found him oiling a disc harrow.

Walker spent Thanksgiving with friends at Helvellyn, picnicking on his "nature estate" above the winding blue creek. He later recopied a manuscript, for which he had been paid by a St. Louis editor who had lost it, along with two more articles. "His carelessness has cost me a lot of extra labor!"

Abby Milton invited him and Wendell for Christmas Eve, but they were bound for the Davidsons'. He collected two packages at the post office, one containing empty walnut hulls, which he suspected nephew Perry of sending. So he repacked them and sent them off, not mentioning the prank when Perry picked up him and Wendell for the holiday.

Chapter 6

1929–1935

1929

In January, he and Wendell began keeping company with Abby Milton and her daughters, who lived on Fort Wood. Abby often allowed Wendell use of her car. A writer herself, she assisted Walker with "incisions and amputations" of his poetry.

Bailey Clark, Elberta's youngest brother, and his daughter Sarah, thirteen, visited from Savannah. Bailey had recently lost his wife, coming with Ida and Ves Polk, and Henry Clark and wife, these representing most of Elberta's remaining family. Walker had not seen Bailey since 1906.

In times of loneliness, he struggled against depression, adding that a walk in the woods or mountains would clear it up. Besides the loss of most of his immediate family, he suffered isolation when absent from his siblings. Many of his friends had also died, and when he thought of them, he "shuddered to see the earth grasping so many in its soddy hands."

He was teaching nature students Harry and Gussie Goldstein, describing them as fine naturalists and ten-year-old Gussie as "wise as a tree full of owls."

He was troubled with an ulcerated stomach, a condition left from his 1902 battle with typhoid. "Today finds me in bed with manuscripts lying all about like a sick child's toys, and in the sight of Creator, just as trifling." His cousin George had prescribed a diet of cream until he recovered. Despite his condition, he visited his father, finding him pulling up fence posts, and so he helped.

His minister friend Dr. Myers sent a note saying, "Damn your illness, which threatens to keep us apart this summer!" Walker thought it one of his finest sermons, proving what he had always believed: sometimes preachers feel like swearing.

By May, Walker was gradually recovering. He wrote to Abby that he and Wendell might move to the great Northwest if they could ever sell their house. But that drab relic on Greenwood Avenue remained a permanent anchor. His niece Dona expressed a wish to buy it but did not have enough income. Wendell was interested in pursuing literature and journalism, with archaeology for a hobby, hoping to pay for college with photography.

As Walker considered moving, even as far as California, he was encouraged by friends, including Mrs. Milton, to sell all and make a living writing and lecturing, as he was now. In case he should follow this route, he stored all his scrapbooks in the Tennessee Room of the public library.

He was writing Abby as she traveled. She said she would not return to Chattanooga without a plan to leave it permanently. She claimed to be moving to California with her children, inviting Walker and Wendell to join them. He reproved her for claiming her faith in God was dependent on her faith in humanity, saying, "Long ago I learned never to depend on humans for anything but disappointment. I have concluded nature's beauty represents a childlike trust in God that no science or cult can destroy."

He also drew strength from his singular sense of humor, which included the world of the winged and four-legged. Heading home, he heard a woodpecker drilling a light pole above him. "I caught his rhythm, and with my pocketknife repeated his picking on the pole. He stopped at once. When I did this a few more times, his red head popped out, and he looked down on me as if to say, 'You old plagiarist! How dare you copy my poetry!'"

He visited Mrs. Sallie M. Connor near Tyner, reporting that she had a pair of dog irons and tongs first used at Brainerd Mission in 1817. She gave him some plants, descendants of ones brought by Brainerd missionaries to Hamilton County one hundred years before.

A trip through Birchwood recalled his days at Morris Hill School, which required that he attend a County Normal for Teachers in Birchwood: "I hitched up old Dan, a western pony having a 'U' on his hip. He resisted all our attempts to fatten him, but was spirited, and would run if the harness broke. My old buggy was well repaired with baling wire so I felt safe alone, staying the first night in Harrison with my father's friend. I then stayed a week with the Smiths, who had a handsome daughter. I took her on a buggy ride, but a pair of brothers attending the institute, nudged me out of the running…I returned home in my buggy, alone."

He and photographer Wendell collaborated on an article and planned to divide the check. Walker was much pleased by the new telephone dial system that began in early May.

The library gave him a scrapbook to compile as a Brainerd book. Ninety-eight pages later, he returned it to the library, where it should repose "until a real history of the Mission is written."

Walker skipped a Decoration Day address because the orator was "an atheist and drunkard." He sympathized with Sequoyah, who regretted compiling his alphabet when it was used to propagate a false Christianity among the Cherokees. Hypocrisy, he said, is the true enemy of Christianity: "Indians recognized the difference, the contrast offending their own strong moral principles…A man must practice what he stands for, or keep silent."

He collected June wildflowers with Abby, presently returned from her travels. She brought Walker home and showed him antiques; they made more excursions, taking her daughter wading. She hired Wendell as her chauffeur; he was teaching her oldest, Corinne, to drive their Chrysler.

Bailey Clark stopped by briefly with another daughter, Evelyn. Walker loved company when he was not working. His son went out most nights with friends now but had screened eight windows to ward off summer's mosquitoes. Wendell's ulcer had not returned, but Walker was now living on a diet of milk and egg products.

While lecturing scouts on robber-flies, which devour houseflies, as he spoke, a robber-fly lit on the back of his hand. "The little fellow darted out, caught a housefly and returned to my hand to devour it. One would have thought I had paid him for the demonstration!"

He was trying to sell magazine rights to two of his books to raise money for Wendell's college. He acknowledged his son's unsuccessful efforts to find employment and hated to see him discouraged.

Wendell had been riding horseback at his grandfather's several times but was given permission to use Abby's auto while she was gone to Atlantic City. Walker spent several afternoons with her before she left, and they corresponded again.

Another publisher lost the entire manuscript of "The Beechblock Circus." Undeterred, Walker completed an article on the Lenoir compass, made in 1793 by Lenoir of North Carolina, by which Lenoir's son, A.S. Lenoir, laid out Chattanooga.

Walker was an astute observer. On a hike, he saw a rattlesnake that had never before been found near the old farm. Hiking with Scouts, they encountered a man with a wagonload of sugar and meal, bound for whiskey making. But his discovery at the Read House lobby disgusted his conservative soul.

A good-looking redhead on the mezzanine took a seat where she could look down on the room below. Smoking a cigarette, she eyed a few men. After a sporty-looking fellow wearing scuffed shoes and prostrated socks got up a flirtation with her, she rose and walked away, beckoning him to follow, which he did. Said Walker, "It was an unexpected glimpse of humanity that I did not wish to view."

Wendell, realizing he would relinquish Mrs. Milton's car on her imminent return, "became inflamed" to purchase an older Chevrolet coupe for $150 but needed a loan. When Walker first declined, Wendell, who had gotten a job with the *Times* as copy boy, took it philosophically, saying better men than himself had walked. That good nature got the best of his father, who signed the note.

Wendell drove his father in his "new" car to Aviation Field, where he was shown how to operate a plane, declined to take a ride for three dollars and met the pilot of a mail plane. Walker never flew.

Wendell, now twenty, applied for the University of Chattanooga. Then, to his father's disgust, he brought home an old Harley-Davidson motorcycle in his car, "so old and worn out it looked like we were operating a junk business." Soon the car was stolen on Wendell's last night at the paper. He resumed his position as Abby's chauffeur.

Abby had been in Canada and the eastern states, bringing back a whole set of dishes to have soup plates for luncheons. Walker was perplexed by such extravagance. He gave her a sack of pears from his backyard tree.

They were working together on a book of poems by late Tennessee poet Emma Bell Miles. Abby had a scrapbook full of them. She was also helping Walker with his poems for another book.

Walker hiked to the Walnut Grove School site, remembering Arbor Day 1892. The children had dug and planted sugar maples from the bottom land around the barren schoolyard, and Walker had named his tree Robert Young Hayne of South Carolina, reading Hayne's brief biography as it was planted. The naming of trees would take on special significance for Walker in years to come.

He was disturbed that cows still browsed the Brainerd Cemetery, visiting the attorney whose client owned the property. The son of one of its missionaries, John Vail, was interviewed by Wendell for a feature in the Sunday *Times*. Walker assisted in obtaining several interviews for his son with local people of interest, and Wendell was becoming a skilled reporter.

In editing Walker's poems for a proposed book, *The Sea*, Abby harshly criticized one poem on the sea lion, claiming it was worthless and would spoil the others. Walker later learned from her daughter that a sea lion in a zoo she visited had frightened her. Walker accused her of letting prejudice affect her judgment of his poem, then admitted he did not care for the piece either.

He attended a country funeral, at which one song declared, "There will be no taxes in heaven." As he considered this piece of "lyric poetry, a yellow jacket investigated my neck and head, and when I objected, went off to visit a woman in front of me. She apparently could not stand the buzzing bee jazz, slapping and clawing at it. When it lit on her ear lobe, she almost upset her chair, and I laughed out loud, despite the solemnity of the occasion. I am not sure what people thought of us."

While banding chimney swifts on the roof of Central High School, Walker met its Negro janitor, William Augustus Banks, author of *Beyond the Ricks, and Other Poems*. Banks, who was studying for the ministry, gave Walker an autographed copy of his book, Walker promising a volume of *Anchor Poems* in return.

Walker brought back some birds for children and friends to release. He brought one for Abby, who had been in low spirits when he called, and came over. After releasing the bird, she took him home, where he helped arrange things in her dining room for a meeting she was hosting for the Daughters of the Confederacy. They later worked some more on Emma Bell Miles's poetry before driving to the homeplace of Chief John Ross, now operated as a chicken restaurant and miniature golf course by Mrs. Robert Cooke.

At Lizzie's, he knocked down some apples, accompanied by an old white sow, so he gave her a core. He could not collect any more apples until he ran her off. She took offense, went away and lay down. When he brought six apples and laid them at her nose, she scorned both them and Walker. "For the first time in my life, I discovered a hog could really be offended."

The rains of October were so severe that Walker was reminded of 1898, during the Spanish-American War, when sixty thousand troops were stationed at Chickamauga Battlefield. Men and horses were trapped in mud, horseflies swarmed and troops died by the thousands of typhoid. "It was the most unsanitary place I have ever seen."

He recorded the Wall Street panic but was not particularly affected, having no stocks. On Arbor Day, he complained there were too many holidays, stating, "To give up a day to idleness seems folly." Wendell had reconditioned his motorcycle and was now riding it with adventurous friend Howard Pack. "He is so proud of that thing, it is pitiful," said Walker, who clearly disapproved.

He continued working with Abby on Miles's poems. Abby had been a good friend of the unfortunate woman, who often visited at the Miltons'. Walker contacted publishers, hoping to get the book out. They also read 250 poems submitted to the Elberta Walker Poetry Contest.

Abby was planning to leave Chattanooga, and Walker had long considered the same but wondered if he ever would. "I am so deeply rooted here, as if a golden cord connected me to this red earth itself...There is much for me to do here."

He was again tackling *Breakfast Stories*, with little enthusiasm, as the complete manuscript had been lost, but was spurred on by the excellent photos he had purchased to illustrate it. He mailed out manuscripts that he "hope[d] not to see again until they are in print." As usual, Wendell returned home late "after a wild goose chase on his motorcycle."

Walker was incensed by Arthur Brisbane's claims in a magazine that man would be better off if all animal life were dead. He fired off an editorial in protest over this "absurd statement from a man who is an ignoramus, yet bears the reputation of being the highest paid American journalist." Walker seldom censored what he was really thinking.

The death of Captain A.J. Gahagan, Chattanooga's oldest citizen, provoked Walker's recollection that Gahagan and two other men running for county office in 1878 had all stayed at his father's cabin when he was an infant—more of the many visitors Tom hosted during his tenure on the creek farm.

On Thanksgiving, Walker took a sack of peanuts to the National Cemetery and fed hungry squirrels. Acorn and hickory nut crops had failed, and they were living on roots and mushrooms.

By year's end, his booklet *A History of Chattanooga* had come out, receiving many compliments. The city had its first white Christmas in years, and record-breaking cold temperatures reached as far south as Miami. He received a fine diary for 1930 from Abby and gave her several dozen postcards of her Fort Wood home made from one of Wendell's photos. He then sent two Japanese art calendars to the Hotel Patten, where she was presiding over a Woodrow Wilson peace meeting.

Although Walker spent Christmas alone, he joined his family the next day at Lizzie's for a sumptuous meal. After building a fire, he sat at the piano and "blasted the atmosphere with sacred songs for a full hour." Music and walks through the country were vital to him. "The association of faces and roads with song is difficult to explain…yet I never hear an old hymn but that my mother comes to me…Song holds the key for me to the door of memory."

1930

New Year's Day came and went. Walker's fifty-second birthday found him still recopying a manuscript lost by Mr. Newsom, a New York editor who dropped dead in 1928. Wendell, who experienced a bad skid and slide into some woods on his Harley, traded the beast for an old Ford, which turned out to be a bad deal. Nevertheless, Walker, who abhorred motorcycles, felt relieved.

Abby, out of town again, wrote that she wanted him and Wendell to go to California in July, while another friend wanted him to move to New York. Walker found himself torn between two coasts without setting foot out of town.

His son, who had all but abandoned journalism, decided to travel the world after one semester and presented a paper before a recent meeting of the East Tennessee Archaeological Society, where his interests now lay.

On a visit, Walker found his father plowing with a disc harrow, working three horses. "Not bad for a man almost eight-three!"

Abby returned in March, she and Walker spending time together again. He had begun a romantic novel, new to his pen, while Abby was planning a book on the history of women's suffrage. Their friendship perplexed Walker. "It is strange to have a friend of more than ten years, who seems to admire one's writings, but unconsciously builds between them a barrier composed of superlative adjectives."

The local DAR chapter installed a marker on Market Street Bridge commemorating John Ross's store and ferry, when Chattanooga was known as Ross' Landing. The chief's grandson, Robert Bruce Ross of Oklahoma, was present for the occasion, his grandfather being the real founder of Chattanooga, which did not take that name until 1838 after the Cherokees were driven west. Senator Newell Sanders presented a work order to Walker, expense paid, to write a local history of the Cherokees and, in particular, Brainerd Mission. This led Walker to travel again to sites of the old Cherokee Nation.

Walker liked a good joke, even on himself. His entanglement with a collie in a shop doorway furnished so much amusement for both store and sidewalk witnesses that laughter echoed down the street. "So much happened to me that a garter dropped from my leg!"

Tom Walker's eighty-third birthday was celebrated with over sixty guests at his home, "the ninth year we have held this dinner in my father's honor." This family occasion was the source of Walker family reunions in years to come, though its origins were forgotten.

On a journey to Georgia, researching for his book, he stopped with a friend to briefly visit Annie Bare Puryear, commenting, "How time does change us all."

When Robert Bruce Ross passed away, Walker was glad the old Cherokee had visited his grandfather's home "before he went away to the other world."

He was still spending time with Abby, who either picked him up or sent her chauffeur. They often parked in woods or fields to work on manuscripts. Walker liked working outdoors, "in spite of speculations that may arise from it." He had succeeded in placing the Miles book of verse, *Strains from a Dulcimore*, with Bozart Press. Although he had nearly completed his first novel, which Abby had encouraged, he was now devoting his time to the project on Cherokee history. But he was grateful for Abby's critique, for "when I tried to read to Wendell and Dona, I had to first tie them to the cookstove."

When the planet Pluto was discovered, Walker, with renewed interest, sent a letter to an endowment in hopes of an observatory being established on Lookout Mountain. It had been his long-standing desire.

Abby went to Uplands Sanitarium near Crossville for a rest and asked Walker to join her a few days. He did, and Dr. May Wharton asked him to do an article on the place. She refused to charge for his brief stay, saying the lectures he gave there had done much good for everyone.

During his visit, he and Abby took walks together and mended some differences on their politics. She rebuked him for writing to her that she should stay out of it altogether, as it strained her nerves. She explained that with women's suffrage settled, she did not feel the need to participate as strongly, no longer having a newspaper for voicing her opinions since her husband's death. This seemed to settle some troubled waters. "Still, this incident has shown me some apparent, and I think, unbridgeable gulfs in our background and beliefs," he wrote.

Walker's Cherokee history now centered almost entirely on Brainerd Mission, as a Miss Penelope Allen was preparing a local Cherokee history.

Susan Weir and Minta Foreman, granddaughter and daughter of Reverend Stephen Foreman, 1938. Walker is shown with the Bible Foreman used at Brainerd Mission.

Senator Sanders brought Mr. and Mrs. Grant Foreman from Oklahoma to Walker's house and to the Brainerd Mission site. Foreman was bringing out a scholarly, researched book about the 1838 removal. Judge Lusk took Walker to Fort Loudoun and then to Chota, site of the old Cherokee Nation's first capital. Walker described it as barely more than a mile wide, with fertile, shiny soil that seemed filled with mica. It was eight miles east of Fort Loudoun, "beautifully situated on the Little Tennessee River." Nearby was the adjacent Cherokee town Tanasi, from which Tennessee takes its name. (These towns are now under water from TVA's damming and flooding of the river.)

Walker hired his son to type his manuscript of Brainerd Mission but was now anxious about Wendell's new interest in flying. Even the death of two young men at Lovell Field had not dampened his enthusiasm, although he was experiencing a return of ulcer symptoms. Walker hoped it was a temporary phase.

Walker's elder brother Will, 1921.

His cousin James E. Walker, a member of the lower house in the state legislature for over twenty years, died at sixty-three. Walker was again sharply aware that friends and family were leaving him.

His brother Will had recently christened his youngest son Robert Sparks Walker III, honoring Walker's firstborn. Walker appreciated his brother's recognition.

The Depression was making itself known in Chattanooga. Walker saw respectable-looking men begging, children without coats in the cold, freight trains filled with hobos and peddlers trying to sell everything imaginable. One young man knocked at his door begging for a bar of soap, asking where he could get a bath, having just come to town on a freight. Walker made meager donations to several individuals and to the Salvation Army, though his own income was puny.

A letter from Abby described the trip around the world she was taking, having the time of her life. A Christmas card from Leila Venable Mason of Atlanta, inviting him to visit, cheered him considerably. Her family owned Stone Mountain, which was being carved as a monument to the Confederates. He finally caught up to his son on Christmas Day at Lizzie's, where they celebrated together. Wendell was now a grown man, and Dona would likely move out soon. Walker was looking into the bleak future of a lonely house, with himself its only resident.

1931

In January, Walker visited Leila Mason at her family's home, Stonehenge, in Atlanta's prestigious Druid Hills. She took him to Stone Mountain, where the Masons also had a summer home. Leila's mother later sent him an autographed book by its sculptor, Gutzon Borglum. Leila had told Walker her family had had such grief over the mountain's carving that she regretted ever beginning it, but work on it would soon resume. The Masons were deeding the mountain to Atlanta.

The Brainerd Mission book was almost ready for publishers, "but there is so much sorrow, tragedy and sickness in its history, that I had to take every bit of cheer and humor to lighten the burden of writing it." He had twice broken into tears before finishing the chapter on the Cherokee Atsee (John Arch). Walker described him as a far better Christian than himself and regretted being unable to find Atsee's picture for the book.

Another chapter devoted to Catherine Brown, a young Cherokee woman of great strength and virtue, touched him deeply. Then, in typing the chapter on imprisonment of the missionaries, he found he had, "in truth, spent that morning tying a noose around the neck of Andrew Jackson. I do not know what readers will think of my frankness, but I am sticking to the truth and laying it bare."

The next-door Gilberts, the longest-residing family in Highland Park, were in Nashville for the time being, and Walker missed them.

Milton Ochs offered him the position of nature director at his newly established Lookout Mountain Park. Walker organized eighteen hiking clubs to enjoy its three thousand acres of trails but found it was taking much time from writing. When Ochs divided the office of nature director from the hiking clubs, without compensation, Walker resigned his position but still hiked there, even after a bad fall that knocked him out for an hour.

Macmillan and Co. accepted *Torchlights to the Cherokees*. Abby returned again with a roomful of exotic souvenirs. She cooked Walker a Chinese dinner eaten with chopsticks, which he commented he would not soon forget, nor would his shirtfront. On another excursion, they botanized wildflowers at Lookout Mountain's Penwoman's clubhouse.

Walker decided to redecorate his shabby bedroom, papering its walls and ceilings, which had last been updated by Elberta in 1922. In June, his heart began to "cut some capers," and he spent three weeks at Uplands Sanitarium again. While there, he met a young woman from Kentucky, Elizabeth Thomassen, who would play a significant part in his life for a brief time.

By fall, he was autographing copies of *Torchlights to the Cherokees*, that name suggested by Leila Mason Etheridge, who had married recently. Both Payne's and Miller Brothers displayed it and reported strong sales, despite the Depression. Social conditions were so bad, Walker said, that there was even general talk of revolution among the public.

Tom Walker, eighty-four, was still farming. The public school, located on land he donated, was filled with students, employing a half dozen teachers. Walker reflected that there once had stood a hog pen there, "in which I imprisoned my first livestock."

He attended Theodore Dreiser's play, *An American Tragedy*, at the Tivoli. Dreiser was now suing the company that filmed his novel for failing to follow the book. Walker had met him in 1903 through Grace MacGowan Cooke, novelist and wife of his *SFG* partner. Dreiser was then an editor.

Walker and his son were at odds regarding Wendell's not returning to the university. He was also upset that Wendell had taken up smoking and was making a long hitchhiking trip to the Smokies with friend Howard Pack. He received one postcard notifying him they had reached Johnson City via a peach truck. Walker feared highway robberies and worried that Wendell would never finish his education, saying, "We have had some lively tilts about it." He was at least comforted that Wendell was writing again.

The twenty-first anniversary of Robert's death found Walker in such depression that he had to cancel plans to meet Senator Sanders. "The human soul is vulnerable to grief that years do not heal." All he could do was walk the floor.

Elberta's nephew Harry Clark married Hannah Wearn and was now editor of the *Birmingham Herald*. But Walker's son was hitchhiking. He hoped for better days.

In late December, he joined Leila Etheridge for a ceremony to place a marker in Fort Payne, Alabama, at the site of the Willston Mission to the Cherokees. Reverend Hoyt, who had taught there, was Leila's great-great-grandfather. As everyone was leaving, Walker slammed the Masons' big Packard car door shut, accidentally cutting off the tail of his overcoat, commenting, "I am now a bob-tailed man."

Macmillan's informed him *Torchlights* had been nominated for the Pulitzer Prize, but despite favorable reviews, sales were falling due to the Depression. He was not given to professional jealousy but declined to publicly comment on Zella Armstrong's history of Chattanooga, citing multiple inaccuracies.

He still resented interruptions of his work by calls and requests for engagements, although they were, for the most part, due to his work. When

Elberta was alive, "she stood between me and the inquiring public." If he did not rise at five o'clock, he declared he would get nothing done at all. While 1930 had been a relatively good year financially, and though he had a book nomination for a Pulitzer, 1931 proved the worst.

He revised his novel *A Drone Takes Flight*, which was being critiqued by Elizabeth Thomassen, the young lady he had met at Uplands. He had disagreed with Abby's criticisms of the story. On a recent visit to Thomassen's home in Fort Thomas, Kentucky, Elizabeth gave him a pen and pencil set.

He recorded his embarrassment while selecting a gift for Dona. A newspaper was tucked in his coat pocket as he walked through crowded aisles, and he became aware of people laughing. He then realized they were laughing at him and looked down. "Lo, a pair of pink bloomers were dangling off my newspaper, and I had been swishing about the store, flinging this garment in everyone's face!" He gave Dona money to buy herself a gift.

1932

Walker's beloved father, Tom Walker, was laid to rest in Concord Cemetery on June 30. After a fall off a ladder, complications developed during the next few days. Walker was in Kentucky visiting Elizabeth when he was notified of the accident and learned his father was asking for him. He returned at once, taking turns with his brothers at his father's bedside, and was present when his father passed. "He leaves behind one of the best reputations of any man I have ever known."

Even in family crisis, en route to Chattanooga by train from Kentucky, Walker reported an amusing incident on himself. The lower berth was empty as he settled into the upper berth. Nearing Chattanooga, he dressed, swinging down to prepare for getting off the train. His left foot struck something hard and sleek, and he attempted to identify it by rubbing his bare sole against the smooth surface. Suddenly a man jumped out of the lower berth, glared up at him and shouted, "Say, did you know you have one foot on my bald head, and another on my shoulder?"

The crowd at Tom Walker's funeral was such that a loudspeaker was set up for those who could not get into the church. Cars were parked on both sides of the highway, over a quarter mile. When Walker and John went to pay the men who dug his grave, they were told, "You owe us nothing! Your father's grave was dug by at least seventy-five men who begged to do it, and well over a hundred more were turned away, who asked to strike at least two strokes with a pick."

At Tom's eighty-fifth birthday dinner, he had confided it would be his last. His older grandsons served as pallbearers, Wendell among them.

Wendell was now home, successfully writing and selling articles. He was proud of a front-page illustrated piece in the *Times Magazine* section and grateful to be selling manuscripts in such hard times. Walker still wanted him to finish his education but was glad for his son's company. He was reviewing two books by Enos Mills, a western naturalist and geologist whom he greatly admired.

But he was lonely. He missed Elberta. He was viewing the friendship with Elizabeth in hopes that it might become something more. They corresponded, and she sent pictures and a rose on his birthday.

He recorded more descriptions of the Depression's impact on Chattanooga and himself. People called on him, asking for work, selling items. A watchmaker and a glassblower came by in one day, followed by a farmer from Alabama the next. He did his best for them, recalling a time when he was fifteen and sold or traded vegetables for nothing—but the family could at least eat the leftovers.

Writing markets remained poor, but despite rising postal costs, "I am shooting bombs of manuscripts. If they hit the editor and disable him mentally, victory is mine!" He was pleased to connect his friend T.J. Campbell with a former publisher of his *SFG*, resulting in Campbell's book *The Upper Tennessee* being published. Campbell was "the happiest man I have ever seen—this transaction taking place at the freshly dusted library table in my front room over glasses of grape juice."

Walker did not win the 1931 Pulitzer Prize. He was beaten by General Pershing's memoirs.

He still hoped to sell his house and overhauled its interior.

It could kill any woman to look after it. Possibly Elberta would still be living had I not kept such a big house. I have painted every room—the first time I had my coveralls on since 1921. But I heard seams ripping while on the ladder before the open window. The strap let go and my coveralls dropped off, leaving me exposed to the neighbors. I crawled off on hands and knees.

I then became a vandal, armed with hedge pruners and hand saw, cutting the fifteen-foot hedge in my back yard.

Walker was primping his house for Elizabeth, her aunt, uncle and another friend from Kentucky, who stayed two days. He pledged to keep it in a clean state when they were gone.

He and Mrs. Richard Walker, wife of the *Times*'s editor (no kin), were invited for dinner at Mrs. Chapin's home on Bluffview, overlooking the Tennessee River. While discussing their mutual purpose of locating bird sanctuaries in the area, Walker learned Mrs. Chapin had all his books.

A recent speaking engagement at Bonny Oaks Reform School reminded him of his 1899 job as captain of the transfer wagon. He was so young, the weight of the pistol strapped to his right side "caused me to walk crooked as a bird dog down a country road." The first morning he walked into jail, the jailer announced he had five white men, any of whom could eat him alive. He found handcuffing repulsive and workhouses gloomy, smelling of grease, slop and soured coffee grounds.

One morning he was given four Negro boys who had escaped from reform school. Walker was to return them, handcuffed—but their hands were so small the handcuffs slipped off. For his month's work—all he ever wanted at this duty—he received thirty dollars. Now his perspective was different: "How glad I was to address these boys on nature, rather than transport them, though I wondered if handcuffs would be necessary to secure their presence at my lecture."

The Lindbergh baby was found dead, but not before the Crossville sheriff arrested four people with a baby answering its description. Despite the Lindberghs' declaration that it was not their child, the sheriff still considered taking the local baby to New Jersey for identification. Walker recorded anything newsworthy that smacked of folly.

By Christmas, he and Elizabeth had agreed to stop seeing each other. She had showered him with gifts, letters, phone calls and telegrams, and he had returned the same. But as possibilities of sharing a future grew, she got cold feet, citing age difference. Walker was saddened, having observed the success of his father's second marriage to a younger woman and hoping his own long isolation was ending. But such was not to be. He told Wendell that although she was not the beauty Elberta had been, Elizabeth had come the closest to mirroring Elberta's sweet character.

Abby called him for the first time in over a year, and Leila Etheridge sent him a gift, as did other friends, which raised his spirits. He was missing his father.

Squire Bates told Walker he still hoped to erect a monument to Tom at the now famous W Road on Walden's Ridge. As he was grinding wheat Tom had given him shortly before he died, Walker recalled his father's strong independence. Tom had left the creek farm to his six children by his first wife, which included Walker.

Walker often had peculiar, sometimes prophetic dreams. He recorded one in which he dreamed he misplaced his favorite pen but had left it at the library. On waking, he had not even known the pen was missing but could not find it. When he went to the library and asked the attendant if anyone had found his pen, she took it from a drawer and handed it to him.

Wendell was still at home, writing for the *Times*. He was doing well in journalism. They discovered that a prowler had moved a ladder to Walker's back porch bedroom window and opened the lattice door but had not broken through the screen. Walker, who slept through it all, surmised that nothing of value caught the miscreant's eye, so he had left.

He watched his diet, believing "one can learn more than a physician about caring for one's health." Dr. Woolford, who had treated Elberta, had recently passed away. Woolford had moved to New Mexico, urging Walker to follow. Wendell had hoped to study archaeology at the University of New Mexico and still talked about it. But their unsold house anchored them to Chattanooga.

Walker voted for Hoover, who lost his second term to F.D. Roosevelt. He recalled his support for Theodore Roosevelt, who was once a presidential candidate for the Bull Moose Party. Walker had sat onstage at the City Auditorium with him at a rally.

He was asked to serve as foreman of the grand jury, replacing Senator Sanders, eighty-two. It was distasteful service, Walker listing as crimes they had to indict drunk driving, murder and administering the oath of sworn testimony to a ten-year-old who assisted a man in a wildcat still. "Afterwards, I took a walk in the pure air. It was so rich and fine to get out among the beautiful things of life after listening to the misery of humanity."

1933

The first half of 1933 was promising for Walker's career. He was visited by Thomas Stribling, 1932 Pulitzer winner. Association Press held two of his manuscripts for three years, but a letter to director William Hearst resulted in the publishing of his book for young people, *Eating Thunder*. He anticipated the coming release of the other, *The Beechblock Circus*.

Local poet Blanche Eisendrath showed him a leather-bound copy of her poems, which had color illustrations by Emma Bell Miles. He was particularly impressed by Edna St. Vincent Millay's poetry reading on the radio, calling her voice "lyrical, imitative of a whippoorwill's."

He received many letters regarding *Torchlights*, among them one from Cherokee W. David Owl, a missionary from Iroquois, New York. The warden of Leavenworth Penitentiary requested a copy. Despite his modest success, the Depression was still ravening the land, cutting into sales, which were half of the previous year.

He was feeding hungry men daily, which affected finances, but he could not see them go hungry. Streets were rife with people pushing all kinds of curious vehicles, selling vegetables, collecting rags, paper and junk. Peddlers were always at his door. Pedestrians were plentiful, having no car fare. Men hid in boxcars and rode on top of coal cars "like buzzards on a rail fence or a dead tree."

He hired a part-time housekeeper, Mary McLain, who told him she sometimes had nothing to eat since most of her work had left her. Walker always sent her home with food.

His experiences with the grand jury were enough to make a book. They sent one "clever fellow" to the penitentiary for life for killing his wife, despite his attempts to play insane by building bird nests during the trial. Judge Lusk accepted a Negro juror, the first in four years, which caused a stir. Walker described the man, Hawkins, as a fine, intelligent retired postman.

Money was scarce, Walker defaulting on his taxes for the first time in his life and unable to collect debts that were due him. He sent seeds of a pink aster he and Elberta had found while hiking to Burpee Seed Company, hoping they might buy it.

Walker not only struggled financially, he also struggled for time. Calls kept coming for hiking and speaking engagements, which he was happy to do, but they interfered with writing. He reported, with some dismay, one phone call asking him to prescribe medicine for a sick parrot.

He lectured in a house once belonging to his brother John's mother-in-law when John worked in a clothing store. John was anxious for Bob to meet his girl Ida, so Walker accepted an invitation to lunch with them. But John thought Bob's clothing too sloppy, and Bob did not wish to buy a new suit. John solved the situation by loaning Bob a new suit left at the store for altering. They planned to return it before the man called for it.

Bob, choking in the suit that did not fit, suffered through lunch but afterward found the man at the store, looking for his suit. He recognized it on Walker immediately, who claimed he barely escaped a lawsuit over that suit.

In August, Wendell took a position at the *Chattanooga News* after looking for work for almost two years. Wendell had published many articles freelance, and Walker reiterated that his son could be an accomplished writer if he wished.

Federal Bank Examiners determined that First National Bank in Chattanooga violated the law, borrowing over $10 million without collateral. Walker was revolted by the greed, stating that close to two thousand people were suffering for it, saying it hurt the area more than the Depression.

Peddlers were still appearing. One young woman appeared at his door asking for the lady of the house.

"I am she," replied Walker.

"Here is a free bar of soap," she said, handing it to him.

"Is this an insinuation?" he asked, in all seriousness.

"No. It's an advertisement," she replied pleasantly.

More humorous grand jury incidents happened. When Walker requested a subpoena from one witness, the man handed him his hat. A second request brought the same results; then the man laid his hat on the floor. Said Walker, "I could not get that subpoena until I asked for the yellow strip of paper in his hand."

He was signing so many indictments that he was concerned about reprisals, causing him to sleep upstairs one night when suspicious-looking people prowled around his bedroom near midnight. Another prowler interrupted a lecture on Lookout Mountain, but it was four-legged: a wildcat drawn to their campfire with meat cooking.

In October, *Eating Thunder* came out. Walker was offended that the main character's name was changed from "Wendell" to "Dick," though he liked its cover and was in general pleased with the book.

Brainerd Cemetery was rescued by the DAR taking it over, restoring markers and setting iron entrance gates. Walker was glad, after spending fifteen years trying to save it "from the inquisitional snouts and browsing mouths of hogs and cows." He credited Mrs. Bashie Martin and Mrs. Willard Steele for the accomplishment, saying his name was kept from negotiations, as his association with restoring the place had created a barrier. "I am proud of the women who put it across!"

Western dust storms created haze in the sky, resulting in colorful sunsets. But Wendell was now out with friends at night, and Walker missed him— and his father.

As winter approached, he found McBroom, his old poet friend, shivering in the only sunny spot on the block, lightly dressed, holding an armful of *Times*.

Walker at Dr. Worcester's marker in Brainerd Cemetery, 1934.

He told Walker he meant to patch his ragged overcoat but was ashamed to wear it. Walker took him to a discreet doorway and made McBroom put on his overcoat, saying to keep it. Walker said he would rather have the gratitude in McBroom's eyes than a window display of his books. McBroom later presented him with a poem dedicated to Walker and Wendell:

Friends, your presents are inspiring
My enthusiasm firing!
By your kindness, I'm acquiring
Clothing fit for a king!
Nothing could have clothed me better
Than this overcoat and sweater
I'm eternally your debtor,
So my gratitude I sing...

The four-stanza poem was signed "Your grateful friend, Henry D. McBroom." He had won prizes for his writing, and Walker was an ardent admirer of his work.

Walker described his views on Christmas as controversial. He knew that some well-intentioned people deplored cutting cedars for Christmas. "As for me, I say, though it be the only tree growing in the wild, slay it, if it can make a child happy!" He believed a tree could serve no higher purpose than to gladden a child's heart. "Thus does my conservationist nature dwell in peace with this outlook."

On Christmas Day, Abby showed him her new book of poems, but he recommended she reject the publisher's poor work, which she did. They were visiting again, taking drives together and enjoying each other's company.

1934

At Lizzie's, Walker befriended a small pig that followed him to the orchard, crying for apples, which Walker gave him. Even after this treat, he tugged at Walker's feet until he was picked up and stroked. "I am extremely fond of pigs...they vibrate like an electric motor when held."

Confederate veterans again gathered in Chattanooga, their numbers significantly reduced from the ten thousand who had encamped in Jackson Park in 1913. They met in the Read House, and Walker, when asked to write them a welcoming poem, complied.

He described a "Golden Dust Storm" made from dust and pollen gathered by winds from the parched fields of Kansas and Nebraska. It was the first such colorful storm of the many that occurred. Concerned about Midwest drought, he considered making a trip to the stricken areas. At his suggestion, Blanche Eisendrath wrote a poem describing it and another poem to honor McBroom, which greatly pleased the newspaper seller. Walker bought him overshoes, saying he had no right to buy his own unless he got some for McBroom.

There were several days each year when he was "crushed almost to the earth by a weight of sorrow…I have to quit everything and lie down." He attributed this to memories of Robert's death and Elberta's. "When I considered what could remove this depression, two things presented themselves: the sound of Robert's and Elberta's voices." Yet he was grateful for the family that had been left to him.

Wendell had become a field boss with the University of Tennessee, supervising forty-five men hired to open an Indian mound above Norris Basin at LaFollette, Tennessee. He was making three times his salary at the *Times* and was responsible for charting and photographing their findings.

Walker visited the proposed site of Norris Dam at the confluence of the Clinch River and a creek. The dam was expected to take two years to fill. Wendell then moved to Clinton, where two more mounds were to be opened, but when federal funding was cut, he was back writing for the *Times*.

Walker was still on the grand jury, dealing with cases "spanning the lower strata of humanity, from arsonists who burned down the Warner Park Roller Coaster in 1931, to five different murderers with guns, knives and poisons their respective weapons of choice." He declined an invitation to enter the race for county judge—the fifth time he had refused. "Politics are repulsive to me. I would rather spend my life meeting with nature and writing of beautiful things."

He purchased several volumes of *Anchor Poems* in a secondhand store. "There they were—soiled, dirty, with greasy spots—my snotty-nosed children! How could I possibly abandon them? But seeing the wear marks of use, how much better to have them like this, than never purchased or read at all."

Walker, who seldom entertained, hosted a backyard party for some of the writing club. He dug a hole, placing in it a jug of juice, preserves and wheat cookies, covered by a small tree. He tunneled under his peanut plant and buried a pound of salted nuts, finishing off with fig leaves pinned to paper napkins. The ladies' reactions were never recorded.

Walker began defending the ailanthus, or Tree of Heaven, outlawed in Chattanooga in June 1879, following the yellow fever epidemic. Its offensive pollen smelled like decaying flesh to attract the carrion flies that cross-pollinated it. Walker called it a good shade tree that could tolerate city smoke and dirt.

In June, two thousand homing pigeons were released in Warner Park. Walker and Wendell went to watch the birds burst forth as a "big, bluish billow, circling to get directions before disappearing like floating leaves."

Books were selling, and Walker was at last out of debt—not bad for an author during the Depression. Encouraged by sales of his children's books, he began revising another one, hoping to "put it over, after a nap of fifteen years."

When plumbing issues struck, he drew parallels between humanity and offending tree roots: "If they would crawl politely into the pipes and not fill them, they might go unnoticed. But greed robs them of reason, and now I must pay a plumber a generous sum."

The Beechblock Circus was displayed in Payne's window. Walker had told the stories to his boys, finishing them in 1916 when a young Wendell was in Florida with his ailing mother.

On December 1, Walker and the Cumberland Hiking Club observed a meteor pass over Lookout Mountain. He described it as fish shaped, a beautiful shade of green fading into silver, "the most remarkable thing I have ever seen in the heavens." Newspapers reported it barely missed an airplane over the airport.

1935

While hiking Missionary Ridge, Walker recalled that fifty years earlier it was a wilderness inhabited by wild turkey, deer and rattlesnakes. The only venison he had ever eaten came from the deer his father killed there. The former hunting ground was now grown up with houses.

After meeting with Professor T.M.N. Lewis of the University of Tennessee, Wendell accepted the position of supervisor over archaeological work to take place in seven counties around Knoxville. The new job was not permanent, so Wendell continued feature writing.

He and Walker went downtown to help McBroom pay room rent. McBroom again wore no coat, ashamed that it needed cleaning. Walker told him to have it cleaned at his expense. A few days later, Walker returned, finding McBroom still shivering. He took McBroom to the dry cleaners and paid the cleaning bill. It was wrong, he said, for a man of sixty to go half-clad in winter.

The nature poetry contest Walker had founded ten years earlier still received many entries. This year author Archibald Rutledge, writer for *American Magazine*, chose finalists.

Walker was treated to bear meat at a dinner with Will, pronouncing it fine—though he felt he was eating another brother. His brother Charlie came from Johnson City to attend. As Charlie left for home, he checked his bags to make sure Walker had not slipped any ridiculous articles into it like rocks or bricks. (These are Walker brothers, remember.) But a paper sack went undetected containing apple peelings, coal, a feather and a sweet potato. Confident of no surprises in his luggage, Charlie carried it all away.

Walker was working on a snowflake essay. He had purchased four hundred snowflake photos a few years back from (now) late Professor W.A. Bentley of Jericho, Vermont, who discovered a means of isolating and photographing them. When asked why he did not charge more for his work, Bentley had said he wanted everyone to enjoy them.

Walker described a failed effort at merging two manuscripts into one as "crossing a dodo bird with a phoenix." He discarded the piece and began *The Pyramids of Chickamauga*, about the battlefield's stacked cannonballs, "tragedy lying behind everyone one of these pyramids." He was selling articles to the *New York Herald Tribune* and hoped to continue. Meanwhile, Wendell published an illustrated article in the local paper detailing work on the Chickamauga Dam.

The public constantly amused Walker. A Crossville woman brought him a box containing a skeleton she thought was a bird with teeth. It was a rat. When she asked if she could burn the thing on his grate, he replied she might, if she could produce the rat's will proving it desired cremation upon its demise.

Walker expressed a wish to build a log cabin on Helvellyn, but sale of 808 Greenwood was an obstacle. It always would be.

He purchased a new tropical hat shaped like a helmet, which he declared made him look like an explorer. It did not protect him from an attack by an Airedale, which grabbed his leg. The dog was removed by its owner. He was then given a young nighthawk that could not fly well enough to be turned loose. Walker fed it grasshoppers and moths, and it soon became a pet, roosting on brush Walker placed in his window until Wendell came in late and stepped on it. Both father and son were devastated.

Walker recorded that six years of drought had turned land between Missouri and the Rocky Mountains into an American Sahara, its soil blown as far as the Atlantic. He believed man had a hand in this destruction. Then he launched a diatribe against the *Nashville Banner*, which offered a cash bonus for the most crows killed in one year, promoting the National Movement to Exterminate the Crow. "When this bird is gone, these fools will see their fields ravaged by every insect pest known on earth," he concluded.

Walker was still working on his Chickamauga Battlefield story but had to work incrementally, as the subject matter sickened him. At one point, he became so depressed that he threw the book down, vowing he would not undertake any more stories that affected his state of mind.

When some longtime neighbors moved to Michigan, Walker commented it was surely not because he had laid watermelon slices over his yard to study yellow jackets. Another neighbor placed a motion picture camera by the nest, while the inflamed insects stung it repeatedly. Walker experimented further, stomping a piece of melon into their hole, which they ate through. His curiosity was roused.

In one-hundred-degree weather, he donned hiking gear, buttoned up his coat and put on his explorer's helmet, preparing to study their evening behavior. As he was about to cork their entrance with another slice of melon, a man approached and asked to use the telephone. Walker did not explain his attire; the man made a hasty call and left, clearly frightened, undoubtedly believing he had disturbed a crazy man. Shortly after, a car that Walker took to be police parked in front of his house and watched for some time as he stomped watermelon slices into his yard.

Chapter 7

1936–1941

1936

A whirlwind Florida trip to see the Pleases resulted in learning that they had lost everything, the bank taking house and farm. But a kind neighbor had bought it and invited them to occupy it as before, without cost. Mrs. Pleas was making her husband shirts from flour sacks. Walker was touched by their plight, good spirits and ongoing generosity. He hoped to get some of Pleas's nature articles out to publishers.

In August, he learned of Wendell's marriage to Frances Richards by reading the announcement in the *Times*. Wendell and his longtime sweetheart had eloped to Atlanta on June 27, 1936, keeping it secret to avoid expense to either family. Walker gave them Elberta's silver spoons for a wedding present.

"My son just turned twenty-seven, and is gone from my roof forever, I guess. Yet I have much to be thankful for, as fathers usually lose their sons to marriage much earlier…I am so glad to see him happy."

His son and new daughter-in-law took him to the Dallas archaeological site, across from Dallas Island, twenty miles north of Chattanooga. He had been premature in thinking Wendell gone from his roof forever, as the newlyweds frequently spent nights in his home. They and Walker often hiked and picnicked together, and when they finally moved into their own apartment, Walker frequently dined with them.

He was disturbed by exploitation of the Dionne quintuplets, whose expenses were subsidized by the Canadian government. "Human beings

An archaeological excavation trench in Dallas Island, 1936. *Photo by Wendell Walker.*

are the silliest of all animals," he wrote. "I know many a Bobwhite who has raised a family of fifteen or more—but instead of assisting her, man is permitted by law to shoot her and her children in cold blood."

In September, he declined an invitation to Gatlinburg with the Cumberland Hiking Club, as it was the thirty-first anniversary of Robert's death: "Still children are killed! Thirty-five thousand men, women and children last year alone, slaughtered by automobiles! All the caution signs in Chattanooga around schools are written in the blood of my boy, for not until he was killed did the city wake up and establish these zones." But, encouraged by Wendell and Frances to go with them, he did visit the Smokies and was glad to have gone.

In November, he observed his yellow jackets still keeping out pickets, despite the cold. He greatly admired them, appreciating their presence on his lawn. "They have just as much right to live on this piece of land, although according to man's laws, I have title to the property. Yet in fact, it belongs to God and not man, so whatever creature he sends here to make its home is just as entitled to occupy it as I am."

He pressed leaves from his big persimmon tree to give out as souvenirs and calling cards to friends who knew his home as Triple Tree Tangle.

He continued frequent hikes with Wendell and Frances, bringing many others, including Jessie Turner, club editor of the *Times*. He recorded a joyous Christmas and spent a lively New Year's Eve in town with Jessie Turner and friends riding in an auto parade on Market Street—his first such "wild night" on the town.

1937

He was selling articles to the *New York Herald Tribune* with regularity, glad to have finished his last Chickamauga Battlefield story concerning Lincoln's brother-in-law, Confederate general Ben Helm.

In March, funding for Wendell's position was cut, while the unskilled laborers were retained. Wendell thoroughly enjoyed archaeological work, and Walker regretted having no business for him to "step into, as other young men had."

He was still having lifelike dreams of Elberta and agreed with poet William Lytle that a man loves only once. He also had vivid dreams of his father: "Someday I shall join him…laws of the spiritual world drawing me as surely as gravity pulls my feet to the ground in this natural world."

As he forged ahead despite loneliness without Elberta, he had almost completed another book, *Nature Ghost Stories*, but was sending the tales out individually to various publishers. His story "I Like Yellow-Jackets" gained a full page in the *Tribune*.

Will asked if he would sell the creek farm belonging to himself and five other siblings for $5,000. Walker hedged; he wanted the place as "a keepsake," fearing someone new might tear down the cabin.

As he was borrowing some photos and material for research, the clerk cautioned him not to lose the articles. Walker replied there was no danger unless his house caught fire. Returning home, he found remains of the Wardlaw house beside his home on fire and his beginning to catch. Fire engines came, but one side of his house was already blazing. He tried to shut windows, but the heat was too great and panes were cracking.

He collected manuscripts, stacking them in the front hall, but firemen told him they would soon have the fire extinguished. The old house next to his took two hours to put out, and the next day his was filled with repulsive odors of water-soaked, charred coals. Over one thousand people came to see it burn.

Wendell repaired and painted their house, making it decent again. He also made "fine nature pictures" for his father's articles. Walker noted, while walking with Wendell to photograph Indian hemp, that tramps were collecting it. "Likely they believe it is the Marijuana plant, outlawed for narcotic properties." But Indian hemp was used by Indians for string.

Walker's cousin Dr. George Walker was unjustly accused of violating the narcotic law, and Walker and J.E. Walker made George's bail. George was trapped by a legal technicality when he was hoodwinked by a Dr. Ellis, who asked him to give a prescription for a friend. But it came out that the "friend" did not exist. Ellis wanted the drug for himself and gave George a bogus name and address.

As the world awaited the fate of Amelia Earhart and her co-pilot, Walker was receiving calls from people asking for menus for a hawk, a black widow spider and a six-foot snake of unknown species. He was constantly requested to lead hikes, though transportation was sometimes an issue, as he did not drive.

He entertained his good friend E.Y. Chapin, president of American Trust and Banking, by dumping sand and two doodlebugs on his desk. For over an hour, Chapin observed their ludicrous backward antics plowing across his desk, providing hearty laughter for a busy banker.

On a trip to Mount Oglethorpe in Judge Lusk's car, another car struck them head-on, giving Walker a concussion and severely wrenched right side. Walker noted it took place exactly twenty-two years after the very day when Robert was killed. While laid up, he had the rest of the house's fire damage repaired. His Negro housekeeper of many years, Mary McLain, brought him flowers from her own garden, "the most touching gift sent me due to my injury…I will long remember Mary for her kindness."

His latest hawk, Theophilus, entertained him considerably during recuperation but eventually took flight through an open screen door. "He joined the winds that were blowing, and disappeared into the heavens towards Missionary Ridge. I miss him, but am happy knowing he is in his native element."

November 11 recalled Armistice Day 1918, when Walker was working at the *SFG* on Chestnut Street:

> *Such a world of confusion and shouting! People went wild over news of victory over Germany. Junk piles, long dead and voiceless, suddenly sprang*

to life as if by magic; items rusty, battered, split, spoke with a glib tongue,
clanging, banging, dragging, a shrieking mass of old kettles, dishpans,
crosscut saws, washpots, sledge hammers, lard cans, and other devices from
the garbage. Every conceivable noise-producing object was pulled from its
hiding place and brought onto the streets throughout the day, the noise equal
to a parade. Screams of joy rang wildly, and booming firearms beat upon
human ears.

The *SFG* office did not participate but was proud the war was over. At intervals during the day, processions passed to the cemetery, bearing bodies of soldiers who died at Chickamauga training field. The war's end saved the *SFG*, as wartime rules were being employed that would have strangled it, and other agricultural papers, to death.

A rumor of Walker's suicide came several weeks before his accident. A friend reported hearing it from someone who had his name confused with Richard E. Walker, the *Times* editor who had taken his life two years before.

Walker celebrated Christmas with Wendell and Frances, who put a tree in the south front room and piled gifts beneath it. He was unusually happy, commenting that if he had grandchildren, it would make Christmas all it should be. Will brought him a jar of "cheese-apple sauce" made of the big yellow cooking apples from their old farm. These required less sugar to sweeten the sauce but were seldom grown anymore. "In them, I heard the voice of the Chickamauga flowing past limestone ledges and red soil, the same lyric sound it has made since we were all boys, laboring on the farm together."

In winter snow he noted outside his window tracks of a wild country rabbit "who had wandered all around my house with his lovely little feet." Rabbits had lived in the limestone bluff near his house for years, and Walker felt their presence made the city more livable.

1938

Walker was given some wild mushrooms but had to find someone who knew how to cook them. Mushrooms, he believed, were a study in themselves, and he had long ago stopped giving advice on poisonous and nonpoisonous types. He feared people might not take time to notice the subtle, distinguishing marks between the two.

He went with Methodist ministers to meet a Negro man, Mark Thrush, who claimed to have turned 117 on Christmas Day. He read without glasses, had all his teeth and sold a pamphlet for twenty-five cents, telling that he had personally known Lincoln, Grant, Lee and all the Civil War generals. "Amazing, if true," said Walker.

In June, Wendell and Frances left for Blythe's Ferry, Hiwassee Island, to begin his work as photographer for removal of the mound before its flooding by the new dam. They came home on weekends, so Walker was not entirely alone. The work was slated to take a year to complete, but Wendell told his father they expected to explore only a tenth of the site. With the flooding, Walker bemoaned the loss of the best agricultural lands in the area.

He hosted a dinner for eight of his closest kin, who missed the big reunions for Tom Walker's birthday. He hoped to make the gathering an annual event.

Walker was suffering from vertigo since his auto accident but was working on a history of Lookout Mountain, interviewing old residents. He spoke with Mr. Linn, a photographer who lived on the mountain and had his studio at the Point. He learned plans were underway to develop the 256-foot waterfall inside Lookout Mountain, later known as Ruby Falls, named for the wife of Lambert, its discoverer.

He visited the Stratton sisters at their home in North Chattanooga to obtain a book Cora Stratton had written about Grassy Cove. She was also an artist, painting china and landscapes. Walker once ordered a set of dishes from her for Elberta, which he gave to Wendell and Frances.

People brought him many creatures, but he was delivered a slobber-soaked baby chicken by a terrier. The dog had taken care not to injure it, seeming to value it highly. Despite the dog's protest, Walker took the chick to his sister's farm.

Since the publication of *Torchlights to the Cherokees*, he had been contacted by others interested in Cherokee history. "Publishing a book guarantees a whole new circle of acquaintances," he said. He also noted selling a previously rejected manuscript to the same editor who had rejected it, simply by changing its title—proving the importance of a name.

In October, he visited Mrs. D.F. Ellis, taking her to the site of Blackwell's Chapel School, which she had attended. They walked to the location of the Cherokee Council House and big spring. She described how it once was, having not seen the spring in fifteen years, though her wash pot was still there. Mrs. Ellis, eighty-three, told of whites taking charge of the council house, calling it Blackwell's Chapel. They turned it into a Methodist Episcopal church and school until 1873, when a new Methodist church was built in Graysville.

She gave Walker much history of Chickamauga and Graysville, telling him the big spring at Graysville had been the home of Cherokee Chief Scrapeshin, the spring bearing his name. The ridge running north to Ryall's Spring is known as Scrapeshin Ridge. She also said there had once been an old log house where Lizzie's house stood. It was home to a close relation of John Ross, the man's two daughters having ridden on horseback to school and church at Brainerd Mission.

Walker celebrated Robert's birthday by attending, with many locals and 125 Cherokees from North Carolina, the placing of markers at Brainerd

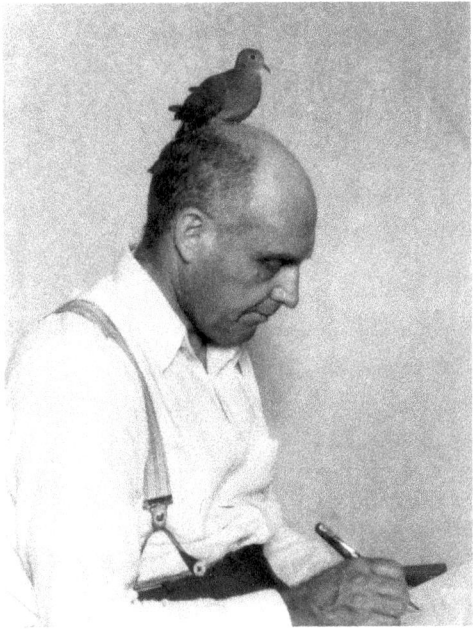

Walker with Noah the dove, 1938. *Photo by Wendell Walker.*

Cemetery. The tablets honored Reverend Stephen Foreman, other missionaries and staff. Cherokees from Oklahoma were present also, taken by Walker and Dr. Steele to the Cherokee Reservation in North Carolina. There they met Cherokee Chief Blythe and took a short hike over Clingmans Dome before boarding the train in Knoxville to head back west.

Walker now had another bird: a dove named Noah that liked to ride the carriage of his typewriter and sit on his shoulder.

Wendell, whose wife taught English at Tyner High, was still working at Hiwassee Island, where both resided most of the time. Walker and his son proposed a Cherokee museum on Lookout Mountain, which never materialized due to financing. Wendell had given his father a book from the Smithsonian Institute, *An Archeological Survey of the Norris Basin in Eastern Tennessee*, by William Webb. Wendell's name was listed in several places, several of his photographs and charts being included.

Walker and family members took a motorboat to the lower end of Hiwassee Island, landing at Blythe's Ferry. There a truck unloaded a band of WPA workers, who climbed onboard with them and rode up the Hiwassee to the Indian mound being opened. They also saw Colonel Benham's vacant

Colonel Benham's Home, Hiwassee Island, 1938. *Photo by Wendell Walker.*

home. Benham had once owned the island, and his brother-in-law, author Opie Reed, spent time there. Walker was sad to think of all being lost beneath the flood.

While researching his Lookout book, he learned that Chattanooga National Cemetery has soldiers from every war the United States has fought. The place was once known as Shrubbery Knob, but General Thomas chose it in 1863 as a burial ground for Union soldiers.

Walker accepted a rattlesnake offered by a caller to "keep up my reputation as a naturalist" but gave the snake to a friend, Fred Cofer. A few days later, he took the hiking club to Graysville, the hike terminating at a large campfire, where Cofer had cooked the rattler. Skinned and cut in pieces, it was tasty, the first snake Walker had eaten. Everyone enjoyed it, though its true identity was not disclosed, Walker describing it as terrestrial fish.

He took his friend McBroom a less exotic edible in the form of peanut candy. But he was murdering flies with a plant from his backyard called "apple-of-Peru" or "fly poison." He crushed a piece in a dish of milk and watched flies fall by the score in half an hour. He remembered his mother used it when he was a child. (One would assume there were no pets around that liked milk.)

Walker thoroughly enjoyed his three fig trees. He climbed among them, picking fruit, giving away what he could not eat and sharing the plentiful crop with birds. He and Dona also cooked them, storing the jars in the pantry. Discovering two jars from the previous year's crop that looked fine, they set them out to eat next. Walker awoke to a terrible racket of missiles striking the ceiling and crashing on the floor. Jar tops had blown off, broken at the neck as smoothly as if cut. Walker felt their lives had been spared, since no one realized the fruit had spoiled.

Lizzie provided him with a young skunk that he named Provided. It was an American skunk—or *skee-unk*, so named by Canadian Cree Indians—that Walker wished to study. He was also temporary custodian of a puff adder, commenting that while he was growing stinging nettles, poison ivy, fly poison and poison oak in his garden—and keeping spiders, snakes, lizards, toads, hawks and a polecat as pets—people must wonder what kind of mortal he was. "But…all creatures and creations have a useful purpose, and I am determined to find it, and in so doing, get a new vision of my Creator!"

A short time later, describing their raccoon as the best pet they ever had, Walker wrote that the skunk had escaped and the puff adder was relocated to a place in the mountains where he was unlikely to encounter the human race. Noah the dove had taken flight out an open screen door but returned weeks later with a wing wounded by birdshot, though Walker had requested in the paper that he not be shot during hunting season. Under Walker's care, the bird recovered.

His Christmas gift this year, he said, was publication of his poetry book *When God Failed*. It was so personal and full of grief that he felt he should not have put it on the public, wondering what their reaction would be. By the close of 1938, he was also wondering, with the rest of America, if Germany would make a move toward Czechoslovakia and, if so, how far the bloodshed would reach.

1939

A terrific January storm sent Walker's chimney crashing onto his back porch, where it broke the roof in and crushed the ceiling. He called Harry Holder, a Negro brick mason, to rebuild the chimney. Walker called him a rare breed—an honest man, adding that he had been swindled by every profession but, "of all damnable professions, that of lawyer is the worst." He could not believe he once considered it for his life's work.

He was obliged to sue his friend Judge Lusk (who insisted he do so) for injuries resulting from their 1937 auto accident. The experience was unpleasant, the opposing attorney portraying him as an ungrateful friend and faking injuries. His own lawyer then changed the jury's opinion, resulting in a small settlement. Walker was glad it was over.

Wendell's Hiwassee Island work terminated. The mound revealed eighty burials, many of the deaths attributed to arrow points and a few missing their heads. He left for Paris, Tennessee, to work on the Gilbertsville Dam

Wendell's "office," Hiwassee Island, 1938.

site. Frances stayed behind with Walker until her school term was out, and Walker hated to see them go. Paris was too far from Chattanooga for weekend visits.

Only minutes after he had been in conversation with brother John concerning his elderly friend Senator Sanders, he received a call from Sanders's nurse telling him of the senator's passing.

In May, Walker suffered a serious heart attack at home and was unable to reach anyone. It was the second such event, the first occurring while he was carrying heavy books upstairs. Hours later, Dona came home and found him a doctor. He was told to remain quiet and not resume his regular activities—perhaps ever—a discouraging diagnosis.

People brought gifts of food and flowers, which cheered him, though he was never a cut flowers fan. "I would rather see an old, rough-skinned toad on my dresser—or a bird, or chameleon…But all are works of the Master Artist who for some good purpose, placed us here."

He could not conceive of a man being more pious on Sundays than any other day. "To attend church on Sundays and live like the devil the rest of the week won't keep a man from hell—here, or hereafter." He usually spent Sundays on the creek farm, which always drew him back to the days of his youth.

He took quiet walks after dark to hear crickets fiddling. "If God can so perfectly orchestrate a cricket symphony, then I can surely trust him to attend to my life hereafter." He was awed by the orderliness of creation. "God's hand is so visible, I do not see how any man can be an atheist. Man's life is also orderly, when he practices the principals Christ taught."

He discussed a peculiar fungus known as "punk" found in hickory and buckeye trees. "It transforms wood into a tough, leather-like material that holds fire until it burns up, but never blazes openly." It was the only substance he knew that could be wrapped and carried safely, sometimes for a day. One could unwind the ball of punk, blow on the encased spark and start a fire. As a boy, he carried pieces of punk to light firecrackers.

May had little rain, reminding Walker of his father's philosophy on growing wheat that he had so loved. Tom had said, "It takes a dry May to make a good wheat year." Few farmers in the area grew wheat anymore. "But my father's smiles would ripple over his cheeks like the winds would ripple over his field of ripening wheat."

Walker caught a cardinal in his hedge, asking a friend to photograph it. Awaiting him, Walker placed the bird's cage in the closet for darkness to calm him. Almost instantly the bird began singing. "What a discovery! What a miracle!" he reported, considering song might be the cardinal's prayer for deliverance. He wondered if humans would be better off if they sang when overtaken by adversity.

A woman called asking if scattering sassafras leaves would keep mice and rats away. Walker replied if her mice were as smart as his, they would soon be making tea of the stuff. He added that rats did not respect such superstitions either.

After many years, he was finally writing about the unpleasant, long-standing circumstances involving him, his *SFG*, the acting assistant postmaster general and a patent medicine company. The postmaster had tried to put him out of business from 1908 to 1910, and there were further attacks from 1914 to 1916. Walker had refused to accept advertising from patent medicine companies and, in fact, spoke out against them. He was somewhat vindicated a few years later when the *Journal of American Medical Association* published unflattering articles about one of the men involved.

According to Walker, in 1908 the American Propriety Association, an organization of patent medicine companies, paid the third assistant postmaster general a bribe to dump Walker's *SFG* from the mails.

He related the story to *Times* editor Julian LaRose Harris, who expressed interest, so Walker brought him copies of the 1915 *Harper's Weekly* containing articles on the lawsuits revolving around the events of those years. He had titled its first chapter "Capturing a Human Skunk." In subsequent chapters, he exposed other conspirators, some involved in the founding of Pilgrim Church. Walker titled his booklet "When I Tried to Be Honest," having waited all this time to put the story in writing until many of those involved were deceased.

"I won't publish it in my generation, as some of the people still living might think I was doing it for retribution. But after a lapse of twenty-five years, I carry no malice for anyone—not even those who persecuted me and the church I helped found. But I will leave it behind when I am gone." The manuscript has not been published.

He mourned the loss of "some of my finest friends" when horses in the Fyffe Barracks perished in a tragic fire. Walker had often brought them apples.

He reflected on his Uncle Preston Walker, who, with brother Lieutenant John and others, tramped through the Cumberland Gap to enlist in the Union army. Preston was a lieutenant in the Eighth Tennessee Volunteer Infantry, and Walker recalled his visit to Chattanooga in 1906. He had to help his uncle out of the car due to his bad shoulder.

At the Battle of Atlanta, Preston received a serious shrapnel wound in his left shoulder. His outfit hauled him around in an ambulance vehicle for a week before the wound was dressed. Gangrene had set in, and flesh dropped off his shoulder bone. They then hauled him to St. Louis, Missouri, and put him in a hospital. He was so ill he picked out his own coffin from the many stacked there.

On top of his wound, he came down with smallpox and was placed in a boat and taken downriver to an island where smallpox patients were quarantined. That hospital was also stacked with coffins, and he saw the dead being placed in them. Feeling sure his time had come, Preston again picked out his own coffin. "But a miracle happened," said Walker, "he recovered and lived to be over eighty-four!"

Walker's uncle told him that while in the hospital, he promised himself if he ever got back to Hawkins County, he would never leave. He clung to that promise until he was nearly eighty, when he visited Chattanooga with his wife, Ellen, to see younger brother Tom and his large family. Walker hired an auto for three dollars a day to take them all around the town.

By summer, Walker's health was again an issue. He checked himself into Uplands Sanitarium, spending two months, the first half of it nearly bedridden. But the beauty of the Cumberlands inspired him, although he wished they had not been renamed for so bloody a man as the Duke of Cumberland, who had massacred the Scots in 1746. He preferred they be "rightfully known by their Cherokee name, Ouisoto, or Otali, Mountains."

From his window one morning, he observed what seemed to be a specter blowing kisses beside a gate post and then entering the grounds to walk through its flowers. She seemed like a woman at first but now appeared as a child. He was unnerved when a second girl appeared beside her and vanished before his eyes.

The first girl then waved as if bidding goodbye and came slowly toward the building, and he heard her knocking on the door. As she turned to leave, Walker coughed and the girl stopped, looked at him and then continued down the road and disappeared. He questioned Uplands' director Dr. Wharton about it and was only told the girl was very bright, about eight years old. The experience was without explanation, but Walker was apparently not the only one to see her.

He observed the emergence of a beautiful moth from its cocoon, encouraging his faith that God could change him "from the clumsy animal I am in the flesh, to something glorious."

By July, he was recuperating at Alexian Brothers on Signal Mountain. He very much liked the Catholic brothers, becoming friends with several. The view from his room was spectacular: "From one of nature's cavernous wombs, I see daily born a lovely white cloud. The majestic mountains rise above it, and how calm is the famous Suck in the Tennessee River, made so by the lock and dam below. The Suck, 'Untiguhi' in Cherokee, or 'Pot-in-the-Water,' is one of nature's obstetric rooms, where the cloud of mist is born each morning."

He met there many retired men who did not know what to do with themselves. He was thankful for his interests and the endless supply of subjects for study, which always recharged his optimism. Among the mountain residents, he met Dane R. Walker (no kin), seventy-two, who helped build the Signal Mountain Hotel, which had become Alexian Brothers. The man had some Cherokee heritage and brought a copy of *Torchlights* for Walker to sign.

Walker was often asked why he named one book *When God Failed*, yet he saw no contradiction between it and his Christian faith. Even Jesus on the cross had voiced a similar cry. "I have waded grief up to my eyes through the dark valley of death more than once. I know what it means to yearn for death, that I might join the family I have lost…but when all seemed hopeless, one of the great mysteries of life took place—resurrection of my faith in God and humanity." Through the message of nature's beauty, he found he had not finished the work assigned to him.

His conservative morals caused him a dilemma, as he terminated a long-standing friendship on learning the man had been cheating on his wife. In a heated conversation, Walker informed him that he did not condone such betrayal and could no longer be his friend, ending their formerly cordial relationship. Whether one agreed with his decision or not, or judged him as stiff-necked, did not matter. His early training in morality had formed his character, and he was prepared to answer for it.

In September, Wendell drove from Paris to take Walker home. He returned to a damp, dreary house and unkempt, tangled yard but was glad to be home. When a new bathroom was installed downstairs and most of the rooms repapered, he could defer to his heart condition and now work downstairs. He would seldom need the upstairs again. He resumed writing, sending articles to Walter Johnson of the Newspaper Publishers Association, who hoped to place them with a syndicate.

Walker, as much of the world, received news of England's declaring war on Germany with grave concern. "Poor Poland! Germany and Russia, like two sheep-killing dogs, are eating her alive, having made a pact to slaughter and divide the carcass. The flesh and bones of her citizens are sticking out of the mouths of two tyrants, Hitler and Stalin."

He hired Rudolph Shutting, whom he had known in his early years at the *SFG*, to make a map for his history of Lookout Mountain. Shutting, once Cook's commercial artist, had a drinking problem that almost ruined his life. Although he had not overcome his problem, he delivered the map a few days later, "fairly good, but full of fingerprints, as if chickens and rabbits had tracked over it." (Shutting's map can be seen on the inside cover of *Lookout, the Story of a Mountain*.)

He continued to mark Robert's birthday, reflecting on that day's cool weather, requiring Walker to build a fire in the downstairs room, which was now his office. He had gone to work at the *SFG* in the Chamberlain Building, only to be informed by Byron Gager, whose office was next to his, that he was wanted home at once. He rushed home to meet Robert and was "thankful we had him for eight years…I believe we will meet again, when I slip out of this mortal body."

He was slowly returning to health despite the heart condition that had kept him flat on his back, unable to travel for nearly eight months. He went to Dr. Bibb, who fluoroscoped him and reported his aorta enlarged. He was prescribed daily nitroglycerin tablets, to be kept with him at all times.

By late October, he had completed his book *Lookout, the Story of a Mountain*, saying, "Now God will have to find me a publisher." He said that if he had money, he would publish local works just for pleasure. He was seeing friends again, among them William Webb, whose father founded Webb Camp for Boys, where Walker often gave nature talks. The younger Webb had written a book to prove Sequoyah's father was a white German trader, Gergat, Webb having researched and lectured on the subject.

But according to Judge Samuel Williams, one of Webb's sources, Sequoyah's father was Christopher Gist, a friend of George Washington who married a Cherokee woman. Sequoyah, an only child, neither read nor wrote but spent twelve years inventing the Cherokee Syllabary. William Webb's brother operated a school in California, one of his pupils having been comedian Will Rogers. Rogers had promised to write the introduction to Webb's book but was killed in a plane crash in Alaska. Walker hoped Webb would get it published, as it would spark debate.

The week of Elberta's birthday, he had two vivid dreams of her. He read *The Life of Samuel Patton*, written in 1854 about a Methodist preacher in the Holston Conference of East Tennessee and a relative of Elberta's. Her brother Henry Patton Clark was named for him.

He reported a remarkable story told by the National Cemetery's superintendent, Captain Henderson. In August, a Negro soldier was buried there. The man's dog came in with mourners by car for the burial but refused to leave. No one could catch him, and he lived wild in a rock cave near the grave. He resisted all attempts of people to approach, remaining half starved, guarding his master's grave. When Henderson recounted the story to a *Times* reporter, the reporter told him of a dog in Georgia whose owner gave him a nickel each morning to go to the meat shop and buy food. When the dog was not hungry, he would bury the nickel, digging it up when he was ready to shop for dinner.

Walker bemoaned the loss of the *Times*, which issued its last paper on December 16. It foundered due to poor management, he believed, of George Milton Jr. and his stepmother, Abby Milton, whose inability to cooperate with each other contributed to its demise. The *Chattanooga Free Press* had signed up for the majority of its stock. Alf Mynders, the late paper's editor, told Walker that George Milton planned to start a new paper. Mynders had signed a charter with Milton, Nicholson and Walker's nephew, Harry Clark, to publish the *Evening Tribune*, though they were incorporating on optimism, having no money.

Walker visited a frail McBroom, giving him money for Christmas dinner, though he spent both Christmas and New Year's Eve alone for the first time in years, as Wendell and Frances were attending an archaeology convention in Chicago. Knowing how much the event meant to Wendell, Walker insisted on their going, despite his son's protests. Later Christmas Day, John took him to Lizzie's, where a holiday dinner cheered him considerably. Afterward, he and his siblings read over old letters, some to his father in 1886, causing him to reflect, "He had the keenest sense of justice I have ever known." He was glad Tom's children had persuaded him, at age seventy-five, to return to his first love: farming.

The county had then offered Tom Walker the position of road commissioner, which he agreed to accept if they reduced the salary, as he felt they paid too much of the people's money for services rendered. "This set politicians to fingering their hair," said Walker. It could set a precedent that might have to be followed in other departments! Tom Walker's acceptance was rejected.

Walker reflected on his father's generosity. When measuring grain or produce, he heaped it into a peak, quoting scripture. As he was a tall man, Tom's Hardshell Baptist Church once threatened to strike his name from its rolls because his feet were too large for its foot-washing vessel.

Walker's grandfather, Edward Walker, was of similar stature, and he recalled their first meeting at Tyner Station. Bob, John and their father took their new spring wagon to meet Edward Walker. The historian in Walker's blood recalled that Tyner was once prominent during the Civil War, being the army loading place when General Bragg evacuated Chattanooga. By the late 1800s, it consisted of a church, general store, blacksmith shop and occasionally a photographer's tent.

The ticket agent had met them, carrying one red and one white lantern. Bob had been excited by the fiery, wood-burning passenger train, spitting embers, wheels creaking and rattling. When it stopped, the silhouette of a tall, straight man descended the platform. He was wearing a broad, stiff-brimmed hat, his face whiskery as he bent to kiss Bob's cheek.

By then, Tom Walker had not seen his father in almost twenty years, and the boys were eager to see this man in the light of the oil lamp. An hour later, they got their first look: "His eyes were bright with a twinkle, few lines claimed his forehead. His beard was shorn close...he wore a home-made grey shirt, possibly homespun. His old-fashioned trousers opened on the right instead of in front. He handed me a pocketknife. I loved him at first sight."

Edward and grandson Bob became staunch friends, pulling the crosscut saw together to cut firewood. He taught Bob to use a frow in splitting boards for the smokehouse they were building. They hung hog meat from scalded yucca leaves grown in the cabin's yard, as the Cherokees had done for bear meat—hence yucca was also known as bear grass.

Walker recalled Edward Walker telling jokes on himself, how he mistook the first bunch of bananas he ever saw for a string of sweet potatoes. He paused beneath an overpass while a freight rumbled overhead so he could say a train had run over him without causing pain.

Walker recorded that Edward was born in Otes, Hawkins County, on May 29, 1819, and married Elizabeth Bryant. Edward's father, John William Walker, was born on February 20, 1797, probably in Hawkins County, and had four wives, the first, Miliah Phillips, being Walker's great-grandmother. (John William was widowed three times.) According to family lore, John William's father was also named Edward and his father John Walker, likely from Virginia and had fought in the Revolution.

When Walker had returned home after his long recovery, he found a chipmunk residing in his kitchen. He hoped to capture it, naming it Sir Walter Raleigh and leaving it food, and before long, the chipmunk came when called.

He appreciated how much work Wendell had done to the house. Three windows in his bedroom faced south, keeping the room so warm that he believed it possible to heat one's home with sunlight. If it had windows facing south, east and west, that natural warmth would be preferable to artificial heat from coal or steam, and he wished he had such a house.

Walker hired a new housekeeper, Addie Walker (no kin), after Mary McLain suffered a stroke and was moved to the county infirmary. Walker described Addie as a mother of nine once living near Gadsden who paddled a boat daily across the Coosa River to the farm she and her husband cultivated. Walker found her very honest, commenting that while some cleaning women carried off food, "perhaps we whites are to blame. We pay them so little, and most white women are so exacting…The Negro race must be able to look up to itself, not down. Most I have known have been very compassionate people, deserving of far better than their lot."

1940

Sometimes Walker was compelled to shut off water to keep pipes from freezing. During that cold February, Will succumbed to meningitis, leaving a wife and two children, and was buried at Concord Church. Walker commented, "It is that deep silence…which brings the sadness. As I reflect on my brother who has meant so much to me…I realize one day someone will reflect on my silence, as I do now on his."

Later that month he received the Boy Scouts' Silver Beaver Award at a banquet held at Hotel Patten. He was honored, despite doctors' advice against undue exertion. He took this warning as a sign to put his manuscripts in good order. He was revising old poems, many of which he had sold in the past, finding them now so flawed he couldn't understand why editors had bought them.

Finances were strained again, requiring him to pay his 1939 taxes late, with penalties. He began a question and answer department in his nature column, but it did not cover his bills.

When Mary McLain died in March, he gave a donation toward her funeral. They had spoken on death often, and she was not afraid. He wished to have known her better, despite the division caused by their different skin colors. These thoughts provoked some angry observations: "We really are a stingy race of people! We feed slop to hogs, give livestock polluted water, and spoiled bread to birds. When our clothes are ruined, we become quite generous and give them to the poor, especially Negroes.

Then we pat ourselves on the back and delude ourselves that we are most Christian and charitable, feeling satisfied we have done our duty to our needy brothers and sisters."

Wendell and Frances were living in Rockwood but came back on weekends to stay with Walker. Wendell showed his father photographs of the excavation at Watts Bar, revealing a roundhouse, the only one found in East Tennessee. They drove to see the vast new Chickamauga Lake, which flooded much of the old lands, Walker admiring its many teals and ducks.

As Europe became a battleground, Walker noted that the birds had not given up hope, behaving as if they were still confident of the Creator's world. A man now in his sixty-second year, he often reflected on the past in his personal writings.

He recalled first seeing the Tennessee River when he was eight. He had gone with his father to the end of Market Street, impressed by a ferryboat moving across the river, propelled by a mule walking in circles. He had previously only seen mules turn the rollers of a cane mill to make sorghum or run a wheat thresher. The new Walnut Street Bridge cost the mules their ferry job, just as electricity soon released them from the streetcars.

Walker remembered he and his brothers, after disposing of their produce, taking the streetcar for Hill City (later North Chattanooga) to see an animal show where an educated horse was star performer. Sometimes they got off at a dance hall called the Valombrosia at the summit of Stringer's Ridge above the tunnel. There they could buy fancy soda in bottles with wire-mounted corks and look down on Dayton Pike below.

"The Bell Distillery used to be at the mouth of the ravine between Cameron and Reservoir Hills, owned by a Mr. Snyder who moved his business from Petersburg, Kentucky, to avoid the Civil War. But when General Wilder brought his forces to Chattanooga and commenced shelling the Confederate fort on top of Reservoir Hill, one-third of the ammunition landed on the distillery, ruining Snyder's business. He returned to Kentucky to make a fresh start.

Hill City was a clutter of cheap houses and shacks, hogs and cattle roaming the streets. When modern homes and streets were later built, I was asked to suggest something to hold soil in such steep surroundings. I recommended kudzu, the vegetable kingdom's race-horse, also suggesting it along highways to Lookout Mountain. But kudzu proved too ambitious, left the banks, struck out through the woods, invaded yards—making it liable for prosecution for trespassing. I have ceased such recommendations.

In National Cemetery, he encountered a young boy with a bunch of snowball blossoms plucked from a nearby bush. Walker pointed out he had violated the cemetery's rule not to pick its flowers, suggesting he might put them on a grave. He pointed out a newer section, but the boy said he preferred taking them to a closer grave and then ran off. He said his name was John Price. Walker did not see where the boy placed the flowers. A few days later, Walker passed the grave of a Civil War soldier, noting the headstone said "John Price, Ohio." He wondered if it might have been the boy's ancestor.

Walker retained fond memories of Walnut Grove. The school was built on two acres donated by Arthur and Jane Steels. Its first teacher was Sam Julian, followed by William Milkens and, later, B.K. Reynolds, who remained ten years. The building was removed in 1912, but its site was still visible in 1940, a foot higher than surrounding ground. Walker earlier attended Mackie School on Mackie Branch, or Tsula Creek, as the Cherokees named it, meaning "red fox."

Walker recalled, "Girls swept the schoolhouse at noon, and boys brought dead wood to feed the large, ugly stove. They carried drinking water from Mackie Spring, which bubbled up from a limestone rock beside Tsula Creek." In 1889, it was abandoned for the larger Walnut Grove.

"Mackie School was built by Wallis Gray, but later torn down, its lumber used by T.O. Dudley in building his two-room residence near the home of Thomas Sparks Lowe at the Graysville state line. Mr. Dudley brought his bride there, and as their family increased, added more rooms." Lowe had come from Pennsylvania around 1849. His wife from South Carolina was of Cherokee descent and knew much of the early Cherokees once living in the Chickamauga area. Lowe was a close friend of Tom Walker and gave much information about their creek farm. When Lowe died, Walker erected a marble tombstone over his grave on the old church farm in Tennessee, about a mile west of Graysville.

Walker wrote his poem "Fairmount" in recollection of his ride on horseback with John and their father in 1893. They had camped for the weekend at the foot of the mountain. Tom Walker was finishing the W Road, and debris was scattered from top to foot of Walden's Ridge from the blast that blew off Hanging Rock. Tom, not wanting to risk anyone else's life, touched off the dynamite himself, raced up the mountain and crouched behind a boulder. Tom said even before the sound, he could feel the mountain pushing his feet backward. Over five hundred spectators on a nearby cliff had watched the spectacle.

Walker learned that the faithful dog keeping watch over the Negro soldier's grave had died during the zero-degree weather. "Despite cold, hunger, and grief, the man's dog kept watch over his beloved master, until he froze to death…What loyalty!"

Spring came at last, turning the vacant lot beside his house into an arbor with vines and wildflowers. Former *SFG* secretary J.M. Carroll paid Walker a surprise visit after twenty-odd years. Carroll was now a judge in Dade County, Georgia.

Elberta visited him again in dreams, stirring memories of their first meeting, when she was seventeen and he had finished teaching at Morris Hill. "The youngest daughter of a Methodist minister, she was educated, cultured, refined, and beautiful." Walker had been tongue-tied but over time saw her again at his sister Mary's.

"Although she never attempted creative writing, she was my most valued critic, and excellent Latin scholar…On our wedding trip, when we discovered the Washington Monument's elevator disabled by lightning, it was she who proposed we climb it on foot."

She loved to take Walker's checks from sales of articles and poetry and purchase some special object to serve as reminder of that particular manuscript. Even her eighteen-karat gold wedding ring was bought from the sale of a magazine essay. Elberta had been the favorite in her large family for her pleasant disposition. "There are some whose voice and presence can inspire and cheer others out of despondency, and such was she. Whatever success I may attain in life…she is largely responsible."

They planned to spend two years in England after World War I but postponed the journey until it was too late. Much later, they planned to move somewhere on the Hudson River, where Walker would become associated with a New York City magazine, but Elberta's last illness prevented this.

In contrast to these treasured memories, he at last described his ill-fated friendship with Abby Milton, who had given a recent reading from her book *Ceasar's Wife* to the writers' club. Ten years earlier, Walker had edited the book, found a publisher and read the galley proofs. Her reaction when he suggested she dedicate the book to her late husband shocked him. "She turned up her nose as if I had offered her a skunk, saying she wouldn't do anything of the sort." Nevertheless, he stayed up nights finishing it, mailing off the book and paying its postage, for which she never thanked him.

"But fool-like," he continued, "I helped with her next book of poems, *Lookout Mountain*, spending weeks taking her on hikes, teaching her wildflowers." Again, he read proofs and got not even a complimentary copy.

But as I had learned by then she was silly and foolish, I acknowledge that of the two of us, I was the bigger fool…I have since shunned her as a pestilence.

She has utterly charming traits, but conducts herself in…a shallow manner. I found her dishonest, for three times she tried schemes to get me to marry her. The last proposition she made, had I been fool and degenerate enough to accept it without marriage, would have sunk me into the gutter and sacrificed my character decidedly. I calculate she owes me ten thousand dollars for time and help, but it is worth twice that amount to be free of her, and so I join with others who view her in similar light.

Walker was a true Victorian, coming from a rigid, conservative background, while Abby Milton was an early suffragette, socialite and liberated woman for her day. Both were strong personalities, much aware of their different views regarding life, and the amazing thing is that they got along as well as they did as long as they did.

His Aunt Mary Walker died in July at ninety-four. The widow of his uncle Lieutenant John Walker, she had been a teacher. "What a beautiful soul," he wrote. "I would love to know how many lives she has touched." Joe Morris, for whom Morris Hill was named, passed away, and the school where Walker and his siblings once taught had become Morris Hill Baptist Church.

When brother John fell ill with a severe kidney infection, Walker climbed stairs to his room, despite his heart condition, to stay with him. Fortunately, John recovered.

On September 2, the Chickamauga Dam officially opened, President Roosevelt presiding. Thirty thousand people showed up, the only casualty being a man who drank from a whiskey bottle and got a wasp in his mouth.

The government enacted the bill conscripting all men between the ages of eighteen to sixty-five, including Walker and Wendell. Walker described himself as willing to serve but, in his present condition, only fit to fight with his pen—"but the pen is mightier than the sword." Despite his son's eligibility for the draft, Walker favored it, citing the possibility of Germany's plan to strike the United States from Mexico.

Walker was fighting his own war with publishers, who paid him half what he was owed. None could be trusted, despite their glossy reputations.

The proposed newspaper the *Tribune* was running at last, with Walker's friend Alf Mynders now working for it and nephew Harry Clark its managing editor. George Milton Jr. was out of the picture.

Walker visited Dr. Steele's new home under construction on Crest Road on the Ridge. "He has a fine view from both front and back yards. He is one of the best friends I ever had."

Avian friends also held place. Wendell photographed the blue jay Hamlet that lived on Walker's back porch and sometimes shared his bedroom. But Walker had noticed a lady blue jay outside that was "in love with him, so I plan to free him."

He wrote an essay on the American Balm of Gilead tree that had grown in the front yard of the creek farm. Neighbors collected its resinous buds to make healing salve, Walker recalling his mother making a remedy from it for sores, burns and insect stings.

He recorded a trip to Rock City Gardens with J.A. McConnel of *Kingsport Press* to see Garnet Carter. They found him friendly, jovial and "a beautiful cusser who could fit 'damn' and 'hell' as perfectly into his conversation as punctuation in a manuscript." Walker had hoped for an order for his Lookout Mountain history but instead received a tentative order to write the history of Rock City.

He spent Christmas with Wendell and Frances, exchanging gifts. Wendell returned to Rockwood with a subscription to the *American Journal of Archeology* from his father and a year's membership in the organization.

1941

Walker was given a picture of Cherokee botanist Tooan-tuh, Spring Frog, by a university librarian. Tooan-tuh had fought with Jackson at the Battle of Horseshoe Bend and went west around 1817, when he was thought to have joined the Arkansas Cherokees, taking part in the Osage War. He had supposedly occupied the creek farm's cabin. Walker greatly admired him.

Addie Walker sent two of her seven daughters over to work, but they did a poor job—and Walker was hardly particular. His solution was to meet them at the door when they came again, telling them he preferred doing the job himself. But since Addie, deserted by her husband, needed money, Walker offered them a second chance, showing them what to do. The girls, with his training, did a fine job, for which he complimented them and paid extra. Next week Addie sent over two other daughters, "and I was compelled to repeat my training program."

In May, *Lookout, the Story of a Mountain* was released and displayed in store windows around town. Walker was given a tea by Miller Brothers Book Department to meet fans and autograph books. He was much pleased by its positive reception.

Forbidden to do the yard work he loved, he engaged Thomas Seals, a Negro man, to keep the place in order. "I seem to have given him the understanding that dinner is included, but he is so nice and gentlemanly, that I get much pleasure from his enjoyment of my cooking. So I put on an apron and give him luncheon, and he eats it all."

The *Times* mentioned Walker's suggestion that Monroe County be changed to Sequoyah County, "in honor of the great Cherokee who was born there." Sequoyah's fame was growing, and Walker felt the world would beat a path to the site of old Tuskegee town near Fort Loudoun to see his birthplace. (Walker was always forward-thinking. There is now the Sequoyah Birthplace Museum, situated on a forty-seven-acre tract on the shores of Tellico Lake, opened in 1986, owned by the Eastern Band of Cherokees. It is located off Highway U.S. 411 on Highway 360 in Vonore, Tennessee.)

He decided to liberate Hamlet, setting him on the windowsill, but Hamlet would not go. The bird picked up peanuts Walker placed to lure him out but hopped back into his room. Hamlet had made his decision, choosing to stay. Walker later found Hamlet had gone through articles in his room, taking those he liked to his quarters on the back porch.

Coming home from town, Walker was astonished to overhear much anti-Semitic talk in people's conversations. "There seems to be a growing sentiment hostile to Jews, and I am sorry to see this race hated. It is a bad sign indeed."

Financial distress forced him to attempt something he hated: ask the Chattanooga Writers' Club for release of his $500, placed at their disposal for the poetry contest awards. He was afterward confronted by a box of five hundred entry poems: "They stared at me so, I could not move a finger towards [reading] them. They had me completely hypnotized, as if a rattlesnake was looking me in the eyes."

The club voted to return his money, but the bank attorney who set up the trust fund declined its return, saying poets of America were its beneficiaries— the contest must run eternally. Walker accepted the news in stride.

He brought McBroom some clothes and wound up giving him money for rent. McBroom was again wearing a summer jacket, although it was thirty degrees out; Walker put his overcoat on him again. "If one cannot give something one needs, there is no sacrifice involved," he commented.

An October 19 earthquake struck the southeastern tip of Tennessee, shaking Walker's house so badly he thought it had collapsed brick pillars beneath his bedroom. Yet he found no damage. He then turned on the radio to hear soothing music but had to cut off several preachers "whose method of delivery was driving away all my pious spirit. To keep from losing my religion, I denied them my ears. I cannot understand why a man would deliver a message to civilized people in a voice befitting a cattle driver. Jesus never preached in such manner!"

He could not vote in the local election because his precinct voted on the fire hall's second floor, with a tremendous stairway to climb. But he voted in the national election, with little enthusiasm, for Roosevelt.

In November, brother-in-law John Davidson lost his barn and two mules in a fire. He was seventy-two, with no insurance, his loss totaling $3,000. Walker and John visited him to cheer him, going afterward to the nearby creek farm, where they waded the icy Chickamauga barefoot. Walker found the old submerged log from which he had slipped as a boy and learned to swim. It had been in the ford over fifty years. He once hunted fossils there while his mother did laundry nearby. "The past, now embalmed in memory, seems like a dream."

His heart still troubled him some, but he was careful of diet and activities. Wendell, Frances and Dona shared his house much of the time and could be of help if trouble struck.

He recalled the secret wildflower garden he once kept on a hill above the Chickamauga. As a child, he felt a wildflower was a creature with personality, the only difference between it and himself being that its feet were anchored in the soil. In truth, he had not diverged from this belief very much.

He read about a man singing a solo in church whose trousers dropped as he reached for a high note. The minister hastily told the congregation to bow their heads in prayer while the man hauled up his pants. Walker reflected on a similar incident in his childhood when a girl lost her petticoat while playing a game of "handkerchief." The mishap was so shocking that it furnished conversation for weeks. This was timely, for as he was speaking at the writers' club, both ends of his suspenders let go, compelling him to slip both hands in his pockets to keep his trousers up before an all-female audience.

Chapter 8
1942–1960

1942

With the bombing of Pearl Harbor, America entered the Second World War. Tires could only be purchased by doctors and other necessary professionals. Among the manufacturers affected, whiskey producers were asked to change their product to industrial alcohol. Not surprisingly, Walker approved of this.

In January, clocks were required by law to move up an hour until the war was over, while sugar and other staples were rationed. Walker was wishing he could serve a useful purpose.

In April, he heard of former *SFG* partner Robert Cooke's death; he was found alone in his small boat in Florida waters. Walker had learned of early partner Elwood Mattson's death the previous February, which opened a cache of memories. He could not think of Mattson without recalling his method of cleaning out their cantankerous wood-burning stove, which intermittently heated the editorial rooms. The thing had chronic throat trouble, its long pipe crossing overhead often getting "croupy." As a last resort, Mattson would dispatch a janitor to the hardware store for zinc scraps. Sometimes burning these relieved the stove's congestion. But when the last zinc lozenge failed to clear the pipe, the janitor was sent for a small bag of gunpowder.

Mattson wrapped this in paper and called in the printer's devil to stand on a chair, asking him to lock arms around the pipe's bend and hold it down hard on the stove. Just as Mattson prepared to drop the powder-filled paper into the burning stove, the printer's devil looked wildly up at Walker and asked what it contained. Someone else in the room uttered, "Gunpowder."

"This man released his hold on the pipe and fled to the back room. As I was fresh from the farm and had broken horses, ridden bucking mules and handled defiant cattle, I was too confident to dread such a puny job. I jumped into the chair, fastened my arms around the pipe and said, 'Let her go!'"

Mattson dropped the package in, leaping onto the stove's loose cap to hold it down. Walker was instantly lifted almost to the ceiling and, through the sooty fumes, made out the dim outline of his partner, twenty years his senior, blown backward and sprawled on the floor. The room looked like a volcano had erupted, ashes and soot so disguising the office force that it became necessary to bathe hands and faces to recognize each other. But the remedy worked; the stove was better behaved the remainder of the winter.

Walker recalled another incident during his tenure at the *SFG*. While he was out, an old bearded teacher who frequented their offices seated himself in the chair behind Walker's desk. Suddenly, a scar-faced stranger appeared in the doorway, swearing and declaring he meant to kill the editor, whom he mistook for the man in Walker's chair. The stranger said he had killed two men before and did not mind a third.

When the old educator tried to escape, explaining he was not Walker, the angry man (an infuriated subscriber) detained him until he was satisfied he was not the target of his wrath. Walker encountered the fleeing educator in the lobby, beard and alpaca coat floating horizontally on the breeze his speed created.

Walker tried to capture him, but he tore free, pausing only long enough to say, "There's an angry man in your office, Bob, and he wants to kill you." Walker entered his office, calm and composed, greeting the man who gradually grew tamer as they conversed. The source of the man's rage was never recorded, but he renewed his subscription before he left the office.

Walker laughed over Woodland Avenue Baptist Church's mysterious seventy-dollar water bill, which was usually seventy-five cents. A compromise of forty dollars was reached, the pastor later learning that neighborhood boys were slipping in, filling the church's baptizing pool and then draining it after their swim to hide their mischief.

Trains rumbling through Highland Park reminded Walker of those that had passed their old cabin. He recalled the gravel train from his childhood, bringing pebbles and rocks to elevate the road bed, and the shiny pay train, with a brass bell like an angel's voice to hardworking railroad men and farmers like Tom Walker. It brought reimbursement for animals lost to the engines, and as a child, Bob thought it carried half the world's gold.

He remembered the weary travelers who used the tracks as a roadway, vagabonds with disappointment on their faces and others with trained animals like bears and monkeys who exchanged performances for food and lodging.

Tom never turned away a stranger, keeping a register of guests' names from year to year. He once showed Walker a yellow-leaved book that was his guest list from 1887. He had entertained 487 people for meals, most of them lodging there, too. That meant there were nearly as many horses to feed and house as people, but Walker's father never asked money for his hospitality. "To do today what he did in those years would break a man with a small income, but our farm was very fruitful."

The Chickamauga's annual flooding left a fresh layer of fertile soil, "the joy of many future crops of corn and hay." Below the cabin was a wooden railroad bridge across the creek, and at either end were water barrels for fires. Mr. Tippens was the bridge watchman, his home so near the tracks that cross-ties ended where his front porch began. Tippens inspected the bridge at all hours, day and night, before trains ran over it. His daughter Amanda often took Bob to her house, keeping him as her baby guest. Passing trains thundered so near that a child could believe they were going to strike the house.

Around 1890, Tom Walker acquired a herd of Angora goats known for their love of adventure. They climbed apple trees and visited the barn loft. Tom afterward got a herd of shorthaired goats that would seem to fall dead if surprised. Bob and his brothers delighted in clapping and screaming wildly behind them, for they would fall to the ground lifeless. But in less than a minute, the goats would twitch and then rise and walk off. To Walker's knowledge, this was the first appearance in East Tennessee of goats bearing the name "Tennessee Fainting Goats."

One night, while the family was out, goats took possession of their sitting room containing the square piano. When Bob entered, the goats left in a flurry, though their odor lingered. He sat in the dark and began to play, but sounds of smacking lips gave him goose flesh. Noises were coming from something in a room where no one was supposed to be besides himself. Bob timidly struck a match, discovering a billy goat on top of the piano, its head almost touching his. The goat leapt over Bob and dashed out to join the flock.

Walker was once involved in theft. Their hired man, a Negro, George Henry, told him and John of an abandoned orchard nearby, so John got a tow sack, and their daylight raid resulted in a bushel of peaches. Returning, they passed the home of another family, the Woods, of sterling reputation.

Their youngest son, Sidney, asked what was in the sack. George Henry, who participated in the raid, said it was Irish potatoes. Sidney, smelling peaches, laughed and said he had been slipping into the orchard too.

George offered to conceal the fruit at his home, saying the boys could get some peaches whenever they wanted. George and his wife, Julia, had one child, a pretty little girl named Susie Emalina Malinda Elizabeth Carolina Jane Henry, who likely never knew a thing about the crime. The next day, Bob and John went to George on a quest for peaches but were told all had rotted mysteriously during the night. Yet for the next few days they noticed, as they ate lunch together, George had some delicious pieces of peach pie.

John was Bob's barber back then, cropping off his hair with glee. As they sought inventive ways to do this, after felling a blackjack oak for firewood, John suggested Bob lie on the ground, as his hair was so long that it could easily be chopped off with an axe. This appealed to Bob, so he stretched out, head on the stump. The first two strokes cut off his hair, but the third wedged it into the softwood, fastening him to the stump. John declared he was thirsty and headed to the house, wishing Bob an undisturbed rest. Bob "rested" for an hour before John returned and released his hair.

Walker was getting favorable reviews of his Lookout Mountain book, the most recent from the *Atlanta Journal Constitution*, sent from old friend Leila Mason Etheridge.

TVA paid Walker $500 to lease a perpetual right of way for a power line across his property, Helvellyn. It cut the land in half, but he had no choice except agree. Eminent domain had won. He and Wendell both thought the power line unsightly.

His coal house lost shingles from high winds, "leaving bald patches like missing hairs from a man's head." Walker, desiring to freshen up his place, painted the back steps and sawed up some hedges without bringing on angina pains. Encouraged, he painted his refrigerator twice, using the last of his paint on the underside of the steps, requiring him to lie on his back on the cold ground. Still his heart gave no trouble.

After this success, days later he painted the front porch and was felled by another heart attack. Fortunately, Wendell and Frances and his housekeeper, Addie, were there at the time. They prepared meals and built fires, Wendell bringing his Morris Hill bell to ring for help, which kindled memories of his teaching days.

Walker recalled Morris Hill's less auspicious name, "Lizard Lope," earned for its abundance of lizards and skinks. A boy once announced a snake in the room, causing pandemonium. During one heavy rain, Walker had to ride to school on a mule. The building had no underpinning, furnishing the only hog shelter for miles around, every stripe of hog congregating under its floor. The steady uproar of squealing, grunting and bumping of heads against sills shook the building. Walker dispatched the largest boy to quiet them, to no avail. Children left their books to pull at tufts of hog bristles sticking through the floor, leaving Walker only the pretense of control over the situation. He later learned of Silverdale School's "Flea-Killing Day," with boys boring holes in its floor while girls poured kettles of boiling water into the sills and ground where flea-ridden hogs had been sleeping.

His daily dread then, spoiling his walk to Morris Hill, was a neighbor's "pugilistic ram, which roved at large, determined to practice his profession on me." After acquiring numerous bruises, Walker carried a pole to place between himself and the beast. Sometimes his father's billy (and bully) goat, with "an ambition to pound people," would lock horns with the old ram, but it always returned home unscathed to seek Walker out the next day. An old woodchopper, J.B. Marsh—who did not mince word with rams or men—settled matters for a few months by nailing the brute a blow on the head with an axe.

Walker taught during the Spanish-American War, when over sixty thousand volunteers swelled Chickamauga Park. Brother John was at the time employed at the only railroad station on the battlefield, known as Lytle, Georgia. Walker sometimes drove a buggy into Lytle with a food basket for John from sister Dona Bell. But none ever reached John, for every vehicle that drove through the battlefield was ransacked by uniformed soldiers. Even dairymen had wagons turned upside down and robbed of milk.

If Army officials knew anything about sanitation, I saw no evidence... As many died there of typhoid as perished in fighting, and during the First World War an equal number died there from influenza. Water stood almost foot-deep around tents, making it impossible to keep anyone or anything dry. In the train cars, ceilings were black with flies; the large bakery filled army wagons with loaves of tasty-looking bread, which in dry weather was left uncovered for clouds of dust to settle over it.

Walker bundled up everything the last day of school, including his bell and chair, which had served his father in the Hamilton County Court for twenty-four years. He often sat by the path at twilight then, "while stars sprinkled hope above me...and I prayed to become an author and poet... Now I hope to regain strength to live long enough to awaken this blind generation to the beauty of creation. The earth looks like it is dressing for a wedding…birds and flowers and all creation are marrying. I want to express this to others…that they not miss it."

The poetry in Walker's soul was interrupted by a call, as usual, this time from a man who needed a snake repellant, as his wife had been awakened by a three-foot snake in bed with her. She had left him until he could promise there would not be others.

Walker admitted Elberta once told him he could not write a love story because he could not sacrifice his ideals to "descend" and lower himself to make characters normal and real. In May, the paper published half of his story "The Thief in the Family," proving Elberta absolutely right. He was sure readers would feel swindled, but a few called to express interest, "although one was frank enough to say I am incapable of writing a modern love story. The piece is too naïve…the characters should swear and be capable of doing anything once taboo yesterday."

In June, Confederate veterans held their fifty-second reunion, with only thirty-seven participating. Walker thought there were about three hundred left in all. Although his family was staunchly Union, Walker felt sympathy for the Confederate soldier "who was duped into fighting to split his country by radicals, whose meetings were secret from the men they drafted. I refer to Jefferson Davis, Robert Toombs, Alex Stevens, and Benjamin, the 'brains' of the Confederacy. Davis had a great dream of empire, to annex Mexico, perhaps Central America, to make one vast empire of slavery."

Walker was rereading Miles's book *Strains from a Dulcimore*, published in 1930 when he was friends with Abby Milton. Miles, a gifted naturalist and writer, had married a man who struggled to provide enough for their family. His wife supplemented their income selling her paintings and writings. Walker had briefly been acquainted with her and her four children and believed she had known much happiness from nature, to which she had been so close.

Miles's first book went into only one edition; her second book on birds did as well. He had administered her estate, recalling the books had not earned enough royalties to pay her funeral expenses, though two thousand copies had sold at that time. Walker wrote a few lines in the preface of her posthumously published book of poems, edited by himself and Abby, in which he compared Miles to the birds and flowers she had loved, saying there was much of mystical wood thrush in her.

Walker believed a writer should not subordinate his profession to another job even when financially necessary. He was willing to rise at midnight to work if he had to. His first book traveled fourteen years and crossed the Atlantic twice before it was finally published by an editor who had seen it ten years earlier. After expenses, its sale brought Walker enough to pay Dr. Steele for removing his tonsils. Steele also required as payment a copy of the book.

In September, he reflected on Robert's birth, remembering how he and Elberta had studied him by the hearth fire. Highland Park back then had a scattered population and was not even part of the city, having no paved streets or sewers. Their house was three blocks from Blue Pond, a huge cavern filled with water, which had been a limestone quarry since the Civil War. Because it attracted boys who liked to swim, causing drownings, Walker asked city officials to fill it in. They turned a deaf ear. But when he witnessed a ten-year-old stumble and fall in and his twelve-year-old brother jump in to save him—and both drown—Walker made another appeal. It, too, was ignored until a damage suit was filed against the city for maintaining a menace, forcing officials to protect the public and fill in the quarry.

Water from his back porch pump thereafter was no longer a clear blue but the color of coffee. George Clark's old well had tapped into the subterranean source that supplied Blue Pond. Walker still used the pump for exercise.

His first eight years of marriage had been "an earthly paradise," when he resented anything taking him from his family. Because his boys loved the woods, he did his best to convert their city home into a country place.

At five, Robert insisted on their reading *Hamlet* and *Macbeth* to him. (Walker recently had such a vivid dream of Robert that he was compelled to take a midnight walk to shake off the sorrow.) His sons peppered him with questions, asking where a light goes when it goes out and if a fly on a moving train is riding or flying. Wendell, eating an apple, once leapt into his lap, and Walker asked what the apple was made of. Wendell had thought a moment before replying, "Sunshine, dirt, and thunder." This gave him the title for his second book, *Eating Thunder*.

Walker and Elberta did not give their boys money without labor. Once, when Wendell wanted to see a movie, he earned a penny for every wild plant he could identify. The result was an elbow-high pile of weeds on their table, botanized correctly. Walker, to raise the stakes, offered fifteen cents for every error Wendell found in his father's articles and others he read in magazines. The number his son pointed out was astonishing. Walker believed this one exercise had made his son precise and accurate in his work as a man.

Walker's choice for punishment, when necessary, was assigning poetry for his boys to copy. He once criticized Wendell for marking his schoolbooks and was presented with a reader from his own childhood whose margins were a mass of scribblings, making Wendell's book neat by comparison. Like an attorney, his son asked him to identify the reader and the culprit who had marked it up. Walker laughed and confessed, saying that taught him to represent himself honestly to his children.

When Wendell became interested in geology and archaeology as a boy, he learned the Smithsonian sometimes had duplicate specimens to exchange for something it did not have. Walker volunteered two hundred-year-old Irish law books, making a trade with the Smithsonian for minerals. Walker then snuck into the alley, gathering common rocks and brickbats. When the real minerals arrived, he removed them and put in his spurious ones, resealing the box. Wendell came home and pried open the box, laying the mongrel specimens on the floor. Walker's conscience was now pricking him painfully. Wendell's initial excitement had colored the ugly rocks with imagined beauty until he took a wholesale view of the lot and, with disgust, said, "This is a cheap lot of stuff for a nationally known institution to send out." Examining them more closely, he recognized them from his own backyard and demanded the genuine articles. Said Walker; "I was glad to see him take this practical joke with good humor, for the average man takes himself too seriously. Walkers have for generations prescribed laughter as part of a healthy diet, essential as vitamins."

He found it puzzling that so few parents found their children's company the most interesting and entertaining in the world. He loved participating in his young boys' lives, even purchasing a bicycle to ride with them. When they persuaded him to take them to a movie, en route, Walker suggested they capture some fireflies, hinting they could release them in the theater. The bugs were loosed, their flashing lanterns the only bright spot in the film. Ten years later, fireflies were still flashing in that theater, the boys having started a tradition. Walker felt if he won the friendship of children and dogs, he gained the most loyal friends to be found.

Wendell the adult had taken a job with TVA as a cartographer, though it was likely he would be drafted. His status was 3A, eligible. He worked in the U.S. Geological Survey office, in charge of photographic work making up army maps of war areas, considered strategic for national defense.

Army wagons loaded with soldiers and equipment passed Walker's house in droves. His youngest brother, Gabriel, a postal inspector, was in India with the troops; his cousin Kenneth had graduated from Annapolis; his nephew John Walker was in a flying squadron; his brother Charlie's two boys were in the service; and his nephew Theodore would soon be drafted.

Walker and Wendell biking, 1919.

At night, he heard bombers passing overhead. In May, Chattanooga had experienced its first blackout, bringing home to Walker and fellow residents the fact that they were engaged in a bitter conflict. "If the human race exterminates itself, I think the next population to dominate will be ants, who are about as intelligent, organized, and ready to put up a fight."

Walker gained a tip from Addie, a surefire method of ridding him of the crick in his neck. She said to go to a tree or post where a hog had rubbed its head, get down and rub his neck on the exact spot. Walker said if his crick didn't get better, he might try it.

While napping in his nephew's car, he was awakened by a soft, sympathetic little voice and opened his eyes to find himself face to face with a Plymouth rock rooster. Lizzie said the bird had both his legs broken once, and Walker felt his reclining position may have roused his sympathy, as he thought both Walker's limbs were broken too.

He kept watch over Dr. Steele's home on the Ridge for two days while Steele attended his son's wedding. Walker called him the finest gentleman he had known, with no hypocrisy about him. The back view from Crest Road showed the mountains on the horizon and lights from the TNT plant in Tyner, where they were making powder "to blow up Germany and Japan." From the front yard, he witnessed the city's total blackout, extending all the way up Lookout Mountain, lasting until 9:30 p.m.

Although the *Times* had cut his column down, he was still receiving calls from it. He explained to one caller that "mast" referred to nuts and seeds, recommending that hogs free-range on it, as they would be plumper and the meat better than slop- and corn-fed hogs. He identified a unicorn plant for an older couple and, when asked his fee, told them it was two of its seedpods.

Sarah Key Patten gave him two boxes of bird eggs collected by her late brother, David M. Key, a young naturalist. Walker gave them a place of honor in his dining room.

Walker recalled a man he met in 1900: Dr. H.S. Chubb of the *Vegetarian Times* from Philadelphia. Chubb had visited Chattanooga, bearing samples of peanut butter, which he found hard to pass on, as no one had ever heard of it and it resembled medicinal salve. It was now a popular food.

Walker had a dream of walking with his father. He had touched Tom's shoulder to see if he had a body, and on exclaiming that he did, his father replied, "Certainly!" telling Walker he remembered his life on earth. On waking, Walker could hardly believe he had not been with him.

On Christmas morning, he wished himself and his pet starling, Winston Churchill, a Merry Christmas. Late that afternoon, Wendell and Frances brought their baby girl, Madeline Alexandra, for a visit. "My old house and I felt happier with a baby granddaughter in it. Wendell has taken me several times to the hospital for a visit. They thought her terribly ugly at first, until I told my son she was better looking than he was at her age…I am so happy to be a grandfather at last…Wendell is excited over his new possession…I told them she is beautiful as a wild flower."

Wendell drove him to Helvellyn, where they pulled a log into the dirt road to discourage trespassers and, in doing, "collected the 1942 crop of beggar's lice." Walker encouraged his son to build on the property.

1943

He recalled a joke his Uncle Gabe played on him in 1916 when he offered to help Gabe shell corn with his ancient corn sheller. He furnished muscle while Gabe fed the ears, and nearby stood his Model T for carrying corn to the Tyner gristmill. Gabe, gifted in the art of jokes, was unusually serious, causing Walker to let down his guard.

Once the corn was sacked, he slid out the door as graceful as a mouse, striking with his walking stick a gallon can hidden behind the corn shucks as he left.

I was immediately besieged by a host of angry bumblebees. How I managed to dive through that small cat-hole door, I will never know. With bees hot on my trail, seeking vengeance, I leaped into my auto and slammed the door. I saw Uncle Gabe safely on his back porch, slapping his hands and screaming with laughter, while I was imprisoned for almost an hour.

Coffee was rationed, and since Walker did not drink it, he purchased and gave his to *Times* editor Alf Mynders, who did. His nephew C.W. Davidson was drafted and went to Fort Oglethorpe, Walker saying Lizzie's farm stopped with his induction. Wendell had not yet been called. Walker had two cousins, one brother and seven nephews now in the army. Metal was being collected for the war effort, including cannonballs from Chickamauga Battlefield. Walker scrounged up twenty-five pounds of metal and was hunting more.

His pet starling, Winston Churchill, often sat on his head while he typed, even remaining there while his "perch" walked around. Walker discovered Winston loved music, sang to the radio and joined in on a violin solo with fervor. Walker brought him fresh wildflowers, "for any bird who loves music must also enjoy the finer things of life."

Walker recalled Thomas Sparks Lowe taking him to Sherman's former encampment to collect Minié balls. Lowe had been absent when the Union army surrounded his home, but the Lowes never harbored hatred for Sherman, as did many Georgians. Sherman dispatched mounted officers to assure Mrs. Lowe that she and her children were safe. Lowe's daughter Hattie told Walker they were treated with consideration, and she did not resent them taking the corn and meat, as this was practiced by both armies.

In October, Walker and two brothers drove to visit their sister Ann Standifer and stepmother, Annie.

All my brothers and sisters were there! Here we sat in the room where I had seen Chess and Dona Bell pass, my mother in the adjoining room, my father but a short while ago. I sensed their presence all around, completing the family circle. We were all together, at one with the beautiful land we had known all our lives.

What is wrong with man that the peace and beauty of Creation cannot pacify him?... When men are led to appreciate the natural world as children, there is less war. "Chickamauga" means slow-moving water, and a walk beside it never fails to quiet a restless heart.

Dragging Canoe, chief of the Chickamaugas, who would not treat with whites, had seceded from the Cherokees in 1776, settling a town on the Tennessee River called Citico. Little Owl, Dragging Canoe's brother, settled a site on the Chickamauga that, according to local lore, was located on its western banks, some said on Tom Walker's old farm.

Calls from readers continued, one man telling Walker he had discovered a cave on the Chickamauga filled with Indian pictographs. Another woman wanted to know if a turtle dove pecking on her screen meant she would have a baby. He mentioned this to his housekeeper, Addie, who replied it meant a death in the family, but he did not pass this on, avoiding the realm of superstition.

Fatigue caused him to miss the wedding of neighbor Betty Gene Gilbert to army officer Raymond Barron. Miss Bonnie Gilbert, taking the place of Betty Gene's mother, who died when she was an infant, had raised her "into a fine young woman, now teaching at Red Bank High." Wendell attended for the family, he and Betty Gene having been childhood friends.

Walker was quietly working on something that had stirred his heart for years and was finding sympathetic souls who shared his vision. Through the rest of 1943 and first half of 1944, he continued writing, hiking and spending time with friends. But he was also meeting with influential folks who were putting together a plan to help make his fondest dream a reality.

1944–1945

Walker never had money. He paid bills and supported himself with writing, having no surplus for extravagant ideas. But among his wide circle of friends were those who did, some seriously interested in turning his father's farm into a wildlife preserve. A serendipitous combination of people, ideas and money was coming together to create a lasting gift to the Chattanooga community and nature lovers at large.

Walker wrote in July, "Today a group of bird lovers, myself among them, met at Topside, Mrs. Sarah Key Patten's childhood home at Fairmount. By late afternoon, the Robert Sparks Walker Audubon Society was officially established. I am uncomfortable with my name so visibly attached to the title, but conceded to general opinion, as it has for years been associated with nature, and our group's intended goals."

Officers were chosen, with Walter Johnson and Sarah Key Patten selected as president and vice-president. Prior to this meeting, a committee had viewed the creek farm and found it appropriate for their purpose. Walker had pored over plans for its conversion to a wildlife refuge. His brothers and sisters agreed to surrender their shares for $1,000 apiece, or $6,000 in total. Walker then donated his share.

By March, the group, at Walker's request, changed its name to the Chattanooga Audubon Society but failed to raise the full amount to purchase the farm. But, wrote Walker, "a hero has come to our rescue in the form of my old friend, E.Y. Chapin." Chapin, having earned royalties from successful books on banking, purchased and donated the property to the Chattanooga Audubon Society. In honor of his wife, the new preserve would be called the Elise Chapin Wildlife Sanctuary.

The derelict condition of the Cherokee-built cabin created a small controversy, some suggesting it be torn down, which grieved Walker. But Sarah Key Patten, who loved historic buildings, generously resolved the issue by paying for its total restoration herself. She also filled it with century-old furnishings, which Walker declared made it like home.

Information that Tooan-tuh, Spring Frog, was born in this cabin had come from Mrs. D.F. Ellis, whose grandparents came to the area in 1834, four years prior to removal. She claimed that the description of Tooan-tuh's birthplace in the *Handbook of the American Indians*, portraying it as near the north end of Lookout Mountain, close to the mouth of the Chickamauga, was misleading. She said it should have stated "near the mouth of the *west* Chickamauga, which empties into the Chickamauga a short distance below the Sanctuary. Wake Robin Hill, bordering the Sanctuary's northwest and western boundaries, is the nearest point to Lookout Mountain." (The accuracy of this information has been disputed, but history from early residents is often as reliable as researched findings.)

Walker, with great joy, was laying out trails threading through the most interesting parts of the old farm. With his hand-embossing "machine," he stamped out common and botanical names of trees, tagging them.

This activity did not harm and, in fact, improved his health. He had decided life was not worth living if he was not active. He remembered the loose dirt in his basement from installing a furnace, so he rose early to shovel dirt out the basement window. If his heart complained, he rested and then resumed. He could soon shovel for an hour without pain. Eventually, he shoveled and scattered all the loose dirt and was "out of a job."

Walker cutting trails along the Chickamauga, circa 1945.

He then took up

> *what Dr. Gilbert warned would kill me—pushing a lawn mower and cutting the hedgerow. Within a month, I could accomplish both with no ill effects, and have been doing them ever since. I did not visit my heart doctor every two weeks as prescribed, but let two years elapse before giving him a call.*
>
> *He flouroscoped me, and I "floored" him. He asked what I had been doing, and I told him exactly. With utter disbelief, he informed me my heart was getting blood through a new passageway. From that day forward, he ceased putting angina patients to bed, and now prescribes daily physical exercise. I must add, my knowledge of which foods to shun has contributed*

to my recovering. While I know I must not run, I can walk five or six miles,
whereas before I could not walk fifteen feet without pain.

Wendell was eventually drafted, leaving by train for what would likely be his induction. But the army decided that his making maps for the U.S. government was more valuable to them, and he was returned to Chattanooga, where he lived and worked until transferred by the government to Colorado in 1948.

1946–1960

In 1946, the Chattanooga Audubon Society began its own magazine, *Flower and Feather*, Walker becoming editor the following year.

In June 1948, a swinging footbridge was constructed across the Chickamauga, which divided the sanctuary in half. Walker invested most

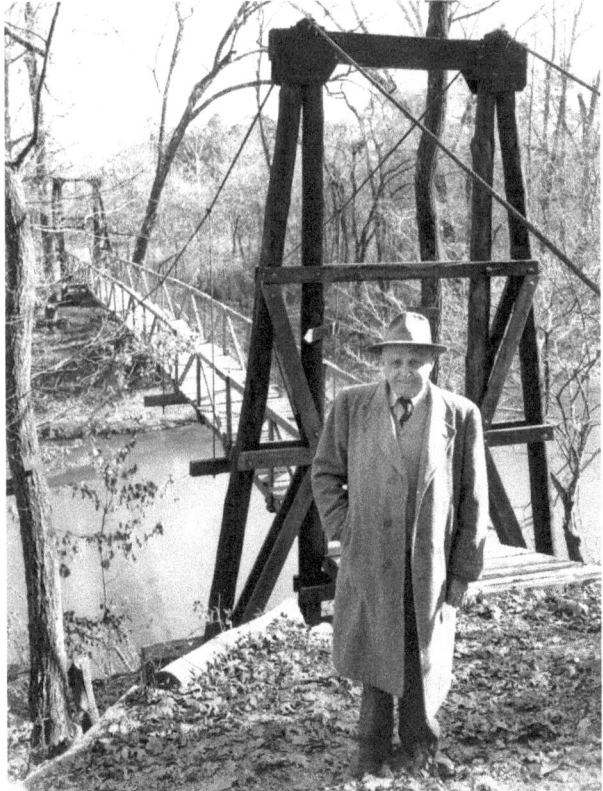

Walker at the Chickamauga Suspension Bridge, 1948.

of his savings in the venture and, when asked who would look after him, replied, "He who cares for the birds and flowers will surely care for me."

Well-meaning friends advised him to accept his son's invitation and move to Colorado. He was sorely tempted but believed he could not abandon the sanctuary. If loneliness in his big, empty house was the price, he was willing to pay it, stating that he could not leave this important job unfinished.

In 1949, he wrote:

> *I am now certain it is my God-given duty to stay in Chattanooga and execute the plans of my Maker...It is important that people, young and old, who visit this Sanctuary, lay aside all cares and burdens to discover their Creator has not retired to some distant planet, but walks along these trails with them, partaking of his beautiful creation.*
>
> *I see that the terrible heartaches of losing my family, and the sufferings that have come from devastating tragedy, have been necessary to qualify me for this work assigned to me. If I am able to make others happy and bring them closer to their Maker through contact with His natural masterpieces, then insignificant as I am, I believe for this purpose, I came into the world.*

Walker continued to develop and share his beloved farm until his death at eighty-two in 1960. The sanctuary, now known as Audubon Acres, still welcomes visitors to its peaceful woods and waters of the Chickamauga.

Epilogue

MADELINE, 1960

H e stood in the doorway, one arm against the jamb, the other raised in parting salute.

"I'll see you soon, if nothing happens," he called.

"I'll be back for Thanksgiving," I promised, believing life would continue predictably. I had no way of knowing I would never see him again. I was leaving for the University in Knoxville.

He had given me a graduation gift: a gold ring with an oval of seed pearls, its central stone missing.

"This was Elberta's. It once had an opal. What would you like in it?" His eye held an expectant twinkle. "Inside are her maiden initials I had inscribed. I gave her this before we were married." He paused, the fleeting expression I knew to expect at mention of my grandmother sweeping like a zephyr across his features. I hesitated.

"I want you to have it!" he insisted. "I can say I gave it away twice, to two people I love. I'll take it to Fisher Evans tomorrow."

In all my seventeen years, I had never seen that ring. Granddad was not one to hoard treasures—quite the opposite. One had to be careful about what one admired in his house; he would likely as not give it to you.

He was sentimental about things once belonging to Elberta, giving me her trinkets: an ostrich-feather fan, a sewing basket, an orangewood box and a bizarre brass and ebony dinner gong. I found it hard to picture my father and his brother summoned by that thing. It had three brass and wood bars strung on an ebony frame like a xylophone. These were struck with a cork mallet, now repulsive from age, bugs having eaten most of it.

Despite illness and suffering, my grandmother had never raised her voice. I studied her pictures, her dark, expressive eyes, the gentle expression. My father bore a strong resemblance to her, and I in turn resembled him. I hoped Elberta's ring might impart her character and wore it all the time, which pleased Granddad.

He was eccentric, I see now. But I accepted his behavior as what grandfathers generally did, believing they rose before daylight, wrote on noisy typewriters until dawn and then went back to bed and rose with the rest of us.

We moved in before I was two. My bedroom had two long, double-hung windows, and I could imagine being a bird in the branches of his persimmon tree. Only a twig when he planted it, it now towered majestically. A male tree destined to celibacy, it bore no persimmons, having no persimmon wife nearby. This parallel to his own life likely did not escape Granddad's observation.

His patience was liberal with interruptions, and I don't recall him ever telling me to go away. He would cease whatever he was doing—usually typing—and involve himself wholeheartedly in whatever concerned me. I believed a grandfather was far better than a pet, which I was forbidden to have since I had asthma.

His outrageous humor always entertained. Approached by solitary, ambling hounds, Granddad would stop, tip his hat and formally address the dog, "How do you do, Sir?" The dogs failed to reply, so I presumed them ill mannered.

"He isn't rude," Granddad explained, "just lost in thought." For years I believed dogs were deep thinkers.

Two squirrels, Hippity and Hoppity, followed everywhere. One scrambling up a tree or a pair chasing in giddy loops inevitably brought, "There goes old Hippity," from Granddad. Old Joel, the rabbit, made fewer appearances but was no less ubiquitous. I was nearly grown before it dawned on me there were many squirrels and rabbits Granddad had dubbed Hippity, Hoppity and Old Joel.

As an only child—a fate worse than death—I was rescued by Granddad. He had me introducing myself to flowers at three. He was my best companion and, I see now, my very obliging babysitter. We Walkers walked everywhere, for by the time I arrived, he had neither owned nor driven a car for years.

Robert's death haunted our family—the lost child hovering over the future, a tragic, benign ghost. I never knew Robert, yet I could retell his death with eyewitness accuracy. I knew it by heart, saw pain in Granddad's eyes when he spoke of Robert, sorrow in my father's at mention of his lost brother. We cherished and passed on the grief like an heirloom, retold the sad tale like a tribal memory around a ceremonial campfire. Robert's loss lived on long after the flesh and blood child departed. In our family, he remained forever eight years old, never forgotten, a sacred part of our oral tradition.

We took frequent romps to the National Cemetery. Granddad said the dead didn't mind if I skipped across their gravestones and in fact they appreciated the company. (This still carries a ring of truth.) It was a good game for a small child, he figured, and did no harm. At limestone outcroppings forming bluffs in the cemetery, we gathered wildflowers, planting them in dirt. A small depression filled with rainwater became a lake—our miniature Japanese garden.

Granddad's backyard grew rabbit tobacco, peanuts, Jerusalem artichokes, fig trees, a mulberry and a large pear tree. He could peel a pear with his pocketknife all in one spiral, without breaking the strip of pear skin, until it hung like a party favor. Beside a brick walkway was Elberta's flower bed, containing mostly wildflowers gathered on their walks together. He kept descendants of the originals, my favorites being bluebells.

He did not cage birds. When caring for injured ones, he gave them the run of the place—imagine the havoc that created. But more memorable was one particular mouse Granddad housed in a cardboard box. I think someone brought it to him—a *singing* mouse that crooned to her dozen bald, pink, squirming babies. The sound was high and plaintive, a tender mouse lullaby. One authoress so admired this mouse that she included it in her book, *The Pink Maple House.*

Granddad showed me how bees climbed into wild potato blossoms to collect nectar and then took naps. He twisted the outer petals shut, trapping the bee, and snapped off the flower, holding it to my ear.

"Hear him carrying on?" he grinned. The bee buzzed furiously, and I asked to hold the flower. He offered it to me with care, but I planted my thumb farther down, taking a firm grasp of Mr. Bee himself. The creature responded by stinging the daylights out of my thumb, to which I responded with hysteria. This left Granddad to explain the situation to Mother, who was certain I had sustained mortal injury. Fortunately, the incident did not drive a wedge in their cordial relationship.

Granddad had two diverse neighbors. One was the Gilbert homestead, an attractive old place, wearing age with refined dignity. Ours, with clapboard covered in gray asbestos, bore a forlorn, melancholy expression, dingy white trim lurking beneath the soot, where coal is primary fuel. Its expression said suffering had taken place within its walls. That was its outward appearance. But inside, in Granddad's presence, melancholy fled. Only joy could exist in his company.

Our other neighbor was an overgrown lot tangled with shrubs, young trees and kudzu, forming a canopy. It once held a house that had burned down, but now the lot was a wilderness, staked out for picnics. The ice cream man came up Greenwood with a pushcart, a hand bell signaling his arrival. Granddad ordered ice cream for himself, a Creamsicle for me, which we took to our "Kudzu Tent." When the lot sold, we watched our haven cleared for a modern dwelling.

Just waking to inspect the front porch was an adventure, where people always dropped things off, seeking information. Something apprehended devouring shrubbery, peculiar weeds, defoliated plants with desperate notes pinned on, dreadful-looking, horned beetles imprisoned in jars and occasionally something good to eat. One needed discernment. One jar might contain a dandy homemade relish, the next a pickled denizen found in a well.

Such things were not confined to the porch. Granddad invariably brought the most unique to his inner sanctum: the dining room. Dankly situated behind the front parlor's portieres, this room—once the scene of refined meals—now served as archives, the massive sideboard obscured beneath manuscripts, dried leaves, gnarled branches, hornet nests, wasp dwellings and serving vessels overflowing with seeds, nuts and hollowed bird eggs. Stacks of publications higher than my head ringed the table. A china cabinet contained classic literature and reference material. Overhead hung a bowl-shaped, leaded chandelier, light feebly glowing through milky green and white tulips. A film, collecting forty years, further dimmed its pallid glow.

The corner fireplace of sponged green tile was enhanced by a mirrored oak mantel; a pair of jewel-toned windows remained the only ornament left in this forgotten room. With futile, determined hope, they bore their vivid hues, colorful brooches on the bosom of an aging dowager.

Granddad made a noble effort at housekeeping, but it was not his forte, and he never apologized. Still, to stay within the parameters of civilization, he kept his parlor free of "interesting discoveries." Couch, tables and chairs were accessible for sitting or writing or whatever well-bred people did. In this room, he greeted guests and conducted business. Another handsome tile and oak fireplace backed up to the one in the forbidding dining room. Dividing these two opposing worlds was a pair of heavy dark green portieres secured to the double door frame. Beyond this feeble divider yawned no-man's land, where all pretense of civilization terminated.

I enjoyed both worlds. Sometimes we played Wig-wag or Trap—hand games passed on for generations. If he was in high spirits, he dragged out the Mission oak rocker reserved for visitors. There had once been two of these, but we destroyed one playing our game. He said it didn't matter because he had another. The damaged rocker remained an ornament in the parlor, never mourned or mended. He had one chair for our game—why be concerned with a broken one?

He'd push back the rug and then shove me in the rocker around the room, pretending it was a train and he its conductor, calling out every stop in Tennessee. More than the game, I appreciated the status—garden club ladies never rode around Granddad's parlor like this! Occasionally, Granddad placed a sock on each hand secured with rubber bands. So armed (or "handed"), he skipped the paintbrush, dipping a be-socked hand directly into a gallon of tan enamel. He could go from application to cleanup by switching hands. He also followed this procedure with the "great serpent" stair railing.

This dark, reptilian thing, terminating in enormous acorn finials, curled around the stairway to the second floor, where Granddad seldom ventured due to his heart. This rail would not permit a child to slide down it. Bracketed tightly to the inner wall, it hung, fat, fixed and utterly useless in my eyes.

Stair treads and portions of the rail he could reach received a dose of tan enamel from sock and bucket. He was never striving for perfection, his mottled paint job giving the appearance of a well-fed, compliant boa. It might even have been his intention.

Following publication of *Torchlights to the Cherokees*, he became acquainted with the Cherokee of the Qualla Boundary and Talequah Reservation. He was invited to the annual Cherokee Indian Feast in North Carolina but could not make the trip. So foods from the celebration arrived, and he shared with me. There was roast bear, deer, wild turkey, trout and barbecued rattlesnake, the bear somewhat greasy but the rattlesnake tasty. There were wild fruits, corn, greens, nuts, pumpkin and several delicious breads, the most outstanding being chestnut bread. I am still seeking its recipe.

The unique bond between grandchild and grandparent allows wisdom to be imparted without criticism or judgment. I recall only one incident requiring his stern discipline, when I was experimenting with slang. He held that a young lady ought to sound like one, but I kept repeating an unacceptable word. It was fairly innocuous—possibly "gosh"—but I repeated it several times.

A sudden thump on the side of my head surprised me. Then he left without a word. I was crushed and completely repentant. Without a cross word, he had expressed contempt for my contemptuous behavior, and I never thereafter sought to provoke him. Dad later told with amusement that this had been his means of disciplining him and Robert. "The thump doesn't hurt," he reminisced, "it's just unexpected and puts you on the same level with a bug. He thumps mosquitoes like that."

There was a time I began, with neighbor friends, to collect broken glass. We'd wait for the garbage truck to churn through the alley and then search the dirt for devastated crystal. Some days we found treasure but sometimes nothing.

Returning from a fruitless search, I encountered Granddad crouched on his kitchen floor, tying creosote-soaked strings around his kitchen table legs. He explained this was an effective weapon in the war against ants, which had invaded his bread. Even fascinating military tactics did not dispel my gloom. I related my failed foray to the alley.

"Wait here," he directed, heading for his pantry and returning with a yellow glass saucer. He set it on his countertop, precariously balanced over the floor so it did not at once fall.

"Feel like jumping?" he asked. He proceeded to perform this exercise with surprising zeal for a heart patient. As we jumped on the linoleum floor, the house shuddered and the saucer trembled, edging its way to certain disaster. I stashed its shards in my Prince Albert Tobacco can. I don't believe we destroyed anything of value—but if we had, it would not equal that fine bit of foolishness.

Aunt Ida Walker, wife of Granddad's brother John, knew Granddad's indifference to material things. After Elberta's death, he and my teenage father were left with her delicate belongings. Ida knew two single men would destroy these things in short order, so she packed everything in a cardboard drum, telling Dad it would be his when he married. Thanks to Ida, Dad and my mother began housekeeping with his mother's finery.

Granddad fancied himself a chef. Wearing an apron, he took on a whole new persona and reckless approach to food. He ate experimentally, having learned which foods made him well and which made him ill, sharing his cuisine with others—usually me.

He kept a wonderful fireless cooker that rendered leg of mutton tasty as a lamb chop. It magically cooked by heating soapstone slabs that were placed with the meat in a metal box. A few hours in this sauna turned meat moist and tender every time. I became a great fan of Granddad's leg of mutton.

One afternoon, I discovered him seated for evening dinner. He prepared the house specialty, so I happily joined him. He emptied a can of Pet milk

Walker takes his granddaughter Madeline on the trails, 1947. *Photo by Wendell Walker.*

over his plate of mutton, peas and some sort of potato, stirring all up with his fork. I questioned this; he replied it all got mixed up anyway, and he was simply saving his stomach the trouble.

Granddad began work on the wildlife sanctuary before I was born. He loved its old cabin, recounting memories evoked by each room. Its steep, narrow staircase led to the loft rooms with low, sloping ceilings. Here, Granddad told tales of his brothers and sisters, for this had been their territory. He never used caution climbing those cabin stairs, as those in his town house. These steps were small, severely pitched, yet he walked right up them as he must have always done.

He kept creek-wading attire in a trunk upstairs, making a show of pulling out this "ensemble." He might have been presenting the latest Parisian fashion, though his wading gear was utterly deplorable. The pants had been worn—how many times?—and might have stood on their own, sized beyond the stiffness of starch by mud and creek water.

Trees at the Ford of Youth rose high, garlanded in grapevines. My friends and I—as Granddad and his brothers had—swung out over the creek on them. While we frolicked, he located the fallen log lying in the water. Here he sat, enjoying our antics, looking much like a man resting on a couch. He was, I think, far more comfortable in the flowing creek on this log than on his parlor sofa.

Walker, Madeline and friends in the Chickamauga, 1956. *Photo by Wendell Walker.*

He delighted in the suspension bridge over the Chickamauga, repeatedly rebuilt after sporadic destruction by spring flooding. Like a demolished anthill, it is soon reconstructed, to the glee of daredevils who enjoy swinging the thing violently from side to side.

Granddad was grateful for his friendship with the Chapins and Sarah Key Patten and other early supporters who championed efforts to purchase the land and open it to the public. He often took me on visits to "important" friends—almost everyone, for Granddad had no friends who were not important. We dined with aristocrats, bankers, doctors, clergymen, salesmen, housewives and farmers. Some were highly educated; others had little education. It made no difference. They were his friends and a superior breed. He might have only corresponded with them. They might have been absent for fifty years. Frequency of contact was no criteria. If someone's name came up with whom he had once been fondly acquainted, he had one standard reply. "Why, I know him [or her]! He [or she] is one of my finest friends!"

In 1950, Granddad, seventy-two, hopped a train taking him west along the route he had traveled fifty years earlier with the Tennessee Press Association.

Walker at Garden of the Gods, Colorado, 1952. *Photo by Wendell Walker.*

We toured him all over the Rockies. At Garden of the Gods, Granddad was photographed where his picture was taken fifty years before.

We drove as high into the mountains as his heart permitted, but at ten thousand feet, he had to lie down. We went to the base of Long's Peak, favorite mountain of Enos Mills, the noted naturalist. Granddad admired this man's work and hoped to visit his widow, who resided in the summer in the rugged terrain she had shared with her husband.

We located Mrs. Mills at the cabin she and her husband built in a lush valley surrounded by snow-crowned peaks. She was a slender, gracious woman, very much an element of the land. She and Granddad blended into that landscape, their faces seemingly chiseled by hands that had formed the craggy peaks surrounding them.

In Denver, Granddad called on writers and publishers. He could travel from Tangiers to Timbuktu and never run short of people to look up. His call to Palmer Hoyt, *Denver Post* editor, resulted in an offer of nature editor—a temptation, the salary more than he made with all his combined activities. But he returned to Chattanooga, having invested too much in the wildlife sanctuary.

Walker and Madeline in the Grand Tetons, Wyoming, 1952. *Photo by Wendell Walker*.

He enjoyed that "romp" so much that three years later he paid another visit. We drove from Denver toward Yellowstone, heading north through Laramie, into a vast expanse of flat, barren desolation, sprouting sagebrush and prairie dogs. The two-lane highway was punctuated by white stripes and an alarming number of flattened jack rabbits. Granddad assured me Old Joel never ventured this far west. We viewed geyser basins, Yellowstone Falls and the Tetons, making note of every moose, bear and elk along the way.

Though we lived in Colorado another five years, he did not visit again. His heart condition required him to keep nitroglycerin pills in his shirt pocket. On learning this was an explosive, I confronted him with my scientific discovery. He stifled a smile and thanked me, assuring me he would not detonate himself.

I took a notion to explore his attic storage room. Granddad expressed an interest in seeing it too, saying if he took his time ascending the stairs, no harm would come.

So we climbed slowly, deliberately, like a sea turtle's heartbeat, two steps on each stair. I held his arm, and he held the serpent railing snugged to the wall, taking care at the tight turn, where treads became triangular pie slices. He yanked open the storeroom door without ceremony. I could almost hear him challenge lurking ghosts to come forth. If one word described him, it is "fearless." Utterly *fearless*.

With flashlights and caution, we made our way to the heap of domestic ruin. There were up-ended tables, broken dressers and the first of several large pictures. Granddad grasped a corner of it, smearing off soot with his fist, wiping the residue on his pants.

"Look!" he exclaimed. "I bought this for your grandmother when we went to housekeeping."

I could faintly make out a sepia country scene.

"This was in the front parlor. She was fond of pictures. We brought a lot of this up here after her passing, your dad and I. Here, what's this?"

He moved on. Next was a long color print of toadstools, and Granddad was pleased to be reunited with it. We plundered the hot, filthy room, unearthing horsehair chairs with fractured legs, Dad's baby rocker, an oak high chair he and Robert had used and Granddad's old trunk, which traveled by train with him to Maryville College. This was mine, he said; he would type out its history to be kept with it. He left little histories on items of interest, as he labeled trees for the edification of passersby. He thought people should know what they were looking at.

As we were leaving, I noticed something under the eaves. As recognition came, Granddad paused but a moment. "Of course," he said softly, "Robert's little rocker. Could you get to it?"

I brought it to him. He gently stroked soot from it. "That's been up here—," he calculated, "close to fifty years. Would you like it?"

"Shouldn't you keep it?"

"It's a shame to leave it here, and I don't think it would fit me," he laughed. "Take it. You'll have children one day, and they're sure to fight over one rocker. You might need two."

He shut the door, studying our sooty loot. "Whatever do people save stuff for?" he mused. "Any of this you don't want, I'm taking to the sanctuary."

I thought, here was a man who had routed his demons without faltering. It hadn't even been a contest.

Not only was he fearless in coping with remembered tragedy, he was bold with present circumstances. At least twice, Granddad wrote, someone roused him from sleep by scraping on his door. This news alarmed Dad, and he insisted his father install more locks. Granddad thanked him but took a more direct approach.

We didn't learn the whole truth until later, Granddad believing such information was best relayed in person. At the first disturbance, he rose, pulled on his trousers and yanked open the door, demanding, "What do you want?" He so startled the perpetrator that, after fumbling a reply, he abruptly left.

By the second occasion, Granddad had enough. Behind his bedroom door were three rifles. One was a long rifle, tall as a man, likely to explode if fired. Another was a shotgun, equally dubious, but the third was his "new" Stevens shotgun, acquired but fifty years before. He snatched up his shotgun, yanked open the door and, through its screen, aimed the business end at the intruder.

"See here! What do you think you're doing?" he demanded.

The startled man blubbered something about wanting to see Delia.

"Delia doesn't live here," Granddad retorted.

"I should be going," was the feeble reply.

Granddad held the shotgun until the man ran down the alley and disappeared. He was never troubled again. Dad did not welcome this tale but was secretly amused, somewhat proud of his elderly father's spunk.

But Dad did not comprehend Granddad's fearlessness purchased in the fire of tremendous personal loss. Once a man has seen the worst, everything else loses power over him. Granddad had discovered this.

A man who appreciated order, Dad sometimes perceived his father as floundering in chaos. But Granddad viewed life as an unstructured laboratory. He saw unexplored trails and ideas and precious little time for important matters. Maintaining artificial order required too much time; order was restrictive, tedious, boring—and, as Granddad had discovered, generally unnecessary. Yet he was far from undisciplined or careless. He simply had a different compass by which he charted his course.

He acknowledged his life as a small piece in a much grander plan. His utter certainty of this permitted his Christian faith to become a liberating, not restricting, force. He did his best with what he deemed important, expecting God to handle the rest.

In 1954, the Chattanooga Kiwanis Club selected him Man of the Year. We were visiting; Dad supervised Granddad's haircut and shave, selected his attire and was more excited than Granddad, who was pleased to attend a luncheon with many of his "finest friends."

They were leaving, but Dad unexpectedly bounded back upstairs. His sharp eye found, to his horror, Granddad wearing one red sock, the other blue. (Let me add, this was not an oversight. Granddad knew the socks did

Walker and his books, circa 1957. *Photo by Wendell Walker.*

not match. He simply did not think it important.) Dad tore into his own footgear. Like a trophy, he held aloft a pair of dress socks.

"He would have gone to that banquet with one red foot and one blue! If he needed socks, I would gladly have bought him some!" He was beside himself. "He doesn't understand the fuss. As long as both feet are covered, why does it matter if they match? Can you beat that?" He flew downstairs, acceptable socks clutched like trophies.

Socks apparently received no further attention, for I found no mention of them in the newspaper.

We loved the Walker-Davidson reunions held at the old cabin or Aunt Lizzie's home. Nephews, great-whatsits, in-laws and outlaws gathered to celebrate. We drove from Colorado. Family friends appeared, now honorary Walkers through osmosis. One man in his nineties, Dennis Corbley, attended with his younger wife, eighty. He had quit driving, delegating this position to her, and, on departure, always called, "Come on, you old woman driver!"

These reunions had sprung from dinners honoring Granddad's father, but the original purpose was forgotten by a younger generation who had never known him. I thought we were just a big family who liked barbecue and catfish. Tables were brought to the cabin, food laid on oilcloth. Men sauntered off to swap tales while women brought forth the conglomerated banquet. I first met up with a tomato soup cake at one of these shindigs; next year someone brought carrot cake, uncommon at the time.

There were casseroles, approached with suspicion by children who prefer identifiable dishes like fried chicken and corn on the cob. Every garden vegetable turned up in some form—boiled, broiled, shirred, stirred, mashed, trashed or batter-fried. Once someone did something so utterly repugnant to green beans that the perpetrator left the dish behind. (A can of soup was involved in this disaster.) One year the menfolk had been a-fishing; fried catfish and hushpuppies abounded.

Children chased across open fields, laying pennies on the tracks for bolting trains to flatten, swinging from ropes in Aunt Lizzie's barn. Had it not been for these reunions, I would never have known most of this side of my family.

Granddad—"Uncle Bob" to many—family patriarch, regaled us with tales and anecdotes. His brothers and cousins relished recounting details Granddad might omit if they showed him in a bad light. The dignity of advancing years did not stifle brotherly rivalry and boisterous Walker humor.

All loved and respected him, proud of this accomplished man who preferred the connecting bond of family over public acclaim. He presided

Walker at his cabin with the Graysville brick chimney, 1955. *Photo by Wendell Walker.*

over these occasions like a great tree whose branches touched a world beyond the limitations of his roots. He never forgot us.

He also never forgot a good prank and once played one on his cousin Professor James Walker involving a fake telescope, its eyepiece soaked with lampblack. Halley's Comet roamed the heavens then, and respectable cousin James stopped to take the street car home with Granddad. He suggested James view the comet, offering the spurious telescope. Because it had no real lens, nothing could be seen, no matter how the eyepiece was adjusted. In disgust, James declared it no good.

Granddad, gleeful, and James walked down the street, shocked faces telling Granddad everyone thought James had been in a fistfight from the black rings around his eyes. James's sister Ethel got on the streetcar; Granddad shook his head, indicating that she reveal nothing. When James and Ethel got off together, she gave him her mirror. Seeing his ghastly appearance, James vowed, "I swear I'll kill that cousin of mine!" For the next twenty years, James repeatedly paid him back.

One Walker devised a postal prank; Granddad denied being its perpetrator. A package tied with twine, no return address, was opened by the first recipient, disclosing a piece of sowbelly. It was swiftly mailed to another Walker, considered most likely to have sent it. Within weeks, this gift (by now rancid) circulated to every sibling at least once until the pork chain letter was terminated by someone as anonymous as its author.

My favorite outrageous joke took place in Granddad's parlor. He had become a lecturer, sought by garden and writing clubs. What his motive was, I know not, except that knowing Walker humor, I think he had a spontaneous idea for a good prank and acted on it.

Ladies were always sending jelly, fruit baskets, poems, doing little kindnesses. Most had happy lives of their own, but some were single, lonely—after all, he was many years a widower, presumably eligible. His parlor was filled with well-dressed ladies perched on his uncomfortable sofa, chairs and one good rocker. I never knew why they came, but it bored me, and I snuck out to prowl the house. It could have bored Granddad too, as he excused himself, slipping from the parlor to join me in the bleak netherworld of the dining room.

"Come here," he whispered, tiptoeing to the curtained doorway, reaching for something in the corner. He produced an eight-foot pole with much accumulated dust. Wiping it with his shirtsleeve, he pointed to its tip, and I realized the pole was covered in a complete snakeskin, head intact.

"A kingsnake!" he whispered. "Someone gave me this. I almost forgot to use it." He was grinning like a 'possum. I was thrilled.

"Tell them I'm looking for something," he commanded, a general ordering his troops. I complied, stationing myself at the parlor's far end for the best view.

Minutes elapsed. I was on the brink of leaving to locate him when conversation suddenly transformed into shrieks of alarm. From the hem of the portieres emerged a snake's head, its body undulating back and forth in a most intimidating manner. Granddad, acquainted with serpentine ways, was putting life into that eight-foot pole. The snake skulked stealthily into the room, darted back under the curtain and then reappeared.

Cries of, "Snake! It's a snake!" split the refined gathering. Women jumped from chairs, and a few stood on them. Granddad fiendishly slid the snake pole across the rug toward the shoes of the nearest woman, and she leapt off the ground. It was disappointing when they realized it was a fake snake.

"Mr. Walker!" they chided. "What a dreadful thing to do!"

But no, they had loved it.

At the sanctuary, he initiated "christening" trees for significant personages. These were located in Literary Acres and Military Acres, families of the honoree often coming for the ceremony. (This likely originated from the earlier practice at Walnut Grove School.)

For almost forty years he lived a widower, yet he seemed to have a secret formula that turned time into vitality. In his book of poetry *When God Failed*, he defined how his perceptions of God had failed in his grief. The last poem describes the redemption he found: "But when I ventured to assuage the grief of others, theirs alone, a Hand appeared and turned the page, and in their cares, I lost my own." He moved beyond his sorrow, instead trying to leave something good behind to account for his time on earth.

Granddad spoke often of Elberta. Through him, I met and knew her. I have loved this woman whom I have never met because she left behind a loving son and husband as living expression of herself.

Walker and Kelly, Greenwood Avenue, 1958. *Photo by Wendell Walker*.

He never spoke as if she were dead but as someone on an extended journey. He was certain of reunion with her and Robert—not in maudlin terms but as fact. He looked forward but was in no mind to hurry it. He was at peace with his circumstances.

When we moved back to Tennessee, I lived at Granddad's, bringing along a roommate of the four-legged persuasion, our dog Kelly. Granddad got on famously with her, giving her the run of the place. She moved into his bedroom, and he made no attempt to dislodge her. I suspected mutton scraps influenced her decision.

We had a Christmas tree that year, his first since we moved away. One gift he loved was candy resembling pebbles. He delighted in these because he could, and did, tell everyone he was eating rocks. He was happy to have his family back, neatly in pocket.

We bought a house in East Ridge, hoping Granddad would move in. Dad would have had better luck convincing an Eskimo to move to Phoenix. He would never abandon his home. Here Elberta birthed two sons and died—in this downstairs room that had become his bedroom, parlor and office. Accepting his decision, Dad began daily visits.

Granddad, eighty-one, never seemed to age, never tired of company, never ran out of stories, never finished writing. He was the most active person I ever knew yet had nothing but time for friends and family.

He made my father executor of his estate, pointing out important papers, "in case anything happens." He continued giving tours of his beloved sanctuary, writing articles, poems and an autobiography, *As the Indians Left It*. We nurtured a false sense of security. Life without him seemed impossible.

On our last visit to the Chickamauga, his brother John came. Granddad wore a pair of ludicrous shoes, tops separated from the soles halfway to the heel. His toes poked out. When wet, the shoe tops flapped as if hinged. He insisted they looked like snapping turtles, effectively frightening off snakes. He could have been right—we never encountered any.

Uncle John was barefoot. They got into a dispute over who had the toughest feet. Granddad, wearing shoes, argued from a disadvantage, so John demanded a rematch. But time would soon divide these brothers.

A few years before our return, until Granddad's death, a baffling incident occurred, and he invited people to help identify it. It was a rapid, hollow sound, its inception just outside the double-hung window beside his bed. In a few years, it progressed to the window frame. By 1958, the sound took place in the air above his bed. Theories varied from house settling and cracking plaster to wallpaper separating; nothing accounted for the phenomenon.

Granddad brought us in to hear it. It was a commanding, summoning sound, between a clap and a firecracker. Dad never ventured an opinion. Granddad casually once suggested it was a reminder his time was short. He did not think it was Elberta but said it would not be long until he saw her again.

So, as people do who cannot face impending loss, we told him he would be with us years hence. Granddad, understanding our fears, tolerated our inept response and changed the subject, speaking little of it again, though it continued.

I was at the university when the call came. Granddad had died the previous day. He had suffered a heart attack at the sanctuary but seemed to be recovering. He was writing, giving reason to hope he was on the mend. Dad visited him that afternoon and was returning with soup. Instead, he discovered his father lifeless on the bed. Always concerned that Granddad look his best, Dad tidied his clothes before calling the undertaker. Mother waited overnight to tell me, somehow thinking bad news is better received in daylight. He died exactly forty-five years to the date of Robert's death, September 26.

People of all ages thronged the funeral parlor; whole families held up their children for a last view of him. Half were unknown to us—but Granddad had known them. They were some of his finest friends.

I forced myself to the viewing, where he was decked out in his best, as if attending another awards ceremony. I stared squarely into his face and felt absolutely nothing. This frail mask bearing my grandfather's likeness might have been a plaster cast. He wasn't here, I realized, and he wasn't dead!

He had abandoned this body for better quarters. It was as he always told me it would be. One day he would receive his wings and would be off. Lines from his own epitaph, written shortly before his death, came to mind: "Let there no trace of tears be found to stain the beauty of the ground where my old chrysalis is laid…But let sweet memories invade the hearts and minds…where I my wings received one day, and like a bird, I sailed away." We thought this one of his best poems, but it was more. A prophetic voice was speaking.

At once I felt the joy that must be his, as he embraced Elberta and Robert after their long separation. This was Granddad's graduation—no time for mourning! Dad was a rock through the wake, funeral and burial, which took place at the sanctuary. I could only imagine his loss, if mine was any indication.

It rained that day, a slow, drizzling, September rain with hazy skies. The cortege proceeded to the sanctuary. But as the hearse carrying his "chrysalis" crossed the tracks, the rain slacked and the sun came out, shining white-hot in a steamy sky. Even Dad commented on the sudden change.

It was a sign he was home. We were to be grateful for knowing him and be about the business of our own lives. That was what he had done—what he would want us to do. There were no unfinished pages. His book had been written, and we knew the story by heart. It now remained for us to complete our lives and hope we did somewhere near as good a job.

It fell to Dad to fulfill Granddad's will. Elberta and Robert were buried in Forest Hills Cemetery, but when his father's farm became the wildlife sanctuary, it was approved for Granddad to be buried there. His wife and firstborn would be beside him, requiring that their graves be moved.

Dad insisted the exhumation take place with his oversight. His background was archaeology, and he would not be dissuaded, so I volunteered to accompany.

There remained of Robert's grave a coffin handle, a few small bones and a folded sheet of corroded copper. Elberta's grave contained coffin handles and few remains. My father tenderly took the crown of her skull in his hand.

"She had long, brown hair," he said quietly and placed it back.

Walker reunion at Audubon Acres, 2000.

The task completed, headstones on the truck, we walked through that peaceful landscape, contemplating our own mortality.

Robert's and Elberta's stones now flank Granddad's arrowhead headstone featuring his bronze likeness and two lines of his epitaph. As with all graves, the real stories lie hidden. Granddad said a man's best and only monument ought to be what he leaves behind for others.

Eight years elapsed until, for $3,000, 808 Greenwood ended its seventy-four years as our family residence. In all that time, going through Granddad's library, papers and correspondence, neither Dad nor I ever heard the mysterious sound again. Weeks were spent in his room alone, sorting personal effects, yet we encountered nothing paranormal. We were left with one conclusion: the rapping had been, as he said, a reminder to complete his work.

We came across a sealed note to be opened upon his death. It described what Granddad termed a "vision" charging him to teach young people the reality of Christ through the Creator's natural world. This had strengthened his desire to preserve his boyhood farm as a wildlife sanctuary. Because people might consider him deranged if he related the incident, he chose to ponder it privately.

A second visitation awakened him days before his death, reminding him to write his message to youth and post it on one of the sanctuary's beech trees. He rose and wrote, briefly stated, that Christian faith becomes richer through the beauty created for man to enjoy. To disconnect man from the majesty of creation separates him from his Creator. By imparting this throughout his life, Granddad fulfilled his mission.

ABOUT THE AUTHOR

Chattanooga is the birthplace of Alexandra Walker Clark, who was strongly influenced by her grandfather Robert Sparks Walker. Together, they hiked the trails at the Chickamauga, where Walker began teaching her, at age three, the names and knowledge of wildflowers, birds and trees. These teachings have remained with Clark, who has made the woods surrounding her home a bird sanctuary, sometimes invaded by raccoons, rabbits and 'possums—all finding an appreciative host.

Walker's teachings have reached a fourth generation, as his great-grandchildren much admire his work and share his passionate love of the natural world. This has led Clark to observe, as her grandfather once stated, "One never knows what will become of an idea dropped into the well of a human heart."

Clark lives in northeast Tennessee with her family.

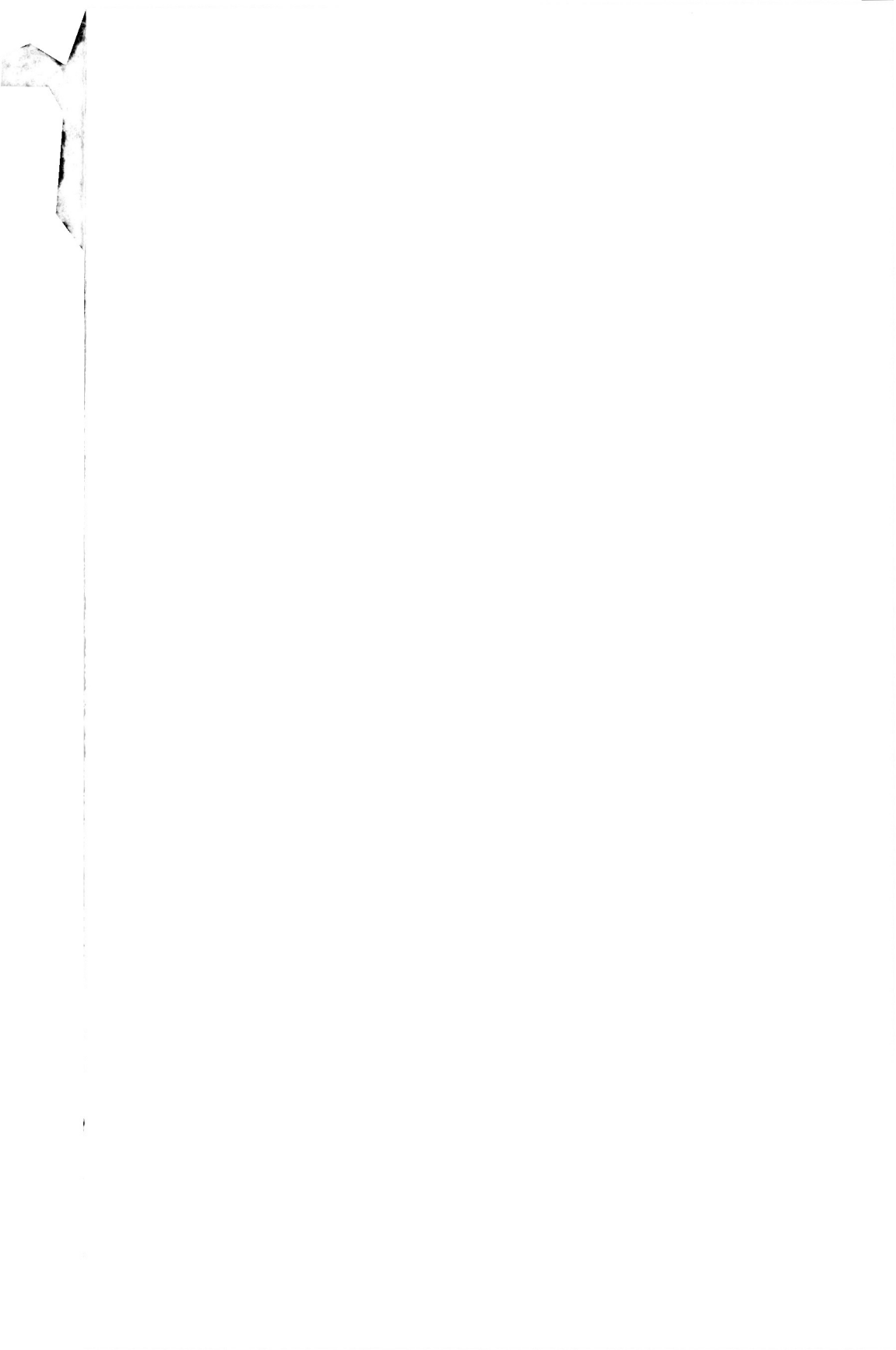

www.ingramcontent.com/pod-product-compliance
Lightning Source LLC
Chambersburg PA
CBHW070927150426
42812CB00049B/1559